B&T
$7.95

W9-BXP-860

This book is dedicated to Queen Hatshepsut, who was the first to record
a voyage of discovery in words and pictures

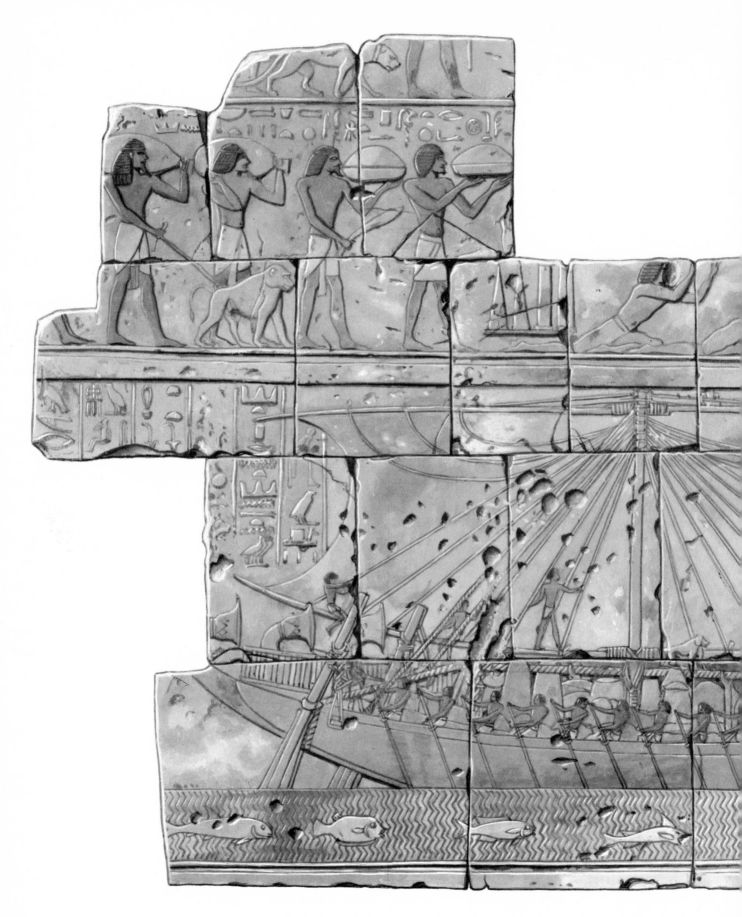

2

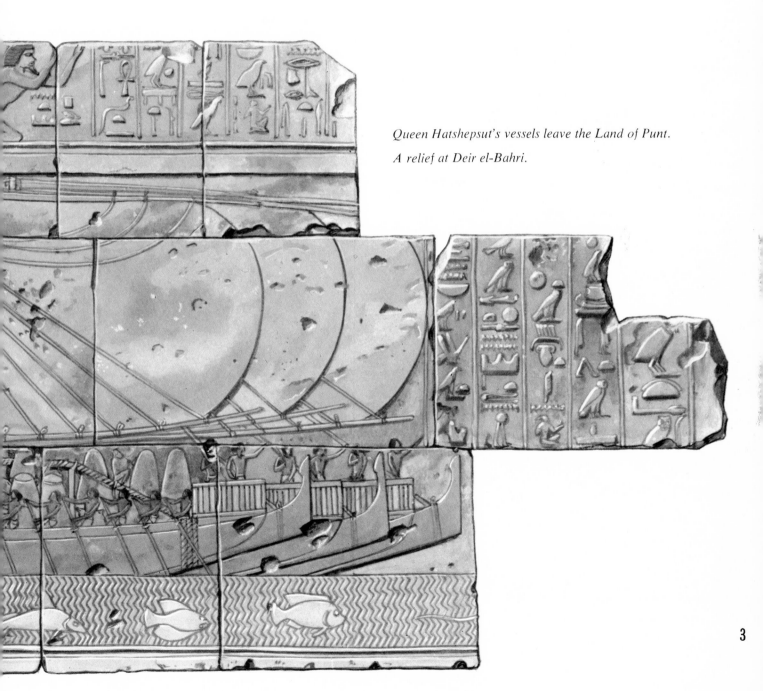

Queen Hatshepsut's vessels leave the Land of Punt.
A relief at Deir el-Bahri.

The map on the end-papers was drawn by Henricus Martellus Germanus in 1489, the year after Bartolomeu Diaz discovered the Cape of Good Hope.

© 1964 BY INTERBOOK PUBLISHING AB, STOCKHOLM. ALL RIGHTS RESERVED
VÄGEN TILL INDIEN © 1964 BY BJÖRN LANDSTRÖM
Sept. 30, 1974
LIBRARY OF CONGRESS CATALOG CARD NUMBER 64—21301
ISBN 0 385 01763 4

Bold Voyages and Great Explorers

A History of Discovery and Exploration
from the Expedition to the Land of Punt in 1493 B.C.
to the Discovery of the Cape of Good Hope in 1488 A.D.,
in Words and Pictures by

Björn Landström

Formerly published as THE QUEST FOR INDIA

A WINDFALL book

published by Doubleday and Company Inc.
Garden City, New York

Wingate College Library

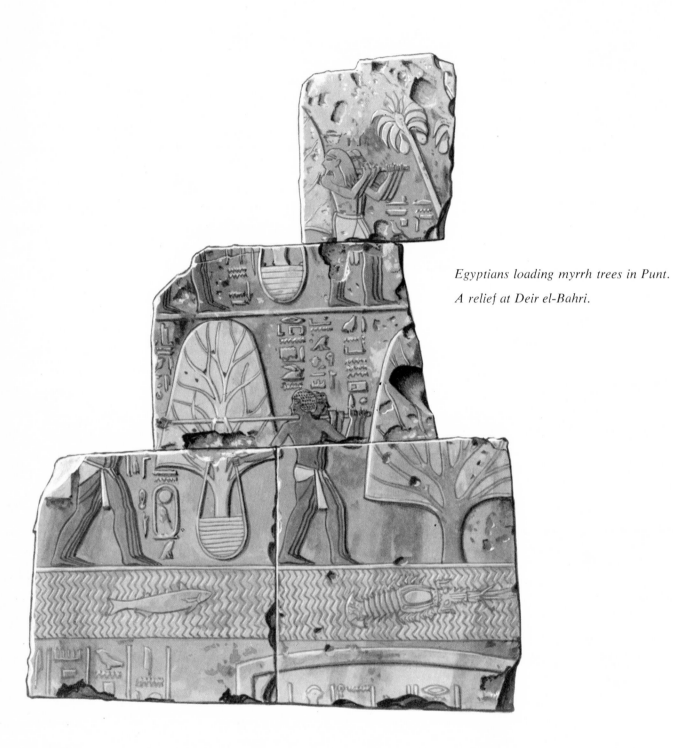

Egyptians loading myrrh trees in Punt.

A relief at Deir el-Bahri.

Contents

063341

A Sinhalese outrigger canoe.

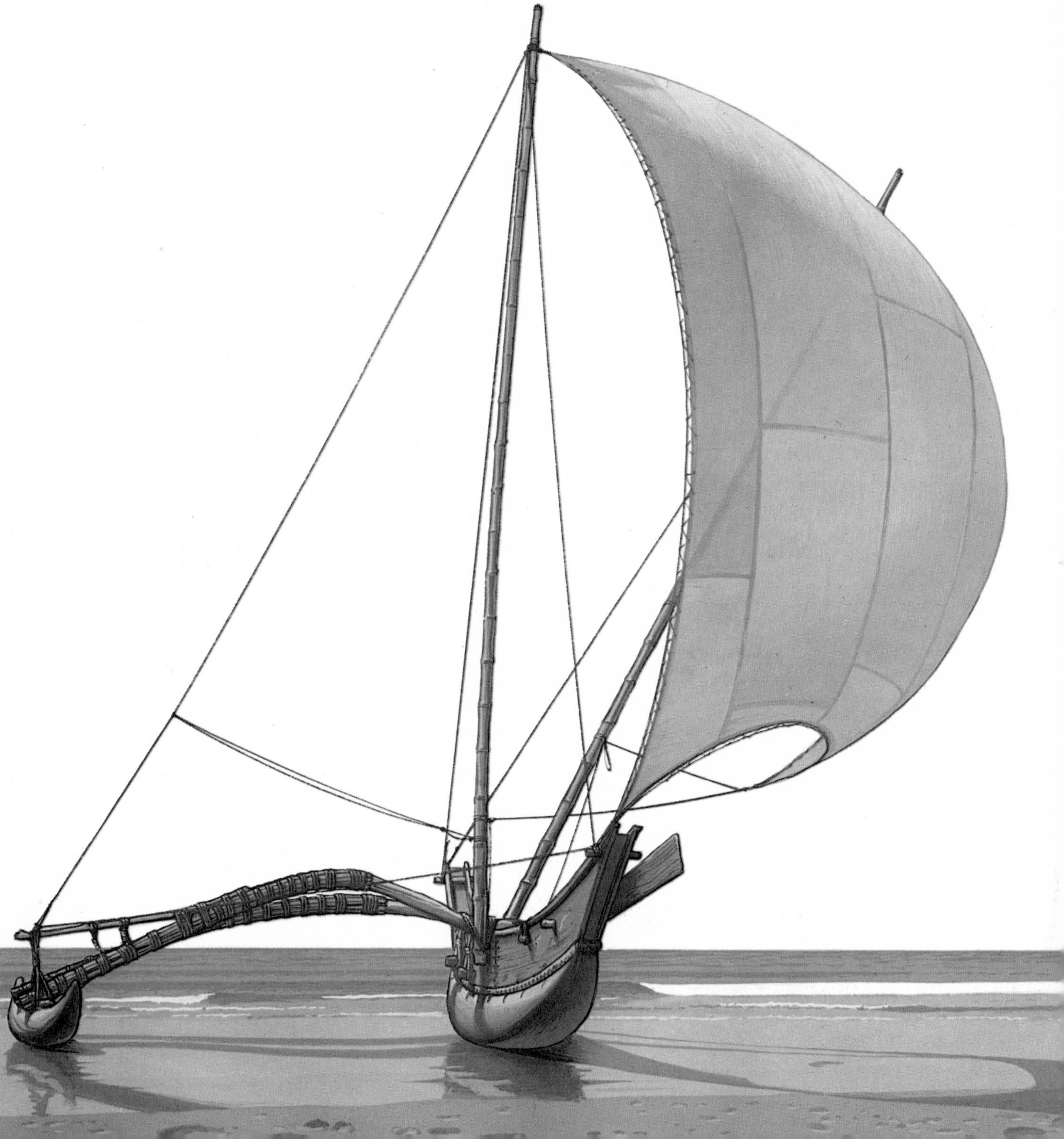

Introduction

This is a tale of explorations by land and by sea, from the voyages to the Land of Punt by the Egyptians, to the circumnavigation of Africa by the Portuguese thousands of years later. The routes were many, but the goal was the same—to reach India, or, more precisely, what medieval Europeans called India. This included not only all Asia east of the Euphrates, but also the Arabian Peninsula and the whole of East Africa. I have confined myself to expeditions which started from Europe and helped to from the European world picture—and by Europe I mean primarily, and perhaps a little inaccurately, the countries around the Mediterranean. In order to connect the era of discovery presented here with later events, I have also told of the Viking expeditions in the north, of the discovery of islands in the Atlantic and of the voyages which eventually brought men to the Land of Gold south of the deserts of Africa.

I have tried to base this presentation on as many facts as possible, and to avoid all speculation and theorizing. May I point out from the very start that I am not a research worker or a scholar. What I tell is roughly what others have told before me, and where it has been possible I have quoted, word for word, what the travellers themselves or contemporary historians wrote about the journeys. My illustrations alone, I believe, may say something that has not been said before.

I have spent many years collecting books about voyages of discovery and exploration. Most of them have been illustrated, and I have found that the same illustrations often reappear in book after book. There are the miniatures from the fifteenth century portraying Marco Polo's journeys two centuries earlier, there are de Bry's engravings from the end of the sixteenth century portraying the voyage made by Columbus a hundred years before, and there is much else which is both artistic and decorative —but which has very little to do with the expeditions as they really were. Just as sixteenth-century artists depicted the Life of Christ in sixteenth-century milieu, so they presented Marco Polo and Columbus and other men of discovery sailing in sixteenth-century ships, wearing sixteenth-century clothes and with a background of islands and countries and habitations which may not have been actually European in character, but had very little claim to historical accuracy.

People of today attach more importance to historical reality and demand a closer adherence to fact. Further-more the artist of today is better situated than his predecessors when attempting to reconstruct any given historical milieu. It has been my wish to portray, as accurately as possible, the men of discovery and their routes, their proper surroundings, their ships and other means of transport and—perhaps more than anything—the countries and peoples they met with, everything they saw. I did not know enough about their vessels, and my studies in that field resulted in my book *The Ship*. It is possible that I still know far too little of what they met with and saw, but I have at any rate tried to fill the gaps by the study of books, by making lengthy journeys into Africa and Asia and by visiting museums in many different parts of the world.

In order to be really complete, our story ought to begin with a scene, many tens of thousands of years ago, when Homo Sapiens set out on his long migratory wandering from his original home. But the migration of a people cannot be looked on as a form of exploration in the proper sense. Our primitive forefathers were nomadic hunters and fishermen and food-gatherers. At a later stage they became keepers of flocks and tillers of the ground, but it was a long time before they settled down. Perhaps ten or twenty thousand years ago some of them may have set up permanent dwelling places beside rivers or lakes or coastal inlets where they had found good, dependable fishing grounds. Five thousand years ago more settled farming communities began to appear in the vicinity of several large rivers. Such was the case beside the Indus, along the Euphrates and its twin, the Tigris, along the Nile, later along the Hwang Ho in China and the Zambezi in Africa—and beside many other waterways. Flint instruments and shells and other objects which archaeologists have unearthed far from their places of origin tell us of trade and travel in times long before the appearance of these cultures. By the time Man began to record decisions and important events in hieroglyphic and cuneiform writing, foreign trade was already vigorous, and it was not long before these civilizations began to import amber from the north, tin from the north-west, bronze and silver from the west, gold, frankincense and myrrh from the south, spices and precious stones from the south-west. But the scribes had more important things than journeys to set down for the benefit of their own age and of posterity, and even though we are able to obtain a little information about significant movements of men or goods from a few short lines or fragments of lines, we do not find any real description of a voyage of discovery until about 1500 B.C.

Egypt and the Land of Punt

The banks of the Nile are really one long oasis, and the boundary between flourishing vegetation and the surrounding inanimate desert is razor-sharp. The peoples that had found their way to the Valley of the Nile from the east felt that there was no need to wander further west into the desert; they settled there and cultivated the land. They dug irrigation ditches and extended the oasis to make better use of the annual Nile floods; and gradually, by fusing with the original African population and other immigrant tribes, they became the gifted people whom we call the Egyptians. At first they lived in a series of small kingdoms, but the river united them, and it was not long before they formed themselves into two large entities which we know as Upper and Lower Egypt. History then tells us that Pharaoh Menes, who was also known as Narmer, united both kingdoms about 2850 B.C. and adopted the title of "King of Upper and Lower Egypt". This is where we set the beginning of Egyptian history, and by custom the age covered by the reign of Pharaoh Narmer and his direct descendants is known as the 1st Egyptian Dynasty.

It is only natural that the boat should become the chief means of transport in this very long country on both sides of the river, but there was no wood suitable for boat-building and so the people made their first craft out of reeds, that is, papyrus. We do not know when they began to build vessels of wood, nor do we know when they first breasted the waves of the Mediterranean from the delta of the Nile, but we do know with certainty that cedar wood was imported from Lebanon as early as the time of the 2nd Dynasty. And a few lines of hieroglyphics tell us that Pharaoh Snofru of the 4th Dynasty, about 2600 B.C., sent forty ships to Byblos in Phoenicia, whence they returned richly laden with cedar wood. The early Pharaohs had begun to import copper, malachite and turquoise from Sinai, and they also began to send expeditions south to obtain ebony, ivory and incense.

Enormous quantities of incense and myrrh were burnt each year on the altars of Egypt for the gratification of the gods. From time immemorial these sweet-smelling gums had come by land from somewhere in the south, and before they reached their destination in Egypt they had to pass through the hands of many middlemen and were therefore inordinately expensive. We do not know which of the Pharaohs was the first to grudge paying such high prices and who therefore decided to send an expedition to Punt, the secret "Land of the Gods", the distant land where the spices came from. This may have already taken place in the predynastic period, before the reign of Pharaoh Narmer. It is recorded that Pharaoh Sahure of the 5th Dynasty, about 2500 B.C., sent a large fleet to Punt. The vessels managed to make a successful return, being laden among other things with 80,000 measures of myrrh, 6,000 weights of electrum (an alloy of silver and gold) and 2,600 logs of costly wood (presumably ebony for the most part). Khnemhotep, steersman on one of these vessels in the following dynasty, tells us in an inscription on his tomb how he, together with Captain Chui, his master, made eleven journeys to the distant land.

Today no one is able to say with exactitude what the Egyptians meant by the Land of Punt. Guesses have been made at Eritrea, southern Arabia, Somaliland and the regions around Zanzibar and Dar-es-Salaam. Personally I am inclined to believe in the last of these conjectures. There the country is so fertile and bountiful that it is easy to understand why the Egyptians called it the "Land of the Gods". Punt might well of course include the entire bountiful region in the south, from Somaliland to the Zambezi, just as India later came to mean all that was desirable east and south of Palestine. But whether the journey to Punt took the voyagers to southern Arabia or Zanzibar, it was a great and laborious and dangerous undertaking. The shortest route from the Nile to the Red Sea passed through a valley which today is called the Wadi Hammamat, and this was an eight-day march through the

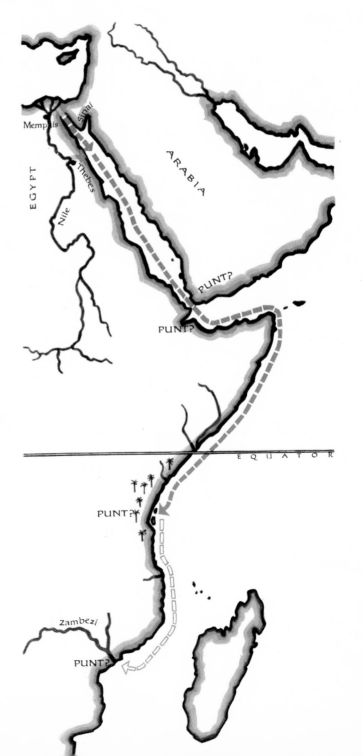

Pharaoh Sahure's ships in the Red Sea on the way home from Punt. — The map shows the route taken by the expeditions to Punt: from the Nile, either through Sesostris' canal or across the Wadi Hammamat to the Red Sea and the "Land of the Gods" in the south.

desert. The Red Sea coast was barren and desolate, and all ship's timber and all equipment for the expeditions had to be hauled across the long desert route. Henu, who during the 1990's B.C. was vizier under Pharaoh Mentuhotep, had an inscription carved into the rock face at the Wadi Hammamat, of which the following is a part:

"My master ordered me to send a ship to Punt to fetch myrrh . . . I left the Nile with 3,000 men . . . Every day I gave each man twenty pieces of bread and a leather satchel, containing two measures of water . . . I dug twelve wells . . . Then I reached the sea, built the ship and sent it off."

The Red Sea is an unfriendly waterway at all seasons; it has coral reefs off its desert coasts. In summertime the days are extremely hot and visibility is often reduced by whirling clouds of sand. The opportunities of going ashore for fresh provisions and water must have been small during the time of the Pharaohs. It is almost certain that the journeys south were made between June and August, when the wind was favourable, and the journeys home through the Red Sea between October and December for the same reason. Even so, the voyagers would inevitably have had to make way against wind and water for longish stretches without the aid of oars. If Punt was in fact southern Arabia, it would indeed be fortunate if an expedition could have been completed within the course of a year. If Punt lay further afield, as I believe probable, the journey out and home would have taken two years— perhaps even more.

The Egyptians were also compelled to sail the Red Sea for the vital imports of copper and stone from Sinai, and it was in all likelihood because of the mines that Pharaoh

11

Sesostris—probably during the 1980's B.C.—had a canal dug from the easternmost arm of the Nile estuary to the Red Sea, so that the ships he sent to fetch the ore could sail directly from Memphis to the ports on the Sinai Peninsula. Then it would have been quite natural for the Punt vessels to take the same convenient route.

During the 13th Dynasty, in the 18th century B.C., the country was weakened by internal strife, and a century later the entire Delta and much of central Egypt was conquered by a people called the Hyksos, warriors from the east, who stormed their way into the country with horse and chariot—a war machine hitherto unknown to the Egyptians. The Hyksos reigned for a century, until the Egyptians regained power under Pharaoh Amasis I. In the meantime, however, Sesostris' canal had been allowed to fall into disrepair—voyages to Punt had not been undertaken for hundreds of years—and the coveted incense and myrrh once again found their

way up to the country by land through the hands of extortionate intermediaries.

Thothmes I of the 18th Dynasty was a warrior king who had extended the boundaries of the country in the south and the east. He was succeeded by his illegitimate son Thothmes II who had to marry his step-sister Hatshepsut, the legitimate heiress, before he could sit on the throne. Thothmes II soon died, however, and Hatshepsut then married her younger step-brother Thothmes III who had been chosen as Pharaoh by his predecessor on the instructions of an oracle. But Hatshepsut was not able to content herself with being a mere Queen Consort. On her mother's side she was a true descendant of Amasis I, the Liberator of Egypt, and she took the reins of power into her own hands and sent her presumably much younger consort to serve as a priest in a temple. It has been estimated that she reigned from 1501 to 1480 B.C.

Being a woman she was not able to win honour on the

Queen Hatshepsut's expedition lands at Punt.

battlefield, and so her term of office was characterized, outwardly at least, by peace. It is said that she was gifted, beautiful and enamoured of magnificence, and to the glory of the god Amon-Ra, as well as to her own, she ordered Senmut, her vizier and favourite, to build a temple at Thebes in a valley which today is called Deir el-Bahri, lying on the west shore of the Nile opposite Luxor. It was quite different from all other temples in Egypt, having open pillared halls and large terraces, and history has it that she wished to build another land of Punt for Amon-Ra. She wrote: "I have made him a Land of Punt in his garden. It is large enough for him to be able to walk there."

Hatshepsut wanted to plant myrrh trees on the terraces in front of the temple, but no Egyptian ship had sailed to Punt—where the myrrh grew—for three hundred years, and no one any longer knew the way to get there. The Queen then let it be announced via the oracle of

Amon-Ra that the route to Punt was to be re-explored. She built and equipped a fleet of vessels, and it is possible that she even dredged Sesostris' silted-up canal so that the ships would be able to leave from her own city of Thebes. It is just as likely however, that the ships' timbers, originally obtained from Lebanon, were hauled as before from Thebes to the Red Sea over the Wadi Hammamat, and that the vessels were then put together there, perhaps near the present-day El-Qoseir. When the fleet returned successfully, Hatshepsut commemorated their impressive journey by having it recorded in text and pictures on one of the walls of the temple cloister.

Archaeologists have excavated the temple from the sand and are still continuing work on its restoration, and

13

Wingate College Library

even though the brightly coloured reliefs portraying the expedition are damaged and faded and still not quite complete, they nevertheless give us a clear picture of the voyagers and the ships and the Land of Punt—a much more reliable picture than the decorative engravings, made in the 16th century A.D., which professed to show ancient voyages of discovery.

We are shown the arrival of the fleet in Punt. Five ships are portrayed, three of them under sail and two propelled

by oars. The number may, however, be a convention, and it may be just as likely that there were twenty or fifty vessels—Pharaoh Snofru had sent forty ships to Byblos more than a thousand years before this time. We see the Queen's representative and his men-at-arms presenting gifts—necklaces, axes and knives—to the ruler of Punt and his prodigiously fat queen, named, according to the hieroglyphics, Perehu and Eti. A hut made of stocks stands among the myrrh trees, in the shade of palms. The natives drive cattle, monkeys and leopards on board the vessels and carry aboard large baskets containing the myrrh trees which are to stand outside the temple at Thebes. The heavily laden ships then sail off again.

The accompanying hieroglyphic text has not all survived, but it is possible to read among other things the following: "Queen Makara [Hatshepsut had many names] made this for her father Amon-Ra. Nothing of its kind has ever been made by any other ruler in this land ...

A vast portion of the Land of the Gods ... which the Egyptians knew of only by hearsay ... As much incense as is needed is taken and the ships loaded as desired ... The people of the Land of Punt know nothing of Egypt ... During the reigns of kings past, back to the time of Ra, its goods were carried from the one to the other ..."

We see the inhabitants of Punt raise their hands in astonishment and ask the Egyptians: "How came you to this land that people know not of? Did you come along the paths of heaven, or have you traversed the sea and the waters of the Land of the Gods? Or have you come on the beams of the sun?"

And the text goes on: "The Queen's ambassador and his soldiers pitched their tents near the terraced mount of balsam in the Land of Punt, which lies on both sides of the sea, in order to receive there the ruler of the country. They entertained them with bread, ale, wine, meat and dried fruits from the land of Tamara [Egypt] as the royal court had ordered them ... The Ruler of Punt came to the shore of the great sea and gave his tribute ... The ships were loaded heavily with all the wonderful wares of the Land of Punt, with the many rich kinds of wood of the Land of the Gods, together with great quantities of sweet-smelling gum and fresh incense, trees, ebony, ivory, pure gold from Amu, fragrant wood, Kesit wood, Ahem incense, sacred gum, mascara, dog-headed monkeys, long-tailed monkeys, dogs, and also with leopard skins and natives of the country with their children."

The expedition had set off during the ninth year of Hatshepsut's reign; if her reign began in 1501, the journey must have taken place in the year 1493—1492 B.C. In 1492 A.D. an even more significant voyage was to take place!

Certain historians maintain that Queen Hatshepsut and Senmut, her favourite, were put to death at the order of the dethroned but still active Thothmes III; and, to add to his vengeance on his grasping step-sister, he carefully destroyed all her portraits in the Deir el-Bahri temple and elsewhere. Around the obelisk she had erected for herself at Karnak he built a high wall, with the result that it is today the most well-preserved of Egyptian obelisks. At the top of another obelisk at Karnak, which she had erected to the memory of her father Thothmes I, she had had a portrait of herself carved. The likeness was preserved, and it is this which decorates the first page of this book.

It has been questioned whether Queen Eti (above left) suffered from elephantiasis or whether her Hottentot curves represented an ideal of beauty. —Many Egyptian warriors, as shown on the reliefs, were probably Sudanese.

14

Crete and Mycenae

Thothmes III, the man of bitter revenge, became Egypt's greatest Pharaoh. He ruled and fought for thirty years after the death of Hatshepsut and created an Egyptian Empire from Nubia in the south to the Euphrates in the north-east. Hieroglyphic inscriptions tell us that at the order of Amon-Ra he had "conquered the outermost bounds of the world and held the compass of the seas in his hand". These words give us some idea of Egyptian views about the size of the world. Rekhmire, his second in command, decorated his tomb at Thebes with pictures showing how all the peoples of the world came to pay tribute to the great Thothmes. There are Semites from Syria and Phoenicia, there are dark-skinned men from Punt and the Sudan, and there are representatives of "the people from the islands in the middle of the sea".

It is possible that by these Rekhmire meant the people of Crete, who are thought to have been the first great seafaring power in the Mediterranean. Their period of greatness began about 2000 B.C. under King Minos who, according to the Greek historian Thucydides, was the first to create a navy. The Cretans were skilled craftsmen and merchants, and the products of their culture found their way to all countries in the eastern Mediterranean and as far west as Sicily. They controlled international seafaring in their part of the world for six hundred years, but it is uncertain whether this world of theirs reached all the way to the western Mediterranean and as far west as Spain, as has often been suggested.

It is also possible that "the people from the islands in the middle of the sea" were the Mycenaeans who at that period held supremacy over southern Greece and the islands of the Aegean. They had adopted Cretan culture at an early stage, and about 1400 B.C. they conquered the whole of Crete and spread their dominion over the seas. They founded colonies and trading stations on Sicily and the Lipari Islands, in southern Italy, on Rhodes and Cyprus, and they kept up a lively trade with Egypt, with Ugarit and Byblos on the Phoenician coast, and with Troy in the north. Then the Dorians came to Greece and swept away Mycenae and its civilization. Cretan and Mycenaean ships had played out their parts on the seas.

Through the Pillars of Melcarth

The Semitic coastal people whom the Greeks called *Phoinikes* were the greatest seafarers of Antiquity. At first they may have been a small pastoral people who had been forced out, by more powerful tribes, on to the narrow strip of land between the mountains of Lebanon and the Mediterranean, a people who by desire or necessity were

15

obliged to turn primarily to trade and seafaring for their livelihood. The Phoenicians lived close to powerful neighbours and were influenced by three great cultures: the Egyptian, the Mesopotamian and the Cretan. Their country lay just where the great trade routes crossed each other, and in this way they came to play an important part in the history of the Mediterranean from quite early times—from perhaps as early as the 4th millennium B.C. Their own great article of export was, to begin with, the cedars of Lebanon, and later they were to become most renowned for their dark-red cloth. It is believed that their trade in this cloth gave them their Greek name, that *Phoinikes* comes from *phoinios,* a word meaning dark red. But they never called themselves Phoenicians, and it is uncertain whether they ever felt themselves to be a united people. Phoenician political life was concentrated in a few more or less independent city-states which joined hands only when the need was great.

But the Phoenicians were also to export something which was to be of far greater value for the future than

cedar and cloth of Tyrian red—namely the alphabet. They had not invented it all by themselves; they had inherited it as the last link in a long chain of development from some other Semitic source. The Greeks probably came into contact with it some time during the 8th century B.C. and immediately saw how very useful it was. And later, via Rome, it was gradually spread over the entire Western Hemisphere.

The first Phoenician city we hear mention of is Byblos, which supplied Pharaoh Snofru with cedar. At that parti-

A Phoenician ship, which has sailed through the Pillars of Melcarth, being repaired on the shore of a bay close to the northern "pillar"—the rock which many years later would be known as Gibraltar.

*A map of Phoenician and Greek cities, colonies and
trading stations (Phoenician red, Greek black).*

cular time it is possible that the trade route involved was
still dominated by Egyptian ships, but later the Egyptians
were to make use of both ships and seamen from Byblos
which was probably never quite able to free itself from
Egyptian influence. More independent and international
was Ugarit, lying further to the north. This city also
traded with the Egyptians, of course, but it went further
than Byblos and tried to maintain connections with Crete
and Cyprus and later with Mycenae. However, it was
only when Mycenaean dominion had been shattered by
the Dorians in the 12th century B.C. that the seas were
laid open to the Phoenicians and their age of supremacy
began. It is true that Byblos had long been weakened by
Egyptian pressure, and had now lost much of its importance; true also that Ugarit had been destroyed by the
"Peoples of the Sea" who had invaded and plundered
Phoenicia from Crete and Asia Minor, who had pressed
on south towards Egypt where they were finally defeated
on land and at sea by Ramses III, the last great Pharaoh.
But in the meantime the city of Sidon had grown up to
power and glory.

The Sidonians perhaps showed even greater interest
than their predecessors in the caravan routes: they extended them and built support stations for their trade
with the countries in the east—at Dan on the Jordan,
at Hamath on the Orontes, at Edessa not far from the
Euphrates, and at Nisibis near the Tigris. It was from
these places that the trade routes ran to the Caucasus
and the inner regions of Asia—and along the rivers to
the Persian Gulf. The Sidonians founded colonies on the
shores of the Gulf of Issos (now the Gulf of Iskenderun)
in the north, and built a series of ports and cities in the
south along their own coastline—Tyre, Dor, Jabneh,
Ashdod, Ascalon and Gaza. It is also certain that they
had Mediterranean colonies on Cyprus, Crete and Rhodes.

By the 12th century B.C., Tyre, twin city to Sidon, had
become the most powerful seaport on the Mediterranean
and was to remain so for four hundred years. It gradually
took over most of Sidon's colonies and founded new ones
of its own until it finally had possessions in nearly all parts
of the Mediterranean. We do not know when the Tyrians
first sailed out of the Mediterranean between the capes
which, in honour of the god of their city, they named the
"Pillars of Melcarth". They journeyed as far as the rich
city of Tartessus, which probably lay at the mouth of the
Guadalquivir; they founded Gades, the modern Cadiz;
and they discovered islands out in the ocean—in all
likelihood both Madeira and the Canaries.

People writing of the Phoenicians often have to use
words such as "perhaps" and "probably", for the Phoenicians were not men to sing their own praises; they were
sober merchants who were well aware of the advantages
of keeping their routes and discoveries to themselves. It
is related that they spread terrible tales of the dangers of

18

the ocean and of the rim of the world, which lay beyond the Pillars of Melcarth, so that they would be able to trade with the silver city of Tartessus all by themselves. And it came about that their tales were to prove more effective than the guns of Gibraltar in our own century. It is said that a foreign ship once tried to follow a vessel from Tyre in order to learn of a secret route, but that the Tyrian captain, rather than betray the secret of the route, ran his ship aground and let it founder.

Of the greatness of Tyre the Prophet Ezekiel has this to say: "The inhabitants of Zidon and Arvad were thy mariners: thy wise men, O Tyrus, that were in thee, were thy pilots. The ancients of Gebal, and the wise men thereof, were in thee thy calkers: all the ships of the sea with their mariners were in thee to occupy thy merchan-

dise . . . Tarshish [Tartessus] was thy merchant by reason of the multitude of all kinds of riches: with silver, iron, tin and lead, they traded in thy fairs . . . The ships of Tarshish did sing of thee in thy market: and thou wast replenished, and made very glorious in the midst of the seas. Thy powers have brought thee into great waters."

One of the most powerful kings of Tyre was Hiram II, who reigned from 969 to 936 B.C. Solomon was his contemporary, and in the First Book of Kings there is much information about Hiram and his relationship with Solomon—reading between the lines we find that the King of Israel was almost a subject of the King of Tyre. Solomon needed wood from Lebanon to build his temples, and he sent a messenger to Tyre to negotiate the purchase. Hiram's conditions of trade were as follows: "I will do

19

all thy desire concerning timber of cedar, and concerning timber of fir. My servants shall bring them down from Lebanon unto the sea; and I will convey them by sea in floats unto the place that thou shalt appoint me, and I will cause them to be discharged there, and thou shalt receive them; and thou shalt accomplish my desire in giving food for my household." — The price Solomon had to pay was 20,000 cors (160,000 bushels) of wheat and 20 cors (1,300 gallons) of olive oil a year. And when the temple was at last completed twenty years later he made a further payment of twenty towns in Galilee. But Hiram was still not satisfied and had to be further placated with a hundred and twenty talents of gold (about five tons).

Ophir, the Land of Gold

We read in the First Book of Kings that "King Solomon made a navy of ships in Ezion-geber, which is beside Eloth, on the shore of the Red Sea, in the land of Edom. And Hiram sent in the navy his servants, shipmen that had knowledge of the sea, with the servants of Solomon. And they came to Ophir, and fetched from thence gold; four hundred and twenty talents, and brought it to King Solomon." — A talent (*kikkar* in the original) corresponded to a weight in the region of 100 lbs. Thus the gold brought to Solomon from Ophir would have been getting on for twenty tons!

There has been much speculating as to where this golden land of Ophir lay. Marco Polo believed it to be in Zipangu (Japan); Columbus looked for it in America. Modern scholars are inclined to think it was in Abyssinia; or near the Zambezi in East Africa; or on the Gold Coast in West Africa; or in India. There are almost as many opinions as there are scholars. Only one voyage to Ophir is mentioned in the Bible, and this was probably made about 945 B.C. The Book of Kings does mention that Jehoshaphat also tried to send ships to Ophir for gold, but his fleet was destroyed in a storm before it had got further than Ezion-geber. So it hardly seems as if it was a question of any organized, joint mining practice by the Phoenicians and Israelites.

After all, the Phoenicians had ancient trade ties with Egypt, a country which imported much gold from the south, and it is probable that they had found out where the land of origin of the gold lay and then started from Solomon's port on the Red Sea coast for a piratical expedition to the Land of Gold. — Ibn Batuta, a Moroccan traveller who made protracted journeys over the entire Arabian world and beyond into Africa and Asia during the 14th century A.D., writes in his *Travels:* "A merchant told me that the town of Sofala lies a fourteen-day march from Kulua, and between Sofala and Yufi in the land of the Limii was a further month's march . . . Gold-dust is brought from Yufi to Sofala." — West of Sofala, about 250 miles inland, lies the mysterious ruined city of Zimbabwe, and around this a number of gold mines. It is believed that the city is extremely old, and many consider that this particular region was Ophir, the Land of Gold—a month's march from Yufi, as Ibn

Batuta wrote. Let us then suppose that Yufi is Ophir and perhaps Zimbabwe. In order to make use of the port in the Red Sea, the Phoenicians, usually so secretive, allowed Solomon's men to take part in the expedition, knowing that they hardly need fear that the less seaman-like Israelites would be able to find their way back there again. Jehoshaphat's failure proved them to be correct. But it is only thanks to the fact that the Israelites were taken along in the first place that we know anything of the voyage at all. There are some who see traces of Phoenician building methods in the ruins of Zimbabwe —but we shall not speculate.

The Phoenicians Circumnavigate Africa

In the 8th century B.C. the aggressive fighters of Assyria began to approach the Mediterranean. They took many Phoenician cities, and threatened Tyre. Since this city was built on an island it had been able to withstand sieges from Egypt and Assyria for a long time, but many of its richest families emigrated overseas to Carthage, founded by the Tyrians a hundred years earlier. Finally, in 666 B.C., Tyre fell, and with its fall the whole of Phoenicia came under Assyrian rule. Ezekiel takes up a lamentation for the fate of the city: "What city is like Tyrus, like the destroyed in the midst of the sea? When thy wares went forth out of the seas, thou filledst many people; thou didst enrich the kings of the earth with the multitude of thy

Ophir, the Land of Gold, may have been the region near the ruined city of Zimbabwe; if so, the Phoenicians would have reached it most easily by sailing up the great Zambezi.

riches and of thy merchandise . . . All the inhabitants of the isles shall be astonished at thee, and their kings shall be sore afraid, they shall be troubled in their countenance. The merchants among the people shall hiss at thee; thou shalt be a terror, and never shalt be any more."

But the Phoenicians were to fill yet another page in the book of discovery. This time it is Herodotus, the "Father of History" himself, who writes in the 5th century B.C.: "For Libya [Africa] furnishes proofs about itself that it is surrounded by sea, except so much of it as borders upon Asia; and this fact was shown by Necho, King of the Egyptians, first of all those about whom we have knowledge. He, when he had ceased digging the canal which goes through from the Nile to the Arabian Gulf, sent Phoenicians with ships, bidding them sail and come back to Egypt. The Phoenicians therefore set forth from the Erythraean Sea and sailed through the Southern Sea; and when autumn came they would put to shore and sow the land wherever in Libya they might happen to be as they sailed, and then they waited for the harvest; and having reaped the corn they would sail on, so that after two years had elapsed in the third year they turned through the Pillars of Hercules [the Pillars of Melcarth] and arrived again in Egypt. And they reported a thing

21

which I cannot believe, but another man may, namely that in sailing round Libya they had the sun on their right hand."

Pharaoh Necho reigned from 609 to 593 B.C. He had the old canal between the Nile and the Red Sea put into order once more, and it was along this route that the Phoenicians sailed out with their ships. It is possible that they made their start in late summer and had to row against the north-east monsoon for parts of the time, but once around Cape Guardafui they would have had the wind with them. Further help round the Cape of Good Hope would have been given by the Mozambique and Agulhas currents. This is perhaps where they made their first halt to sow their corn and harvest it before moving on along the African west coast with the south-west trade-winds. They would have had to have reverted to the oars again to cross the doldrum belt and battle their way forward against the north-east trade-winds before they were once again able to sow and reap their corn somewhere on the coast south of the deserts. From there the route past the Pillars of Melcarth and home across the summer Mediterranean would not have been difficult.

They could well have taken this route, but many scholars have doubted that they did so. Herodotus' remark that they "had the sun on their right hand" must of course be interpreted that they had seen the sun in the north. He entertained doubts about this observation, but it is evidence for us that they at least sailed south of the Equator. Many of the scholars who disbelieve that the Egyptians, Phoenicians and other early seafarers ever did make long ocean voyages state that the ships of those times were not sufficiently seaworthy, even though we know very little about them. However, the pictures of the

Punt ships at Deir el-Bahri have convinced me of the relative seaworthiness of the Egyptian vessels. That few historians of today might be willing to make a long ocean voyage in such a ship is quite another matter. — Let us then believe, with Herodotus, that the Phoenicians were the first to circumnavigate Africa.

Phocaea, Miletus and Carthage

During the period of Phoenician trade supremacy in the Mediterranean, new waves of conquerors had forced their way down into Greece. It was only by the 9th century B.C. that conditions had again become settled and the Greek world had taken the shape which it was, on the whole, to keep through its greatest age. The Greek mainland, the islands in the Aegean, Crete, Cyprus and the west coast of Asia Minor were under the rule of independent cities which, on the whole, kept the peace with each other. The Greeks began to reappear on the maritime scene as much as 150 years before the fall of Tyre, and they were soon to set about colonizing the distant shores of the Mediterranean.

But their colonization, unlike that of the Phoenicians, was not methodically carried out with the intention of creating support stations for the trade routes. The Greeks had not yet become traders. They were mainly farmers, and it was over-population and internal political conflict which caused a great many of them to seek new homes abroad. Ships with emigrants left from almost every independent city—from Corinth in particular—their goals

22

lying chiefly in Sicily, in southern Italy and in North Africa to the east of the Gulf of Sidra.

The inhabitants of Phocaea on the western coast of Asia Minor were of bolder spirit than other Greeks, and they are said to have sailed not in trading vessels but in long "penteconters", warships which were rowed by fifty men. They pushed far up into the Adriatic and reached the mouth of the Po; they founded Massalia (Marseille) at the mouth of the Rhône; they fought an important naval battle with the Carthaginians in their attempts to colonize Corsica; they dug themselves in on the east coast of Spain; and it is related that they sailed out through the Pillars of Melcarth, which they called the Pillars of Hercules, and traded for tin and silver in Tartessus.

The inhabitants of the remarkable city of Miletus in Asia Minor turned to the north-east, forced the Hellespont and the Bosporus, and sailed bravely out into the vast Black Sea—waters which before that time were almost unknown. The classical legend of the voyage of the Argonauts, which together with the Odyssey ranked among the favourite reading matter of the Greeks, did certainly describe an early Greek voyage on this sea, but the narrative related that it was so full of dangers that the Greeks called it *Pontos Axeinos*—the hostile sea. By about the year 800 B.C., Milesian seafarers had founded a colony on the south shores of the sea, and two hundred years later they had colonies all round it, finding it in no way to be hostile. They were in fact to come to call it *Pontos Euxeinos*—the friendly sea. It appears as if the Milesians also traded with people far north and north-east of the Black Sea. Herodotus tells of Aristeas from the city of Proconnesus on the Sea of Marmora who journeyed to the Issedones, and it is believed that those people lived

In the 8th century B.C. emigrants from the overcrowded states of Greece sailed to find new homes, and thus came to establish bases for later Greek trade.

on the other side of the Ural Mountains beyond the vast dominions of the Scythians. And Greek tapestries have indeed been found south of Lake Baikal in Mongolia.

The fall of Tyre also brought about the end of independent Phoenician activity in the eastern Mediterranean, but to the west there was a well-established system of colonies and trading stations which were now taken over by Carthage. The Phoenician Carthaginians were not, like the Greeks, mainly a farming people; they were merchants, shipowners and managers of plantations whose lot it was to supervise the functioning of a ready-made trading system. They built new cities in the south and the east along the Gulf of Sidra as defence against the ever-advancing Greeks, and they took new possessions in the vicinity of the Pillars of Melcarth, on the Balearic Islands and on Sardinia. In their struggle against the Phocaeans they now and again joined forces with the Etruscans who long previously had settled in northern Italy. In order to gain complete control of the trade in silver and tin, the Carthaginians destroyed Tartessus. But it was found impossible to get large enough quantities of tin from the mines in Spain, and so people became dependent on the import of the metal from the "Cassiterides" —the Tin Islands which lay somewhere in the unknown north.

23

The Tin Islands

In order to discover the way to the rich tin mines for themselves, the Carthaginians sent an expedition north along the coast of the Ocean under the leadership of Himilco about 525 B.C. In his *Natural History*, Pliny the Elder mentions the journey in short: "When Carthage was at the height of her power, Hanno journeyed from Gades to the bounds of Arabia and told of his voyage in writing, as did Himilco who at the same time had been sent to explore the outermost bounds of Europe."

Unfortunately almost nothing of Himilco's report has come down to us. The only source we have is in Avienus' *Ora Maritima,* a didactic poem from the 5th century A.D. which is based on Greek legends. He, too, refers only briefly and vaguely to Himilco. He says that the Tartessians used to sail to the land of the Oestrymnians, and that later the Carthaginians and those that lived near the Pillars of Hercules also went there. He allows Himilco to say that the journey to Oestrymnia took four months, that he met with great difficulties in the way of dead calms, shallows, seaweed that impeded the progress of the vessels, seas that sank so that the water hardly covered the keels, heavy mists and all sorts of animals of the sea and monsters of the deep.

A four-month voyage north is a long one, and we may presume that Himilco made careful exploration of the coastline and perhaps even founded colonies before finally reaching the land of the Oestrymnians which without a doubt was southern England—possessing as it does all

the difficulties of tidal flow for a man from the tideless Mediterranean, and furthermore possessing the mists and calms described. It was in Cornwall he found the mines which had long supplied the peoples of the Mediterranean with tin.

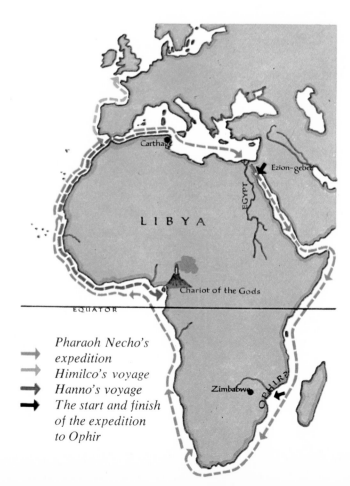

Pharaoh Necho's expedition
Himilco's voyage
Hanno's voyage
The start and finish of the expedition to Ophir

Hanno's Voyage to the Chariot of the Gods

According to Pliny, Hanno the Carthaginian sailed "to the bounds of Arabia" at the same time as Himilco journeyed north. Hanno's report has not been entirely lost, since it has come down to us in relatively unchanged form in a Greek transcription from the 10th century A.D. It is to be found in *Codex Heidelbergensis 398*, and runs as follows:

"1. It was decided that the Carthaginians should send Hanno on a voyage beyond the Pillars of Hercules to found Libyo-Phoenician cities there. And he departed with sixty ships of fifty oarsmen apiece and a total of 30,000 men and women, together with provisions and other necessities.

2. When we had set sail and passed the Pillars, we founded the first city and called it Thymiatherion. Below it lay a great plain.

3. We journeyed from here to the west and came to Soloeis, a promontory in Libya which is covered with trees.

4. There we built an altar to Poseidon and then journeyed on for half a day to the east until we came to a marshy region full of tall, dense reeds which was lying not far from the sea. Here there were elephants and large numbers of other grazing creatures.

5. Having journeyed on for a day beyond the marshy region, we placed new inhabitants in cities by the sea which we called Carikon Teichos, Acra, Melitte and Arambys.

A Carthaginian ship sails out through the Pillars of Melcarth. To the left, Africa and the Sierra Bullones (at modern Ceuta); to the right, Spain and Gibraltar.

6. Passing on from here, we came to the great river of Lixus which flows out of Libya.

7. Beyond them there are wild Ethiopians who inhabit a country full of wild animals. This is broken off by high mountains where it is said that the river Lixus rises. But people of a different appearance, the Troglodytes, are said to live in the mountain gorges, of whom the Lixites had to say that they run faster than horses.

8. Then we journeyed two days to the south past desert land, taking with us Lixite interpreters, and then a further day to the east. There, in a silted-up bay of the sea, we came across a small island, five stadia in circumference. We caused colonists to settle there and called the island Cerne. From our journey, we came to the conclusion that it lay directly opposite Carthage, since the voyage from Carthage to the Pillars was as long as from the Pillars to Cerne.

9. From here we came to a large river, Chretes by name, and to a lake. In this lake there are three islands, larger than Cerne. After a day's journey from here we came to the end of the lake, beyond which rose great mountains. These were inhabited by forest dwellers who were attired in the skins of animals and who sought to stop us from landing by hurling stones at us.

10. Moving on from here, we came to a large, broad

25

The Cameroons Mountain in eruption.

river which was full of crocodiles and hippopotami. Then we made about and returned to Cerne.

11. We journeyed another 12 days to the south, following the coast. There were Ethiopians living everywhere, but they fled instead of waiting for us. Not even the Lixites who were with us understood their language.

12. On the last day we came in sight of great, wooded mountains. The trees had a pleasant smell and were of many kinds.

13. It took us two whole days to sail round these mountains, after which we came into a vast ocean bay, the opposite mainland shore of which was level country. Every now and then during the night we saw the flames of fires, at times in fair numbers, at other times only few of them.

14. We took on water and journeyed on for five days along the coast until we came to a large bay which according to our interpreters was called the Western Horn. In it there was a large island, and on the island was a salt lake with yet another island. We made our way thither. In the daytime we could see nothing but forest, but at night we saw many fires. We heard the sound of pipes and cymbals, the rumble of drums and mighty cries. This instilled fear in us, and our soothsayers ordered us to leave the island.

15. We passed on with all speed and sailed along a burning yet sweet-smelling region where streams of fire ran out into the sea. We could not go ashore because of the heat.

16. In the grip of fear, we made all haste from this place also. On the four nights following we saw land covered in flames. In the centre of the land was a high pyre, larger than the others, which seemed to reach to the stars. In the daytime it proved to be a high mountain which is called the Chariot of the Gods.

17. We journeyed on from here for three days past streams of fire and came to a bay which is called the Southern Horn.

18. On the other side of the bay lay an island, similar to the former. For this too had a lake, and in the lake was another island which was inhabited by forest dwellers. The greater part of them consisted of women with long-haired bodies, and our interpreters called them 'gorillas'. We pursued the men but were unable to seize any of them

because they fled and climbed up steep cliffs and defended themselves with stones. We captured three women, but they bit and scratched their captors and would not go with them. We killed and skinned them and took the hides to Carthage with us. We did not journey farther than this since our provisions were beginning to run low."

Such is Hanno's narrative.

The interpretations of it have been many, but I do not wish to complicate things by going into the matter. A number of misunderstandings and errors in transcription have doubtless found their way into the text with the transcriptions of the centuries. We must thus accept the statement that 30,000 people managed to board only 60 ships as an error and hardly a statement made by the sober Hanno. The entire first section also seems to have been re-drafted in comparison with the rest which is written in "we" form. It is also possible that certain omissions have been made. The Greek historian and philosopher Arrian, who lived during the 2nd century A.D., gives a somewhat clearer picture of the route in his very short version of the voyage. He writes: "Hanno the African departed from Carthage, passed through the Pillars of Hercules out into the ocean, and, leaving Libya on his left hand, sailed for 35 days until he turned his vessel to the east. Having once again turned to the south, he found himself in great difficulties—much lack of water and great heat, together with fiery streams . . ."

Many of the places mentioned in the narrative are today impossible to identify. The promontory of Soloeis is most approximate to Cape Ghir, and the river Lixus is Oued ed Dra in southern Morocco, just as the Chretes is Saguia el Hamra. No one has been able to identify the position of Cerne, Hanno's southernmost colony, but it is known that it was still in existence four hundred years after it was founded. The fiery Chariot of the Gods with its streams of fire was probably an erupting volcano with its streams of molten lava. And the first such volcano we come across on his way lies in the high Cameroons Mountain which is indeed impressive enough to be called the Chariot of the Gods. That Hanno did in fact journey down into the Gulf of Guinea is also borne out by Arrian's summary of the voyage: first south, then to the east, then again to the south where the difficulties were met with.

Pliny's statement that he was to have sailed "to the bounds of Arabia" should not be taken literally. At that time people had no idea of the real size of Africa, and the length of the voyage made the geographers think that he had sailed to the southern extremity of Africa, where the people of those days believed that Arabia ended. At all events, Hanno's feat must be placed among the greatest in the history of exploration, even though it was not to have any practical consequences. In a few summer months around the year 525 B.C. he had explored a stretch of coastline which it was to take the Portuguese, almost two thousand years later, fifty-six years to rediscover.

According to tradition, the two Greek epic poems, "The Iliad" and "The Odyssey", were written by a blind poet called Homer, but later investigators believe that it was a multiple authorship. Although the poems have been dated by scholars to about the 9th century B.C., the events they describe are of much earlier date. The poems contain details which, when taken together, give us some idea of contemporary Greek views about the shape of the earth. — Their world is like a plateau on the top of a mountain; inside this, close to the surface of the earth, lies the House of Hades, the realm of Death, and beneath it Tartarus, the realm of Eternal Darkness. The plateau of the earth is surrounded by Oceanus, the world-river, and from its periphery rises the fixed dome of the sky. The sun, the moon and the stars rise from the waters at the edge of the dome, move in an arc above the earth, and then sink once again into the sea to complete their course beneath Oceanus. The atmosphere above the mountain of the earth is thick with clouds and mist, but higher up is the clear Aether with its starry ceiling.

The Persian Empire

About the middle of the 6th century B.C., Cyrus the Great, King of Persia, began to expand his dominions. His armies crushed the Babylonian Empire and conquered the whole of Asia Minor. Cambyses, his son, continued the expansion and, with the support of a Samian and Phoenician navy, conquered Egypt, whence he penetrated to the oasis of Siwa in the Libyan desert and to Ethiopia in the south. He also had plans for the conquest of Carthage, but since the Phoenicians in his navy refused to fight against their own kinsmen he had to abandon the idea. Darius the Great, his successor, forced his way east as far as the Aral Sea and the countries bordering on the Indus; in the north he invaded Scythia (the Ukraine); this invasion failed, but he did succeed in conquering Thrace,

between the Aegean and the Danube. Then he turned against Greece herself and suffered a decisive defeat at Marathon. Xerxes, his son, continued the war against the Greeks, but after his defeat at Salamis he went home, and with his withdrawal came the decline of the Persian Empire.

Scylax in the Indian Ocean

Sea routes between India and Arabia have doubtless existed for a very long time indeed, but according to history the first Westerner to sail these waters was Scylax the Greek from Caryanda in Asia Minor. He was presumably one of the commanders in Darius' fleet, and, before the campaign against India, he was sent by the Persian king in 518 on an expedition to discover the mouth of the Indus and from this spot to investigate the coastline to the Persian Gulf and the Red Sea.

Herodotus writes of the journey: "Of Asia, the greater part was explored by Darius, who desiring to know of the river Indus, which is a second river producing crocodiles of all the rivers in the world—to know, I say, of this River where it runs out into the sea, sent with ships, besides others whom he trusted to speak the truth, Scylax also, a man of Caryanda. These starting from the city of Caspatyrus and the land of Pactyica, sailed down the river towards the east and the sunrising to the sea; and then sailing over the sea westwards they came in the thirtieth month to that place from whence the King of the Egyp-

tians had sent out the Phoenicians of whom I spoke before, to sail round Libya. After these had made their voyage round the coast, Darius both subdued the Indians and made use of this sea. Thus Asia also, excepting the parts of it which are towards the rising sun, has been found to be similar to Libya."

Certain scholars have tried to identify Caspatyrus as Kabul, but Kabul lies 6,900 feet above sea level, and it is only much lower down that the River Kabul—a tributary of the Indus—becomes navigable. The expedition could have started on its voyage from here. Herodotus' remark that they sailed towards the east most probably did not come from Scylax himself, since the Indus flows mainly towards the south-west. But in Herodotus' time the size of Asia was not known, and he must therefore have concluded that such a distant river as the Indus would naturally have run towards the east, towards the outermost edge of the world, which was envisaged as a disc at that time.

In Egypt, Darius had cleared the old canal to the Red Sea, and it was through this that Scylax and his followers returned to the Mediterranean. Beside the canal Darius erected four monuments, and on one of them we are still able to read the following: "This is I, King Darius, the Persian, who speak. From Persia I conquered Egypt. By my order this canal was dug from the river which is called the Nile and runs through Egypt, to the sea which passes out from Persia. This canal was dug in the manner I willed, and ships sailed through it from Egypt all the way to Persia, according to my wishes."

Scylax sails down the Indus. In the foreground a banyan tree with aerial roots. — The map shows Scylax' voyage from Caspatyrus to Egypt.

For many centuries philosophers and geographers flourished in the port of Miletus in Asia Minor; the first of the Milesian scientists is thought to have been Thales, who was born about 624 B.C. He saw the earth as one vast hollow sphere (1), whose lower half was full of water, Oceanus, on which the disc of the earth floated freely about. The upper half of the sphere consisted of air, and above the air was the aether, in which the sun, the moon and the stars coursed.

Anaximander, thirty years younger than his master Thales, saw the earth as a thick disc freely suspended inside the world sphere (2). For him, Oceanus was merely a broad belt round the mainland, and was itself encircled by the mountains at the rim of the earth disc, which were ʳo distant that no one had been able to sail to them. According to tradition, Anaximander drew the first map of the world, but no one knows what it looked like.

Hecataeus, who is considered to have been the greatest geographer before Herodotus, was also born in Miletus. About 500 B.C. he engraved a map of the world on a copper plate (3), and Herodotus says that Aristagoras, the ruler of Miletus, showed such a map to Cleomenes, King of the Spartans, when discussing plans for an expedition against the Persians. However, Cleomenes saw from the map that Susa, the Persian capital, was three months' march from the Aegean coast, and he would have no more to do with the plan. The map has disappeared, but Hecataeus' commentaries on it have made a reconstruction possible.

The great Pythagoras from Samos, who founded a religious order in the city of Croton in the 6th century B.C., was probably the first to maintain that the earth and the planets were round. At any rate, the Pythagoreans, the members of his order, pictured the Cosmos, or Universe, as a hollow sphere at the centre of which was the central fire, the Hearth of the Universe; this lay so far from the earth that it could not be seen (4). Revolving round this, like concentric globes, were ten ethereal spheres. One was the sphere of the fixed stars, then came the spheres containing the five known planets, the earth, the moon and the sun, and—last of all, to make up the Holy Number, ten—yet another "counter-earth". When the ethereal spheres with their round orbs revolved about the central fire, a wonderful, unceasing harmony was produced—the music of the spheres.

Parmenides of Elea was probably the first to maintain in public that the earth was a sphere; in about 470 B.C. he published a didactic poem entitled "About Nature". He thought the universe to be geocentric—that is, he believed that the earth was suspended in the centre of the World Sphere. It is probable that he also thought that the earth was divided into five climatic zones (5), one broad torrid zone about the Equator, two temperate zones and two cold zones nearest the poles.

The great philosopher Plato, who taught about a

hundred years after Parmenides, combined Anaximander's and Parmenides' views of the world, seeing the earth as an enormous sphere whose surface was covered with large craters (6). The entire known world, Oceanus and all, he placed inside the uppermost crater.

Eudoxus of Cnidus, Plato's contemporary, tried to measure the size of the earth (7). He calculated that the

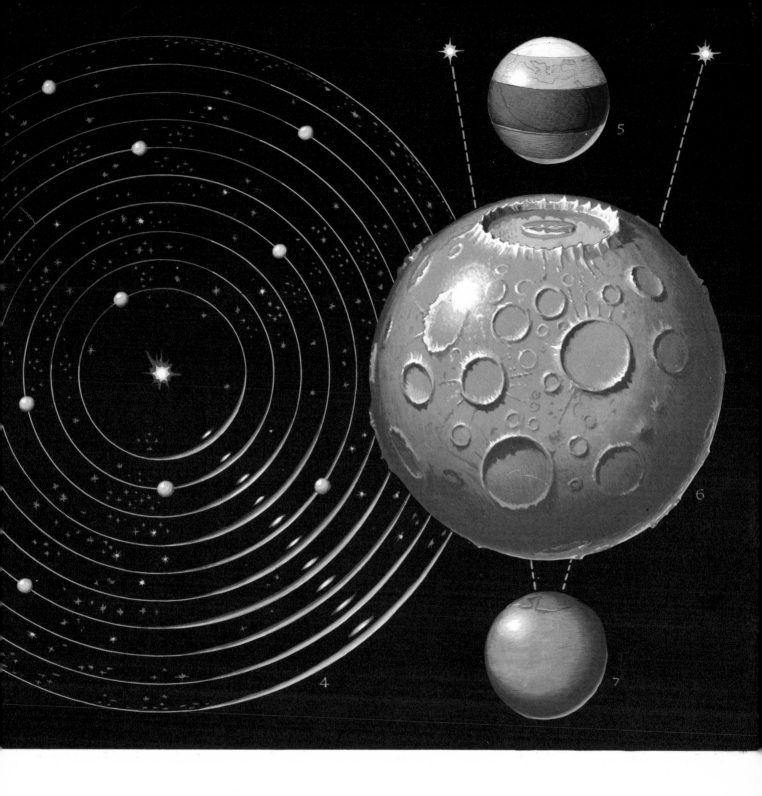

distance from the Hellespont to Syene (modern Aswan) in southern Egypt was 20,000 stades, and then measured the angle between the star in the zenith over the Hellespont and that in the zenith over Syene. His result was 1/15th of a great circle, and thus the distance from the Hellespont to Syene would correspond to 1/15th of the circumference of the earth, i.e. the circumference was 15 × 20,000 stades = 300,000 stades (about 35,000 miles). The real circumference of the earth is about 25,000 miles. Eudoxus' error was not due to his method, which was both correct and brilliant, but because he could not obtain the exact measurements of the distance from the Hellespont to Syene. Nevertheless, he had arrived at an approximation.

31

Herodotus' Geography

Herodotus, the "Father of History", was born at Halicarnassus in 484 B.C. His family was comfortably off and gave him the best possible education, and he was able to increase his knowledge of countries and peoples by much travel. The book he wrote on the Persian Wars has become both a general history of mankind and a description of almost the whole world as known to his contemporaries. Although many of his descriptions and interpretations are too fantastic for us to swallow, he was not entirely uncritical. He saw his surroundings far more realistically than did most of his contemporaries; sometimes he even goes to the extent of doubting the truth of a story he reports at second-hand. We shall have to believe that he was familiar with theories about the sphericity of the earth, but even though he was often critical of other geographers he nevertheless seems to have accepted the old belief of the world as a disc.

Scattered throughout his text is so much information about countries and rivers and seas and their relative size and position that many have tried to draw maps of Herodotus' world from it. Not wishing to be outdone here myself, I shall quote the most important passages which have led to his world picture as I see it.

Herodotus writes: "And I laugh when I see that, though many before this have drawn maps of the Earth, yet no one has set the matter forth in an intelligent way; seeing that they draw Oceanus flowing round the Earth, which is circular exactly as if drawn with compasses, and they make Asia equal in size to Europe . . . I wonder then at those who have parted off and divided the world into Libya, Asia and Europe, since the difference between these is not small; for in length Europe extends along by both, while in breadth it is clear to me that it is beyond comparison larger; for Libya furnishes proofs about itself that it is surrounded by sea, except so much of it as borders upon Asia. [Then follows the narrative of the Phoenician voyage round Libya, see p. 21, and further on the story of the voyage made by Scylax, see p. 28] . . . Thus Asia also, excepting the parts of it which are towards the rising sun, has been found to be similar to Libya [i.e. surrounded by sea]. As to Europe, however, it is clearly not known by any, either as regards the parts which are towards the rising sun or those towards the north, whether it be surrounded by sea . . .

"The Persians inhabit Asia extending to the Southern Sea, which is called the Erythraean [i.e. the 'red' sea. — The Indian Ocean was called the 'red' sea during the entire classical era; it was only during the Middle Ages that the denomination was transferred to the Red Sea proper] . . . This then [Asia Minor] is one of the peninsulas, and the other beginning from the land of the Persians stretches along to the Erythraean Sea, including Persia and next after it Assyria, and Arabia after Assyria; and this ends, or rather is commonly supposed to end, at the Arabian Gulf [the Red Sea], into which Darius conducted a canal from the Nile . . . With respect to the voyage along it [i.e. Herodotus' Arabian Gulf], one who set out from the innermost point to sail out through it into the open sea, would spend forty days upon the voyage, using oars; and with respect to breadth, where the gulf is broadest it is half a day's sail across . . .

"And Asia is inhabited as far as the Indian land; but from this onwards towards the east it becomes desert, nor can anyone say what manner of land it is . . . Then again Arabia is the furthest of inhabited lands in the direction of the midday [i.e. south] . . . As one passes beyond the place of the midday, the Ethiopian land is that which extends furthest of all inhabited lands towards the sunset [i.e. south-west] . . .

"For the Nile flows from Libya and cuts Libya through in the midst, and as I conjecture, judging of what is not known by that which is evident to the view, it starts at a distance from its mouth equal to that of the Ister [Here Herodotus means that the source of the Nile is as far west as that of the Ister = Danube]; for the River Ister begins from the Celti and the city of Pyrene [the Pyrenees?] and so runs that it divides Europe in the midst (now the Celti are outside the Pillars of Hercules and border upon the Cynetes, who dwell furthest towards the sunset of all those who have their dwelling in Europe); and the Ister ends, having its course through the whole of Europe, by flowing into the Euxine Sea at the place where the Milesians have their settlement at Istria. Now the Ister, since it flows through land which is inhabited, is known by the reports of many; but of the sources of the Nile no one can give an account, for the part of Libya

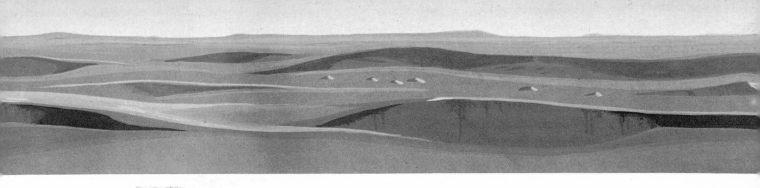

through which it flows is uninhabited and desert . . .

"For all that sea which the Hellenes navigate, and the sea beyond the Pillars, which is called Atlantis, and the Erythraean Sea are in fact all one, but the Caspian is separate and lies apart by itself. In length it is a voyage of fifteen days if one uses oars, and in breadth, where it is broadest, a voyage of eight days. On the side towards the west of this sea the Caucasus runs along by it, which is of all mountain ranges both the greatest in extent and the loftiest . . . while towards the east and the rising sun a limitless plain succeeds . . .

"And taking his seat at the temple he [Darius] gazed upon the Pontus [the Euxine], which is a sight well worth seeing. Of all seas it is indeed the most marvellous in its nature. The length of it is eleven thousand one hundred furlongs and the breadth, where it is broadest, three thousand three hundred . . . This Pontus also has a lake which has its outlet into it, which lake is not much less in size than the Pontus itself, and it is called Maeotis [the Sea of Azov] and 'Mother of the Pontus'."

Herodotus tells of five youths from the country of the Nasamones on the Gulf of Sidra, who pushed down through the desert to the south-west until they came to a great river which flowed east. They had seen crocodiles there, and so Herodotus was convinced that they had reached the Nile, which he believed to rise in West Africa. — It has been suggested that the Nasamones came upon the Niger near Timbuktu, but it is more probable that they got no furhter than to the Fezzan, where dried-up river beds bear witness of large prehistoric rivers, and where carvings of crocodiles have been found on rock faces. The dromedary was not yet in use in Africa in Herodotus' days, and it is difficult to believe that the youths could have crossed the sands of the desert as far as the Niger on horseback.

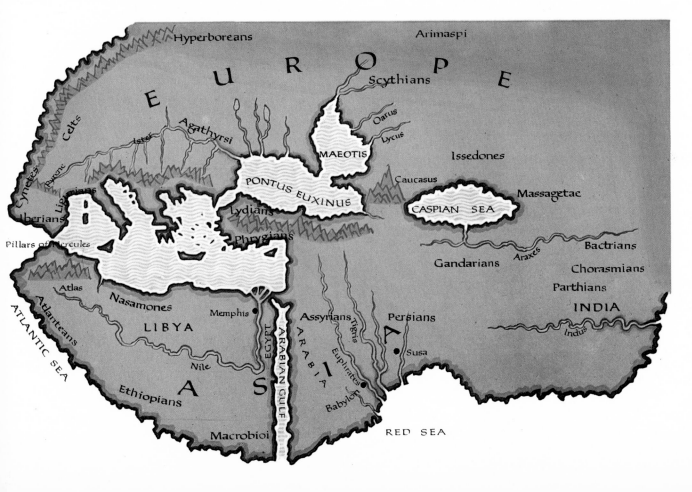

Pytheas' Voyage to Thule

One of the most progressive astronomers, geographers and travellers in antiquity was Pytheas. It appears that he wrote only one book, entitled *About the Ocean*, and only a few quotations from it are preserved in works by other classical authors. But he was often referred to and spoken of, and many geographers belittled his theories and statements in their own works, and it is in this way that we know at least something about his activities and can understand that in many ways he was far in advance of his times. He was the first to suggest that the tides were dependent on the phases of the moon, and the first to observe that the Pole Star was not the true centre around which the stars revolved.

Pytheas was born in Massalia about 380 B.C., and was probably about fifty years old when he made his long voyage of discovery, presumably at the request of the merchants of his home town, to the countries in the north. At that time the Carthaginians had full control of the Pillars of Hercules, the exit from the Mediterranean to the Great Ocean outside, and stopped everyone else from passing through, and we must therefore presume that Pytheas followed the old trade route north along the Rhône and then north-west along the Loire to the port of Corbilo—the Greeks of Massalia had long obtained their tin from the islands in the north along this route. It was from Corbilo that Pytheas really began his voyage of discovery.

He sailed past Cabaion (Cabestan Bay near Brest) and past Ouxisame (Ouessant) to the coveted tin coast. Diodorus, who lived during the 1st century B.C., wrote the following about Pytheas' observations: "The inhabitants of Britain who dwell about the promontory known as Belerium [Land's End] are especially hospitable to strangers and have adopted a civilized manner of life because of their intercourse with foreign merchants. They it is who work the tin, treating the bed which bears it in an ingenious manner . . . Then they work the tin into pieces the size of knuckle-bones and convey it to an island which lies off Britain and is called Ictis [St. Michael's Mount, Cornwall]; for at the time of ebb tide the space between this island and the mainland becomes dry and they can take the tin in large quantities over to the island on their wagons . . . On the island of Ictis the merchants purchase the tin of the natives and carry it from there across the strait to Gaul; and finally, making their way on foot through Gaul for some thirty days, they bring their wares on horseback to the mouth of the River Rhône."

Pytheas then continued north along the west coast of Britain and very likely paid a visit to Ierne (Erin = Ireland), Hebudes (the Hebrides) and Orcades (the Orkneys). Then he sailed for five days over the sea and came to Thule, "the outermost of all countries". And here we can turn to the Greek historian Geminus, from the 70's

B.C., who quotes Pytheas: "The barbarians showed us the place where the sun goes to rest. It so happened at that time that the night in these regions was very short, in certain places of two hours' duration, in others of three, so that the sun rose once again only a short time after it had set."

Most people believe that Pytheas' Thule was the region around present-day Trondheim, but there have, of course, been scholars who disagreed, and the Faeroes, Iceland and Greenland have all been suggested. While in Thule he was told that further north the sea turned solid and the sun never set in summertime; it was for this report, among other things, that learned men in the south derided him as a prodigious liar.

From Thule he sailed back to Britain, followed its east coast southwards—there is a source which states that he made the journey by land—and then crossed the North Sea to the North Frisian Islands and to Heligoland, which he calls Abalus. Pliny the Elder quotes him: "In the spring the waves wash up amber on the shores of this island. The inhabitants use it as fuel instead of wood . . . and also sell it to their neighbours the Teutons."

We must presume that Pytheas had by now completed his mission. He had investigated the route to the country of tin and amber, and so he returned home, possibly by the same route. But it is more probable that he followed the old amber route along the valleys of the Rhine and the Mosel down to the Rhône. Later he recorded his observations and experiences in a book. It may be that this was kept well guarded as a secret document in Massalia for a long time, but authors were gradually to obtain access to it and to quote from it and mock it, so that the

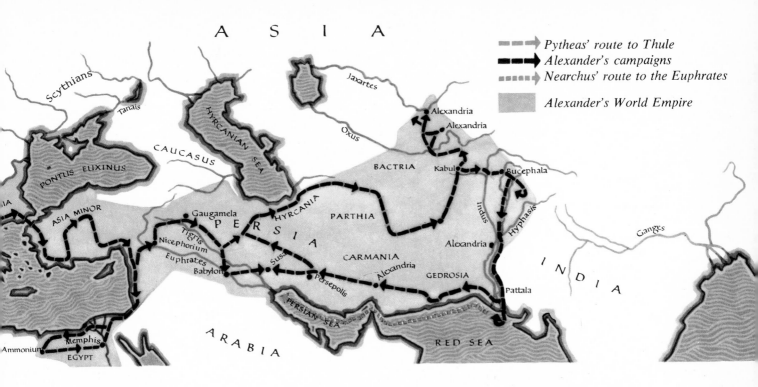

Map legend:
- Pytheas' route to Thule
- Alexander's campaigns
- Nearchus' route to the Euphrates
- Alexander's World Empire

Greeks of Massalia perhaps did not think the secret worth keeping any longer.

Alexander the Great

Without Alexander the Great it is possible that Greek culture and its ideals would never have survived for the benefit of Europe. After the successful defence against Persia, the feeling of unity which had existed between the small Greek states fell off, and, weakened by internal bickering, they were not able to stop the Persian king Artaxerxes II from reconquering the whole coast of Asia Minor. Philip of Macedonia managed to reunite the Greeks with arms and diplomacy, and he was chosen to lead them in an expedition against the Persians. Unfortunately, he was murdered before the expedition set off, and his place was taken by his son Alexander, known as the Great.

Alexander was twenty years old when he came to power in 336 B.C. He, too, needed to take to arms and use all his diplomacy to restore the shattered unity, but two years later he was able to set out with his army of 30,000 infantry and 5,000 cavalry on the long-planned expedition of reprisal against the Persians. In a lightning campaign he defeated the army of Darius III and conquered the whole of Asia Minor, Phoenicia, and Egypt, where he founded the city of Alexandria. Then the Persian king, who by this time had managed to gather together another army, was again utterly defeated at Gaugamela near the Tigris.

The campaigns which were carried out after Gauga-mela may be looked on as expeditions of discovery. One or two Europeans, Scylax for instance, had previously journeyed far into Asia while serving under the Persians, but Alexander's expedition was to afford deeper and more lasting understanding of the countries beyond the Tigris, including India. South of the Caspian Sea he forced his way into Hyrcania and then on into Bactria, and then crossed the rivers of the Oxus (the Amu Darya) and the Jaxartes (the Syr Darya). After a disappointing campaign against the always elusive Scythians he turned south towards India. He crossed the Indus, and it was only at the Hydaspes (the Jhelum) that he first met with any stubborn resistance. This came from the brave King Porus and his army, which included some elephants. Alexander defeated him. He then wanted to push on even further, to the Ganges and the eastern rim of the world, but after eight years of hardship his army had had enough, and he was unable to persuade his men to go any further east.

The speech he made to his army at the Hyphasis tells us of his idea of the world and of his plans for it, and I want to quote a part of the speech as it has come down to us in Arrian's *Anabasis*, our best authority on Alexander: "If, however, by these your labours Ionia is now in our hands, the Hellespont, both Phrygias, Cappadocia, Paphlagonia, Lydia, Caria, Lycia, Pamphylia, Phoenicia, Egypt, with the Greek part of Libya, part of Arabia, Lower Syria, Mesopotamia, Babylonia, Susia, Persia, Media, with all the nations subject to Persia and Media, and those that were not; if the regions beyond the Caspian gates, the parts beyond the Caucasus, and on the other side of the Tanais, Bactria, Hyrcania, the Hyrcanian

35

Sea; if we have driven the Scythians into the desert; if, besides all this, the river Indus runs through territory now our own, the Hydaspes likewise, the Acesines, and the Hydraotes, why do you hesitate to add to this your Macedonian empire the tribes beyond the Hyphasis? Do you fear lest tribesmen yet remaining may withstand your approach? Why, some of them surrender readily, some run away, and are captured, some desert their country and leave it open for you, which we have handed over to our allies and those who have voluntarily come over to us.

"I set no limit of labours to a man of spirit, save only the labours themselves, such as lead on to noble emprises. Yet should any desire to know what will be the limit of this our actual warfare, I may tell him that there remains no great stretch of land before us up to the river Ganges and the eastern sea. This sea, I assure you, you will find that the Hyrcanian Sea joins; for the great sea of Oceanus circles round the entire earth. Yes, and I shall moreover make clear to Macedonians and allies alike that the Indian Gulf forms but one stretch of water with the Persian Gulf, and the Hyrcanian Sea with the Indian Gulf. And from the Persian Gulf our fleet shall sail round to Libya, right up to the Pillars of Hercules; and from the Pillars all Libya that lies within is becoming ours; and all Asia likewise, and the boundaries of the Empire in Asia, those boundaries God set for the whole earth . . ."

We see that Alexander—and perhaps his teacher Aristotle, too—regarded the Hyrcanian Sea (the Caspian) as a part of the great ocean surrounding the world. This was contrary to Herodotus' view.

And so Alexander was forced to make the long journey home. At the Hydaspes he built a great fleet consisting of warships and transport vessels, and with him, as skilled crew members and builders, he had Phoenicians, Cypriots, Carians and Egyptians. The army embarked and sailed down river, and since the spring waters were running high it was an undertaking full of adventures, the vessels often running into obstacles and heeling over at dangerous angles. They came into the Indus and passed down to Pattala, where the river divided into two great arms. Here, however, they met with a storm which came from the sea, and the fleet sought shelter and anchored up against the banks.

Arrian writes: "There they anchored, and there followed the usual feature of the ocean, the receding tide; as

During the early spring of 329, Alexander exposed his army to one of its greatest trials by forcing it over the 11,500-foot Khawak Pass in Hindu Kush.

37

a result their ships were left high and dry. This Alexander's troops had not before known of, and it caused them no small amazement; but it caused them even more when the time passed by and the tide came up again and the ships floated. Such of the ships as the tide found comfortably settled on the mud floated off unharmed, and sailed once more without sustaining damage; but those that were caught on a drier bottom, and not remaining on an even keel, as the onrushing tide came in all together, either collided one with another, or were dashed upon the ground and shattered. These Alexander repaired as best he could, and then dispatched in two of his pinnaces down-stream some of his men to explore the island by which the natives affirmed he must anchor on his voyage down to meet the sea. This island they called Cilluta. The scouts reported that there was good anchorage by the island, and that it was large, with fresh water, so the rest of the fleet put in at the island; but Alexander himself with the best sailers from among his ships went to the far side of the island, to get a view of the outlet of the river into the sea, and see if it offered a safe passage out. So advancing about two hundred stades from the island they sighted a second island right out in the sea . . .

"Then on the next day, passing the mouths of the River Indus, he set sail to the high seas, to see, as he himself said, if any country stood out, near by, in the ocean; but in my own judgement chiefly that he might have voyaged in the Great Ocean beyond India . . .

"After his return to Pattala, Alexander sailed down to the ocean again by the other mouth of the Indus, to learn by which branch the outlet of the Indus to the ocean was safer; these mouths of the river Indus are eighteen hundred stades apart from one another . . .

"Proceeding by this passage he also reached the sea; discovering that the passage by this branch of the Indus was an easier one. He then anchored by the shore, and taking with him some of the cavalry went three days' march along the coast, observing the nature of the country for the coasting voyage, and ordering wells to be dug, so that as they sailed along they might be able to get water. Then he himself returned to his ships and sailed back to Pattala."

There are many contemporary, or almost contemporary, portraits of Alexander the Great, and all of them show the pensive face of a handsome young man. This picture of him on a coin shows him wearing Ammon's horns as a symbol of power; there was indeed a time when he asserted that he was of divine descent and the son of "Zeus Ammon of the Desert". — The most versatile of the classical scientists was Aristotle, the Greek philosopher who lived during the 4th century and who, among other things, was Alexander's teacher. Like Parmenides of Elea before him, he believed that the earth was the centre of the universe and that the planets and stars revolved round it in a complicated system of spheres. He said that all matter that gravitated towards a centre must be spherical in shape,

and he demonstrated the sphericity of the earth by observing the shadow it cast on the moon during lunar eclipses. He also asserted that the stars were living entities made of aether—spherical to be sure, but nevertheless divine and eternal. He saw the universe as a finite sphere with no outer space outside its limits.

But Alexander did not take his army home by sea. Arrian goes on to say: "On this Nearchus writes thus: Alexander had a vehement desire to sail the sea which stretches from India to Persia; but he disliked the length of the voyage and feared lest, meeting with some country desert or without roadsteads, or not properly provided with the fruits of the earth, his whole fleet might be destroyed; and this, being no small blot on his great achievements, might wreck all his happiness."

And so Alexander decided to march overland with the main part of his army to Persia. The fleet he sent under the command of Nearchus to explore the sea route and the coastline. The voyage of the fleet from the Indus to the mouth of the Euphrates took 130 days, 31 of which were spent at sea. It was a voyage of many adventures and founderings, and among the things met with was a large school of whales which were put to flight with trumpet calls. And yet it was the land route through the deserts which proved to be the more difficult, and the army suffered much from heat, thirst and hunger before it finally reached Persia after campaigning for ten years in all. — The Conqueror of the World here wished to make Babylon the capital of his dominions, and he was fully occupied with plans for new conquests when he suddenly fell ill and died in 323, only 32 years of age.

The importance of Alexander the Great for Europe's knowledge of the world and the world's knowledge of Greece can hardly be overstated. Natural scientists, geographers, historians and philosophers had accompanied him on his expedition and were able to record its findings. By wise diplomacy he had won friends among earlier enemies, and so political ties were made and new markets and trade routes came into being. He had founded and built Greek cities deep in Asia. And it was because of his expeditions that Europe first came to be conscious of India's existence.

The Ganges and Taprobane

Alexander's World Empire was, of course, too loosely connected to be able to continue as a single unit, and the confusion and struggle for power that arose at his premature death hastened the process of dissolution. Yet Alexander had founded over seventy cities, and these were colonized chiefly by Greeks and Macedonians from the always overcrowded mother countries. There were Greco-Macedonian colonies in Assyria and Babylonia, and in distant India. The city that rose to the greatest importance was Alexandria in Egypt, a city which was already predestined to become a junction for trade because of its advantageous position. And in fact it was not long before a large section of the Greek scientific and cultural élite moved to the new world city, which thus also came to be the intellectual capital of the age.

In India, immediately after the death of Alexander, King Chandragupta mustered several small kingdoms to fight against the Macedonians in the north-west, and it was not long before he managed to reconquer all the land east of the Indus. King Seleucus Nicator, Alexander's successor in Asia Minor and Syria, made diplomatic contact with Chandragupta about 300 B.C., and among his ambassadors to India was a scholar called Megasthenes who, according to Diodorus, was able to report the following: "Now India is four-sided in shape, and the side which faces east and that which faces south are embraced by the Great Sea, while that which faces north is separated by the Emodus range of mountains [the Himalayas] from that part of Scythia which is inhabited by the Scythians known as the Sacae; and the fourth side, which is turned toward the west, is marked off by the river known as the Indus, which is the largest of all

streams after the Nile. As for its magnitude, India as a whole, they say, extends from east to west twenty-eight thousand stades, and from north to south thirty-two thousand. And because it is of such magnitude, it is believed to take in a greater extent of the sun's course in summer [the part of the earth lying between the Tropic of Cancer and the Equator] than any other part of the world, and in many places at the Cape of India the gnomons of sundials may be seen which do not cast a shadow, while at night the Bears are not visible; in the most southerly parts not even Arcturus can be seen . . . There are found . . . much silver and gold, not a little copper and iron, and tin also and whatever else is suitable for adornment, necessity, and the trappings of war . . . The land of the Indians has also many large navigable rivers which have their sources in the mountains lying to the north and then flow through the level country; and not a few of these unite and empty into the river known as the Ganges. This river, which is thirty stades in width, flows from north to south and empties into the ocean, forming the boundary towards the east of the tribe of the Gandaridae, which possesses the greatest number of elephants and the largest in size."

Megasthenes was also one of the first Westerners to hear mention of Ceylon, which was most often called Taprobane by Europeans during the classical era. Pliny informs us of this: "That Taprobane is an island was established during the reign of Alexander and by his expeditions. Onesicritus, a commander of his fleet, writes that larger and more aggressive elephants are to be found there than in India itself, and Megasthenes says that a river divides the island and that the inhabitants, who are called Palaiogonians, produce more gold and larger pearls than the Indians."

Seleucus Nicator also sent an expedition to see if the Caspian was connected to the outer ocean. We do not

know how this was done, but Patrocles, its leader, reported that it did have an outlet at the northernmost part of the coast of India and that it therefore could be reached by ships from India!

The Ptolemies, the new Greek rulers of Egypt, also sent out expeditions to explore their part of the world empire. They founded cities and trading stations on the west coast of the Red Sea right the way down to Cape Guardafui, and in the south they pushed far into unknown "Ethiopia", mainly in order to hunt and capture elephants. But they also sought contact with Chandragupta's India, and in a short remark by Pliny we learn that their ambassador was a man by the name of Dionysius. This diplomatic contact did not, however, lead to any direct form of trade between India and Egypt. Alexander had never conquered Arabia, and his successors were unable to control the old trade route over the sea from India to the Persian Gulf and Arabia.

The ragged volcanic hills which rise from the low sandy shores of southern Arabia make Aden one of the best natural harbours in the world. It was doubtless used as such in prehistoric times, and under the Ptolemies it was to become of great importance for European trade.

The Ptolemies, like their great predecessors, cleared the canal to the Red Sea, but their ships sailed no further than to the trading stations in Eudaimon (Aden) and on the island of Dioscorides (Socotra) whither the coveted Indian goods came in Arabian, Indian and Sinhalese ships. The merchants in southern Arabia saw to it that no eastern or western power replaced them as intermediaries, and since they themselves produced incense and myrrh they also saw to it that no such goods were brought in from the east or the south.

41

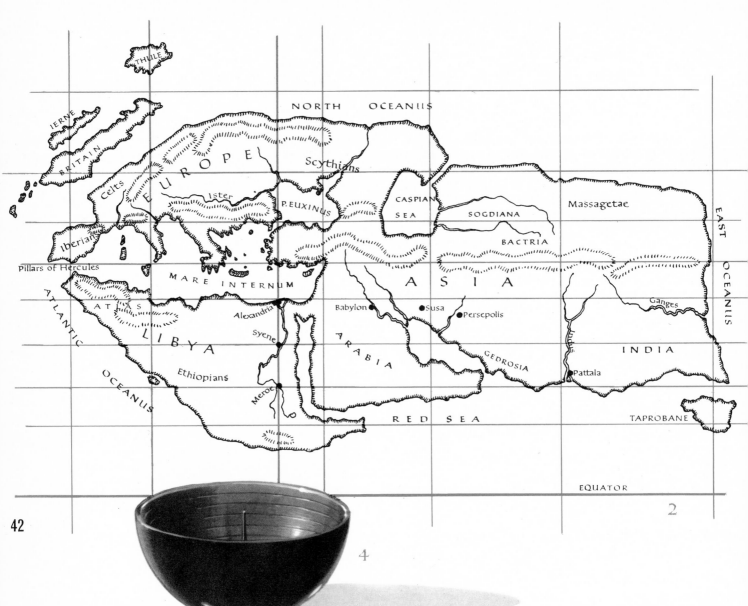

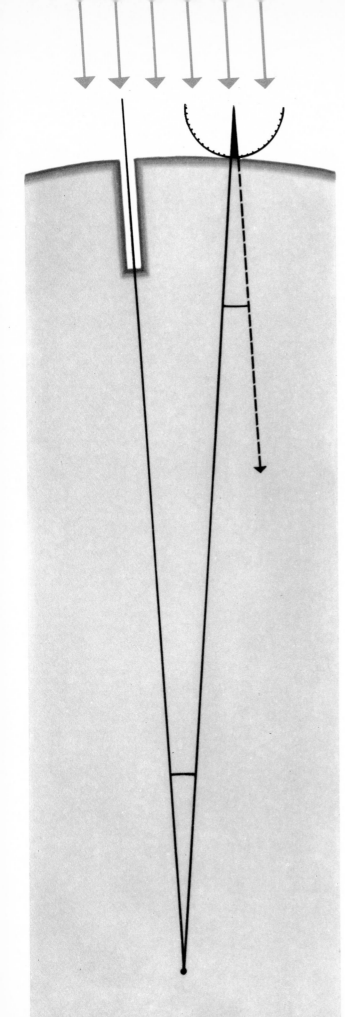

1. As early as 285 B.C., Aristarchus of Samos propounded the theory that the sun, and not the earth, was the centre of the universe, that the earth made a complete revolution round the sun once every year, and that it rotated on its own axis once every day. The theory found some support, but most people thought it was too bold.

2—3. Eratosthenes was born at Cyrene in North Africa in 276 B.C. He became head of the Academy and Library at Alexandria, and by measuring the latitudes of different places and the approximate distances between them he was able to construct a grid on which to draw his map of the world, a reconstruction of which is shown here. It is said that he understood the theoretical possibility of reaching India by sailing west across the Ocean. — Like Eudoxus, he tried to calculate the circumference of the earth. As his starting-point he chose Syene (modern Aswan) in southern Egypt, which was believed to lie on the northern tropic. There was a deep well there, and once a year, at the summer solstice, the sun was reflected in its waters, and was therefore at the zenith. On that very day he measured the angle of the sun at Alexandria, finding it to be 1/50th of the great circle. Since he calculated that Alexandria lay 5,000 stades due north of Syene, it was a simple matter for him to find the circumference of the earth to be 250,000 stades, i.e. $50 \times 5,000$. This is something like 28,500 miles. Since the true circumference is about 25,000 miles, his result is not at all bad.

4. When measuring latitudes, Eratosthenes used a hollow sundial, or scaphe, which had an indicator called a gnomon. The concentric rings inside the bowl marked the length of the shadow cast by the sun, and from these one could reckon the sun's altitude.

5. The first globe we know of was made by Crates at Pergamon in Asia Minor about 180 B.C. It showed the known mass of land and also three hypothetical continents which were separated from each other by the broad stretches of the Ocean. Here in reconstruction.

3

5

Eudoxus and the Hippalus Winds

The voyages of discovery hitherto dealt with were all state-inspired or the result of great joint trade interests. The first private explorer we hear mention of is Eudoxus from Cyzicus in Asia Minor who made his very remarkable journeys about 110 B.C. He was a relatively rich man who was able to spend a fortune on his interests, and he seemed to be possessed by an almost sporting lust for adventure. His story originates with the philosopher Poseidonius, who was somewhat younger than Eudoxus, and it comes down to us via the geographer Strabo, who lived about the beginning of the Christian era:

"Poseidonius tells the story of a certain Eudoxus of Cyzicus, a sacred ambassador and peace herald at the festival of Persephone. Eudoxus, the story goes, came to Egypt in the reign of Euergetes the Second [146—117 B.C.]; and he became associated with the king and the king's ministers, and particularly in connection with the voyages up the Nile; for he was a man inclined to admire the peculiarities of regions and was also not uninformed about them. Now it so happened, the story continues, that a certain Indian was brought to the king by the coastguards of the recess of the Arabian Gulf [the Red Sea], who said that they had found him half-dead and alone on a stranded ship, but that they did not know who he was or where he came from, since they did not understand his language; and the king gave the Indian into the charge of men who would teach him Greek, and when the Indian had learnt Greek, he related that on his voyage from India he by a strange mischance mistook his course and reached Egypt in safety, but only after having lost all his companions by starvation; and when his story was doubted, he promised to act as guide on the trip to India for the men who had been previously selected by the king; and of this party Eudoxus, also, became a member.

"So Eudoxus sailed away with presents; and he returned with a cargo of perfumes and precious stones . . . But Eudoxus was badly disappointed, for Euergetes took from him his entire cargo."

Today it is believed that Hippalus the Pilot accompanied Eudoxus on his voyage to India, and that the route which the Indian pilot showed them in gratitude for their saving his life was the monsoon route. The Arabians and Indians must, of course, have known and made use of the monsoon winds for centuries. These winds blow over the Indian Ocean from the north-east in winter and from the south-west in summer; if a man knows the right season

Of course it cannot be proved that Eudoxus reached right down to the Cameroons Mountain with his three ships on his first expedition, but his fearlessness and stubborn perseverance make it not unlikely.

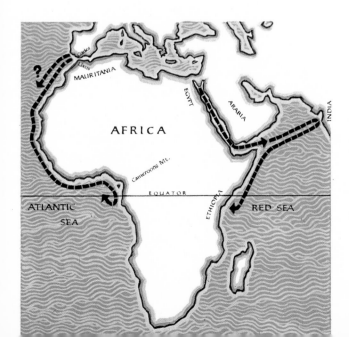

to choose, they will carry him straight across the sea in reasonable comfort. When direct passage from India to Egypt became more common, it was these winds that were used, and they came to be called the Hippalus Winds.

Poseidonius' story goes on in this way: "And after the death of Euergetes, his wife, Cleopatra, succeeded him on the throne; and so Eudoxus was again sent out by her also, and this time with a larger outfit. But on his return voyage he was driven out of his course by the winds to the south of Ethiopia [this presumably occurred while sailing from India with the north-east monsoon. He missed Cape Guardafui and ran too far to the south], and being driven to certain places he conciliated the people by sharing with them bread, wine, and dried figs (for they had no share of such things), and in return therefore he received a supply of fresh water and the guidance of pilots, and he also made a list of some of their words. And he found an end of a wooden prow that had come from a wrecked ship and had a horse carved on it; and when he learned that this piece of wreckage belonged to some voyagers who had been sailing from the west, he took it with him when he turned back upon his homeward voyage. And when he arrived safely in Egypt, inasmuch as Cleopatra no longer reigned but her son in her stead, he was

45

again deprived of everything, for it was discovered that he had stolen much property.

"But he brought the figurehead to the market-place and showed it to the shipmasters, and learned from them that it was a figurehead from Gades; for he was told that whereas the merchants of Gades fit out large ships, the poor men fit out small ships which they call 'horses' from the devices on the prows of their ships, and that they sail with these small ships on fishing voyages around the coast of Maurusia [Morocco] as far as the river Lixus; but some of the shipmasters, indeed, recognized the figure-head as having belonged to one of the ships that had sailed rather too far beyond the Lixus River and had not returned home safely.

"And from the above-mentioned fact Eudoxus conjectured that the circumnavigation of Libya [Africa] was possible, went home [to Cyzicus], placed all his property on a ship, and put out to sea. First he put in at Dicaearchia, then at Massalia, and then at the successive points along the coast until he came to Gades; and everywhere noisily proclaiming his scheme and making money by trafficking, he built a great ship and also two tow-boats like those used by pirates; and he put music-girls on board, and physicians, and other skilled men and finally set sail on the high sea on the way to India, favoured by constant western breezes. But since his companions became tired of the voyage, he sailed with a fair wind towards the land; though he did it against his will, for he feared the ebb and flow of the tides. And, indeed, what he feared actually came to pass: the ship ran aground —though so gently that it was not broken up all at once, and they succeeded in bringing safely to land the cargo and also most of the ship's timbers; and from these timbers he constructed a third boat about as large as a ship of fifty oars; and he continued his voyage, until he came to people who spoke the same words that he had made a list of on the former occasion [by this we must of course understand that he read the words aloud, and that the people understood them]; and forthwith he learnt this, at least, that the men in that region belonged to the same nation as those other Ethiopians, and also that they were neighbours to the kingdom of Bogus [Mauritania].

"Accordingly, he abandoned the voyage to India and turned back; and on the voyage along the coast, he espied and made note of an island that was well-watered and well-wooded but uninhabited. And when he reached Maurusia safely he disposed of his boats, travelled on foot to the court of Bogus, and advised him to take up this expedition on his own account . . . And when Eudoxus heard that he was being sent out, ostensibly, on the expedition as proposed by him, but in reality was going to be placed out on some desert island, he fled to the territory that was under Roman dominion, and thence crossed over to Iberia [Spain].

"And again he built a round ship and a long ship of

fifty oars, his purpose being to keep to the open sea with his long ship and to explore the coast with the round ship. He put on board agricultural implements, seeds, and carpenters, and again set out with a view to the same circumnavigation; his intention being, in case the voyage should be delayed, to spend the winter on the island he had previously observed. to sow the seed, reap the harvest therefrom, and then finish the voyage which he had decided upon at the outset. 'Now I,' says Poseidonius, 'have traced the story of Eudoxus to this point, but what happened afterwards probably the people of Gades and Iberia know.' "

And we know no more of Eudoxus' fate to this day. It is uncertain how far south he reached on his first voyage along the west coast of Africa, but linguists say that the words he had noted down probably came from one of the Bantu languages, and in order to be able to hear such

The pink areas on the map show the Roman Empire at its greatest extent, that is, during the reign of the Emperor Hadrian, 117—138 A.D.

a language on the west coast he would have had to have gone right the way down to the Cameroons. The large island with its many trees and good water supply could then be Fernando Póo. At all events he was one of the most remarkable seafarers that ever lived and the first to try to reach India by circumnavigating Africa.

The Roman Empire

Significant things had been taking place in the western Mediterranean, things which in the beginning did not seem to affect or trouble the Hellenistic states. Rome had already begun to extend her Imperium during the reign of Alexander, and later, over a period of about a hundred years, she was to gain control of almost the entire Mediterranean region. Carthage was crushed after long wars during which Rome learned the need for a powerful fleet, and when Sardinia, Corsica and Spain were also taken, the new world power turned east, took Macedonia and assumed the "protection" of Greece. At a later date, Pergamum, Rhodes and Egypt were also incorporated.

Roman legions also moved north towards the hitherto almost unknown parts of Europe, and the whole of Gaul, the Alpine countries and the greater part of Britain were conquered. The resistance of the Germans in the north made the Rhine and the Danube the natural boundaries in that region, and in the east, where the Parthians had put a stop to the Roman advance, the Euphrates became the natural boundary. Further south the deserts of Arabia barred all conquests. But the Mediterranean had become a Roman sea.

When the wars were over, the relatively peaceful period that followed naturally favoured trade. No longer hampered by aggression from several quarters, seaborne commerce in the Mediterranean flourished more than ever. The Romans had broken the Carthaginian stranglehold on the Pillars of Hercules in 206 B.C., but sixty years were to pass before they dared to grope their way carefully out along the ocean routes. Traffic along the old trade routes through Europe flourished, but most important of all was the Rome—Alexandria route, which saw to the transport of Egypt's cattle and corn and the bringing of spices, silk and precious stones from the countries somewhere in the East.

When Egypt became a Roman province in 31 B.C. the trade with India increased a great deal. Strabo says that before this hardly twenty ships a year had sailed out, but that now large fleets journeyed to India and "to the outermost point of Ethiopia" and returned with valuable

47

cargoes. He states that merchants seldom journeyed as far as the Ganges, and that trade was mainly centred around ports in the Bay of Bengal. Augustus had sent ten thousand men in a fleet consisting of eighty warships and a hundred trading vessels to conquer the western and southern parts of Arabia, but the men were overcome by heat and thirst and had to retire. It was during Nero's reign that the Arabs first came under Roman dominion, and Aden and Socotra became Roman colonies.

From the ports around the Bab el Mandeb Straits it was now possible to sail in a fortnight with the Hippalus Winds to Muziris (Cannanore) in India, where the vessels were loaded with pepper, drugs, dyes and precious stones —many of these goods coming from countries and islands in the East which Europeans were still almost wholly ignorant of. Further to the north at Barygaza (Broach) in the Gulf of Cambay the ships were loaded with the coveted goods that had come along the caravan routes from the country of the Seres (China), silk above all.

Indian ambassadors came to the Emperor Augustus at Samos as early as 20 B.C. with gifts of various kinds, including a tiger and a python. About 50 A.D. a Roman was driven by a storm to Ceylon, and a few years later a delegation was sent from that country to Nero's Rome to establish diplomatic relations. By this time not even the routes to China were unknown to the peoples of the Mediterranean. When the Romans sacked Jerusalem in 70 A.D. many Jews emigrated, and, according to Hebrew and Chinese inscriptions at Kaifeng, the first Jews came to China during the Han Dynasty.

48

In 24 A.D., Aelius Gallus, the Roman governor of
Egypt, embarked an army of ten thousand men to
Leuke Kome in Arabia by the order of the Emperor
Augustus. From there it was to proceed south on
an expedition of conquest along the coast to the
then, fertile region known as Arabia Felix, near the
Bab el Mandeb Straits. Strabo, the historian who
described the expedition (the red broken line on
the map), wrote of many cities which were taken
and destroyed, and he blames the failure of the
campaign chiefly on Syllaeus, the Arab ally who
is said to have led the army through waterless desert
and thus caused many to die of hunger and thirst.
Another historian says that there was a terrible
disease which could only be cured by treating the
sufferers with oil and wine, of which there was a
shortage. After six months' hardship the army had
had enough, and at the city of Marib in the land
of the Sabaeans it turned for home. Leuke Kome
was reached after sixty days. Only seven men are
said to have fallen in battle. The remainder—
exactly how many we do not know—died of hunger
and disease.

The following year, the Roman prefect Petronius
set out from Syene with thirteen thousand men on
a "campaign of revenge" against the Ethiopians
(the grey broken line on the map), reached Napata
and then turned back, for he found that the country
beyond was very difficult to cross. Syene remained
the southern limit of the Roman Empire.

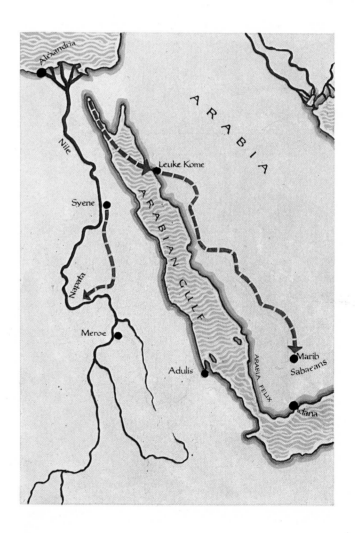

Periplus Maris Erythraei

It has been said that the Romans lacked interest in geography, that they merely counted the mileposts along their roads, whereas the Greeks attempted to map the world. And true it is that one of the most important geographical documents from Roman times, the *Periplus Maris Erythraei*—Navigation of the Red Sea (i.e. the Indian Ocean)—was written by an Egyptian Greek. We do not know his name, but it is believed that he was a merchant from Berenice on the Red Sea who had sailed with the Hippalus Winds in the Indian Ocean for many years, and who had probably also sailed to the Ganges and the Malay Peninsula. He wrote his navigational manual for the benefit of others in 90 A.D., and we are still able to read it in transcription today in the *Codex Heidelbergensis*. Let me quote a few passages:

"Two days' sail beyond, there lies the very last market-town in Azania, which is called Raphta [Dar-es-Salaam]; which has its name from the sewed boats already mentioned [small vessels whose boards are not pinned to each other but are sewn together are still to be found in the Indian Ocean]; in which there is ivory in great quantity, and tortoise-shell. Along this coast live men of piratical

habits, very great in stature, and under separate chiefs for each place. The Mopharitic chief governs it under some ancient right that subjects it to the sovereignty of the state that is become first in Arabia. And the people of Muza [Mocha] now hold it under his authority, and send thither many large ships using Arab captains and agents, who are familiar with the natives and intermarry with them, and who know the whole coast and understand the language.

"There are imported into these markets the lances made at Muza especially for this trade, and hatchets and daggers and awls, and various kinds of glass; and at some places a little wine, and wheat, not for trade, but to serve for getting the good-will of the savages. There are exported from these places a great quantity of ivory, but inferior to that of Adulis [the port of Zula on the Red Sea], and rhinoceros horn and tortoise-shell (which is in best demand after that from India), and a little palm-oil.

"And these markets of Azania are the very last in the continent that stretches down on the right hand from Berenice; for beyond these places the unexplored ocean curves around toward the west, and running along by the regions to the south of Ethiopia and Libya and Africa, it mingles with the western sea."

As to India, we are told that "among the market-towns

Elephant fights have been arranged in India and Ceylon since time immemorial for the entertainment of their princes and people.

of these countries, and the harbours where the ships put in from Limyrica [the Malabar Coast] and from the north, the most important are, in order as they lie, first Camara, then Poduca [Pondicherry], then Sopatma [Madras] . . . About the following region, the course trending toward the east, lying out at sea toward the west is the island Palaesimundu, called by the ancients Taprobane [Ceylon] . . . It produces pearls, transparent stones, muslins, and tortoise-shell.

"About these places is the region of Masalia [Masuli-patnam] stretching a great way along the coast before the inland country; a great amount of muslin is made there. Beyond this region, sailing toward the east and crossing the adjacent bay, there is the region of Dosarene, yielding the ivory known as Dosarenic. Beyond this, the course turning toward the north, there are many barbarous tribes, among whom are the Cirrhadae, a race of men with flattened noses, very savage; another tribe, the Bar-gysi; and the Horse-faces and the Long-faces, who are said to be cannibals.

"After these, the course turns toward the east again, and sailing with the ocean to the right and the shore remaining beyond to the left, the Ganges comes into view, and near it the very last land toward the east, Chryse [the Malay Peninsula]. There is a river near it called the Ganges, and it rises and falls in the same way as the Nile. On its bank is a market-town which has the same name as the river, Ganges. Through this place are brought malabathrum and Ganges spikenard and pearls, and mus-lins of the finest sorts, which are called Ganges muslins. It is said that there are gold-mines near these places, and there is a gold coin which is called *caltis*. And just oppo-site this river there is an island in the ocean, the last part of the inhabited world toward the east, under the rising sun itself; it is called Chryse; and it has the best tortoise-shell of all the places on the Erythraean Sea.

"After this region under the very north, the sea outside ends in a land called This, where there is a very great inland city called Thinae, from which raw silk and silk yarn and silk cloth are brought on foot through Bactria to Barygaza, and are also exported to Limyrica by way of the River Ganges. But the land of This is not easy of access; few men come from there, and seldom. The country lies under the Lesser Bear, and is said to border on the farthest parts of Pontus and the Caspian Sea, next to which lies Lake Maeotis [the Sea of Azov]; all of which empty into the ocean . . . The regions beyond these places are either difficult of access because of their excessive winters and great cold, or else cannot be sought out because of some divine influence."

51

The Routes to China

During the century before the birth of Christ, China had expanded to such an extent that it now reached to the bend of the Jaxartes and to the borders of the Parthian Empire. The Parthians bought all the silk they could that came by this route, and then resold it to the great Roman market. The Chinese wanted to establish direct contact with Rome, but this was not to the liking of Parthian trade policy. About 98 A.D. the Emperor of China sent a deputation under General Kan Ying with the object of reaching Rome, but he turned back in Parthia, and the Chinese annals tell us of the reasons for this. The Parthians had said this to him: "The sea is broad and great. With favourable wind one may reach Ta Tsin [the Roman Empire] in three months. When the winds are unfavourable, however, the voyage may take as much as two years. That is why we supply our vessels with provisions for three years. There is also something about the sea which makes a man extremely homesick. He who journeys out on to the waters is beset with melancholy. But if parents, wife and children are unimportant to the ambassador it will be only natural for him to sail."

Although the Parthians kept watch along the overland routes to the Land of Silk, it is highly probable that one or two Roman merchants managed to elude their vigilance. Ptolemy, the great geographer, tells of a certain "Maes, also called Titianus",—a Macedonian and son of a merchant—who about 100 A.D. was to have sent an expedition to the Seres. After a seven-month journey his men reached the "Tower of Stone"—perhaps the present-day Sian, then the capital of China. They estimated that the distance they had covered on their way there was 90,000 stades or about 10,000 miles.

It is related in the *Hou Han Shou*, the annals of the younger Han Dynasty, that musicians and jesters came to China from Rome in about 120 A.D. and that they performed before the very person of the Emperor. They had probably reached the eastern regions of India by sea and from there up along the caravan routes. The Chinese chronicler states that they themselves said: "We are men from the western Ocean. The western Ocean is the same as Ta Tsin [the Roman Empire]. Ta Tsin is reached via the land of Shan in the south-west."

Further on in the annals we come across a short description of this Ta Tsin: it seems to have been given by certain wily merchants from the West, who had let it be understood that they were ambassadors from Marcus Aurelius, and had thus found a friendly reception. They had arrived in China at the Annam border and brought with them gifts of ivory, rhinoceros horn and tortoise-shell. With regard to these simple presents the chronicler

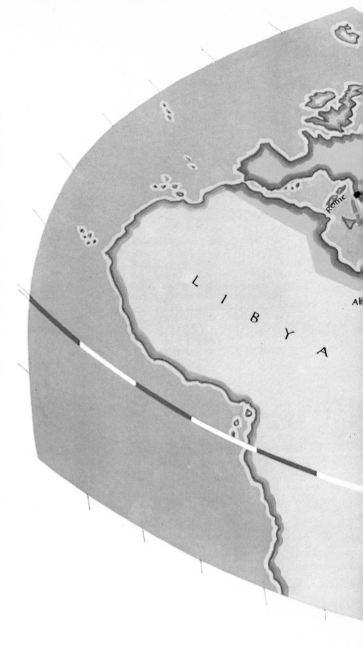

writes: "The list of their gifts did not, however, include any precious stones. This makes one believe that they have withheld them."

The description of the Roman Empire and its people follows: "This land is very extensive and embraces a great number of subjugated nations. The walls of the houses are built of stone, and inns are to be found along the streets. The inhabitants cut their hair and wear beautiful clothing. In warfare they have drummers, standards and tents. The capital is 100 li in circumference and contains ten palaces, all of them at a distance of ten li from one another. All pillars in these palaces are of crys-

52

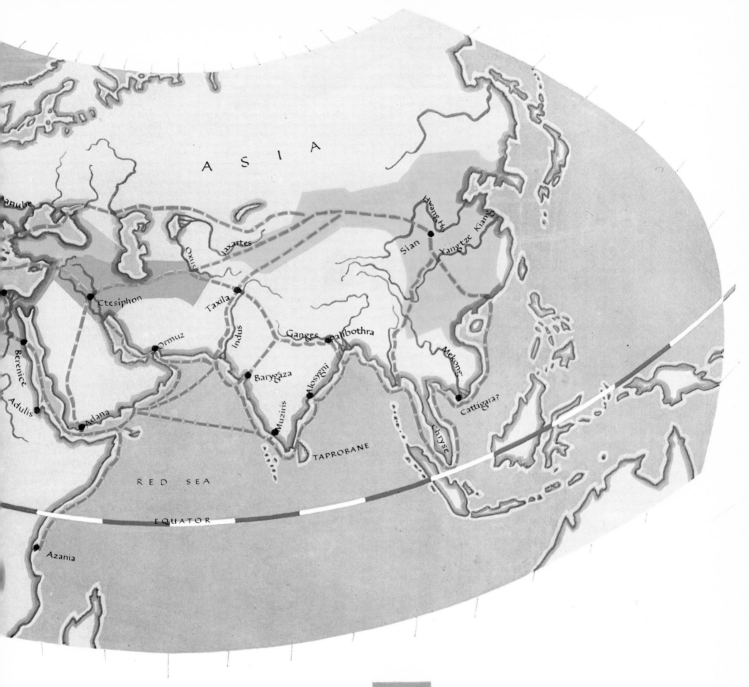

tal. The great council is made up of the 36 generals of the army. The kings are elected. The country has much gold, silver and precious stones, and the inhabitants are very rich, especially by reason of their trade with Indians and Parthians. All that is costly and unusual in other countries comes from this kingdom. The inhabitants are of straightforward and righteous character, and their merchants never have two prices. Grain is always cheap. The economy of the country rests on a well-filled treasury. When ambassadors come to the borders of this kingdom they are taken by guards to the capital, where they are given gold coins as a gift."

The Roman Empire

The Parthian Empire

China

The most important trade routes

This map is based on modern measurements, but for the sake of comparison it has been drawn on Ptolemy's projection. See the next page.

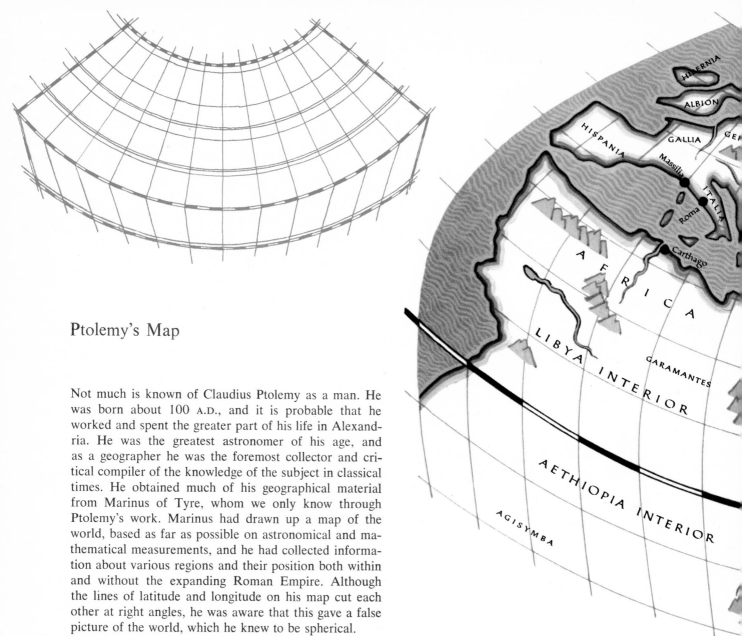

Ptolemy's Map

Not much is known of Claudius Ptolemy as a man. He was born about 100 A.D., and it is probable that he worked and spent the greater part of his life in Alexandria. He was the greatest astronomer of his age, and as a geographer he was the foremost collector and critical compiler of the knowledge of the subject in classical times. He obtained much of his geographical material from Marinus of Tyre, whom we only know through Ptolemy's work. Marinus had drawn up a map of the world, based as far as possible on astronomical and mathematical measurements, and he had collected information about various regions and their position both within and without the expanding Roman Empire. Although the lines of latitude and longitude on his map cut each other at right angles, he was aware that this gave a false picture of the world, which he knew to be spherical.

Ptolemy himself probably never drew a map of his own, but he elaborated a system for the benefit of future geographers and cartographers. He constructed many different projections for use as a basic frame, and one of them was a pure conical projection in which the lines of longitude turned sharply down at different angles at the Equator. In another projection, the lines of longitude curved off towards a centre somewhere in the region of the unmarked North Pole. The projection displayed 180 degrees of longitude, that is to say half of the circumference of the world, rather more than 60 degrees of latitude north of the Equator and only 20 degrees south of it.

His list of places and regions is based to a large extent on the material collected by Marinus. He supplies us with the latitude of 8,000 places, all the way from 67° north to 16° south. Furthermore, he gives the longitude of 180 of them. Marinus of Tyre had calculated that the length of the entire land area as it was then known, i.e. the distance between the Canary Islands and China, was 230°. Ptolemy corrected this length to 180°, which was still 50° too much. For his time his methods were strictly scientific, and it was not until 1,600 years later that satisfactory longitudinal calculations could first be made. He criticized Marinus and ridiculed most observations made by earlier travellers. He was very often quite right, but he made a serious mistake in not accepting Herodotus' description of the Phoenician circumnavigation of Africa. As a result of this he joined Africa to

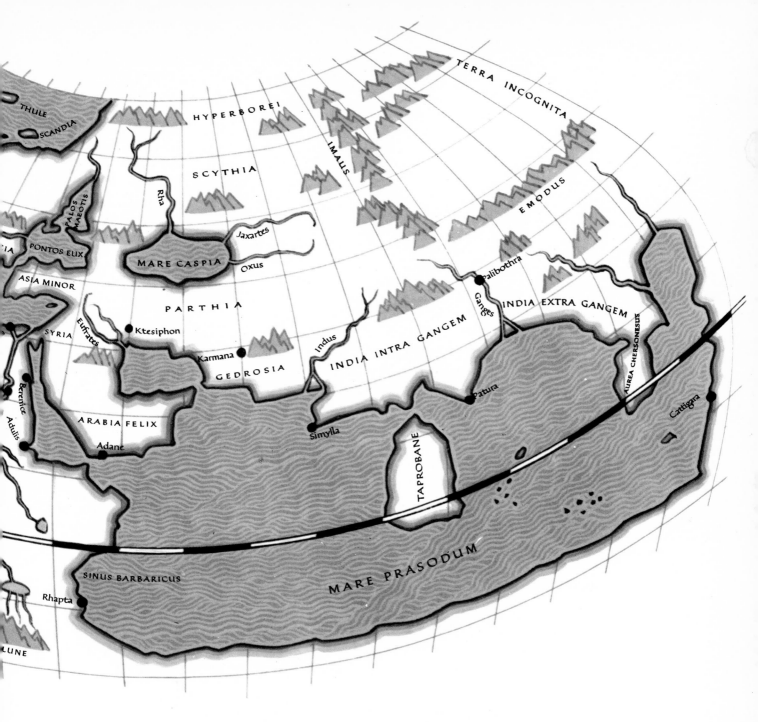

Asia in the south and this made the Indian Ocean into a great inland sea. The mass of Afro-Asian land in the south was allowed to continue downwards into a great, unexplored southern continent.

Since his days, many people have drawn up "Ptolemaic" maps of the world according to his directions. The oldest in existence is from the 14th century. In this version of his map we can see that Ptolemy knew of the Baltic Sea as well as the Danish Peninsula, but the rest of Scandinavia was to him merely an insignificant little island. The Palus Maeotis (Sea of Azov) reaches almost to the Baltic, but the Caspian is correctly positioned and,

for the first time since the days of Herodotus, seen as an inland sea. Taprobane (Ceylon) in the great inland sea of the Indian Ocean is made fourteen times too large, but both the Indus and the Ganges seem to lie in their correct positions on either side of a shrunken Indian Peninsula. It is possible to recognize Indo-China and the Malay Peninsula, but then the coastline turns south instead of north. Ptolemy knew, however, of a sea beyond Chryse (the Malay Peninsula): "Marinus does not tell the number of stadia from the Golden Chersonesus [Chryse] to Cattigara, but he says Alexander [a seafarer, Marinus' informant] wrote that the shore line extends

This picture shows a junk under way on the River Mekong, perhaps at Cattigara.

toward the south, and that those sailing along the shore came, after 20 days, to Zaba. From Zaba carried southward and toward the left [i.e. towards the south-east], they came after some days to Cattigara. He lengthens the distance, interpreting some days to mean many days."

Many have puzzled themselves as to where this Cattigara lay. Guesses have been made at Singapore and regions in China and on Borneo, but if today we sail for 20 days from the Golden Chersonesus, i.e. from the Malay Peninsula, especially its southernmost cape, and follow the coastline as was commonly done in those times,

we come to Bangkok, which might have been the Zaba of antiquity. Prominent ports and trading stations were often situated near rivers. After "some days" sailing to the south-west we reach the mouth of the great river Mekong, and it is here I believe Cattigara may have lain.

The most surprising thing Ptolemy has to tell us is this: "Toward the west [from the cannibals of Ethiopia] are

the Mountains of the Moon from which the lakes of the Nile receive snow water." — It seems as if the great lakes of Africa were known to him, as well as Mount Kilimanjaro or Mount Kenya. We know that Roman expeditions pushed far down into Africa, but there is no evidence that they ever reached as far south as this. We shall therefore have to believe that some merchant who had sailed down to Zanzibar with crew members who knew the whole coast and understood the language, as the author of the *Periplus Maris Erythraei* says, had been told of these lakes and this mountain with snow on its

There is hardly any doubt that the Mountains of the Moon are Mount Kilimanjaro and Mount Kenya.

peak, and that this had later been reported to the geographers.

The great age of classical geography came to an end with Ptolemy. A new era was gradually beginning, an era which was later to be called "the Dark Ages"; an era, which, at least as regards exploration and geographical discovery, was to lag far behind the classical period.

57

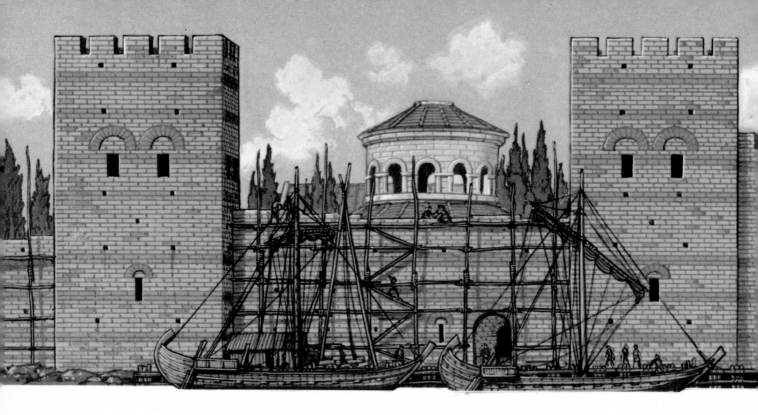

The Fall of the Roman Empire

There are no reports of expeditions or geographical developments from the time when the monuments of the classical era were pillaged, ravaged and burned by plundering Teutons and intractable Christians; all we are able to understand is that early trade connections were broken and that old trade routes were raided, and gradually came to be abandoned and forgotten. Even the hitherto secure Mediterranean once again became a dangerous sea for peaceful seafarers.

Early in the 4th century, Constantine the Great made old Byzantium, on the western shore of the Bosporus, the capital of the Roman Empire and renamed it Constantinople, and towards the end of the century the empire was divided into two halves with the Adriatic and the Gulf of Sidra as a boundary between them. With some simplification it may be said that the onslaughts of the Asiatic Huns into Europe began the great upheaval and subsequent catastrophe which enabled Teutonic tribes to infiltrate into the Roman Empire. The Byzantine Empire successfully managed to ward off the barbarian onslaughts, but the Western Empire gradually fell under their power. The Vandals pushed their way through Gaul into Spain, later to be forced down to North Africa by the Visigoths. The Angles and Saxons conquered England, the Franks and Burgundians took possession of Gaul and various Alpine regions, and Italy and Rome itself were vanquished first by the Visigoths and then by the Ostrogoths. The Huns themselves, however, were also crushed.

The walls of Constantinople began to be built in the 5th century. Two hundred years later, and for hundreds of years to follow, they were to protect Europe from the invading armies of Islam.

In the 6th century the Byzantine emperor Justinian tried to restore the Roman Empire to its previous extent, and it is true that he managed to reconquer the kingdom of the Vandals in North Africa and defeated the Ostrogoths in Italy after a critical battle. But by 568 the greater part of Italy was lost again to the Lombards. This date is usually taken as the end of the Great Migrations.

In the year 380 Christianity became the state religion of the Roman Empire, after much resistance from those in authority. The Church had in fact already been shaken by great internal strife in the early 4th century, when the presbyter Arius won many followers in Alexandria with his teaching that the Son of God was not begotten but created by the Father before the creation of the world. Both the Visigoths in Spain and the Ostrogoths in Italy adopted Arianism, and even though the Church Council of Nicaea declared Arius' teachings to be heretical, Arianism lived on for many hundreds of years. A new controversy arose about a hundred years after Arius, when the patriarch Nestorius, in Constantinople, asserted that clear distinction must be made between the divine and the human natures of Christ. This belief also was censured by a Church Council, but it continued for a time in Syria and spread to Persia, where the Church finally came to accept a completely Nestorian

creed. Nestorian missionaries then carried their teachings into Asia and reached both India and China. — From the beginning of the 5th century the Bishop of Rome had the right to superintend the Church in the West, whereas the Church in the Byzantine Empire was under the Patriarchs of Alexandria, Antioch, Jerusalem and Constantinople. Much dissension already existed between the Church in the East and the Church in the West, and deterioration of contacts during the course of the centuries was to intensify this, leading, in 1054, to a definite division of the Church into the Greek Orthodox and Roman Catholic branches.

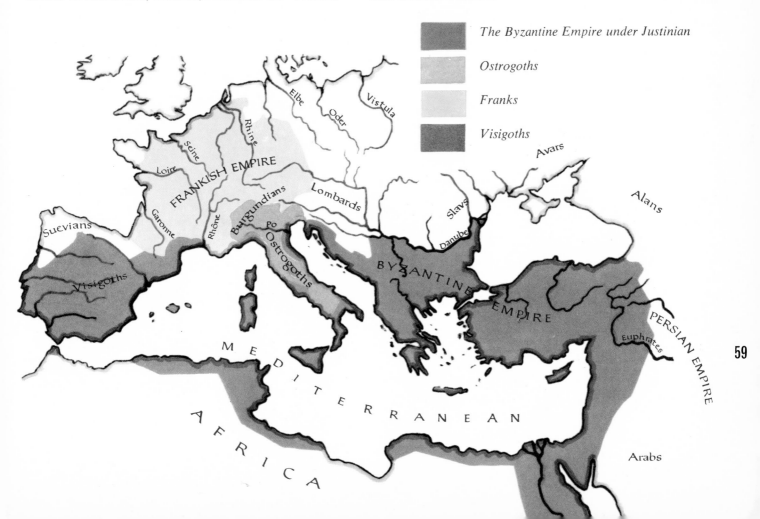

The Byzantine Empire under Justinian

Ostrogoths

Franks

Visigoths

The coin portrays King Azana of Axum, who was instructed and baptized by Frumentius. He reigned from 342 to 351.

Frumentius Converts the Axumites

The journeys described in this chapter are not voyages of discovery in the true sense, but the results of them were, in some strange manner, to inspire other explorers to make new efforts as much as 1100 years later. The events to be related may perhaps sound like some legend, but they are referred to in many old sources, and we hardly have any reason to doubt the truth of the stories.

Towards the end of the 3rd century Rome had lost her direct trade connections with India. The kingdom of Axum, or Ethiopia as we know it today, had extended its dominions across the Red Sea to southern Arabia and taken the Roman trading stations, and all traffic in the Indian Ocean was under the control of Arabs, Axumites and Persians. It was at approximately this time that people in Europe began to refer to all land beyond the Red Sea as India—irrespective of whether it lay in the south or the east. It almost seems as if it were some kind of reaction against Greek—i.e. heathen—passion for accuracy. The past was forsworn and forgotten so quickly and deliberately that one might be led to believe that the Christians, in their enmity towards the world, wished to forswear reality itself.

However, there were still scholars who had dealings with things temporal, who interested themselves in foreign countries and peoples. It is the theologian Tyrannius Rufinus who relates the following at some time towards the end of the 4th century: "A certain philosopher, Metrodorus by name, reached the parts of India lying farther afield to acquire knowledge of the country and to explore the limits of the world. Stirred by his example, Meropius of Tyre, a natural philosopher and explorer, was taken by the desire to journey to India for the same purpose. With him were two companions, young boys to whom he gave instruction in the natural sciences. The younger of them was called Aedesius, the other Frumentius. They

It is not very far from the Red Sea to Axum on the map, but the route winds its way up from the coastal desert, through difficult passes, to the Abyssinian plateau, more than 6,500 feet above sea level.

reconnoitred and made note of the things that were to their liking, and when the explorer later set out on the return journey, the ship in which they travelled put into a certain port to take on fresh water and other necessities.

"Now it was so that as soon as the barbarians who lived there heard from neighbouring tribes of any discord in their relations with the Romans, they were in the habit of putting to death all who came to them in Roman ships. The explorer's ship came into this port, and he, together with all those who were on board with him, were killed. But the two boys, who were preparing for their lessons beneath a tree, were saved, when they were found, by the mercy of some of the barbarians, and they were then taken before the king. This personage appointed Aedesius to be his cup-bearer. But Frumentius, whose intelligence and wisdom he had immediately perceived, was ordered to take charge of his reports and papers. Thereafter the king treated them with great respect and love.

"When the king died he left behind him a wife and a young son as heirs to the kingdom, but as to the youths, he gave them the liberty to do as they wished. But the queen, who had no more faithful servants than these in the entire country, was most urgent in her desires that they should share the governing of the country until her son should reach an age when he would be able to do so for himself. Her desires in this were directed towards Frumentius in particular, whose wisdom made him well suited to govern a country, for the other was merely a fellow of pure loyalty and of sensible character. And to all this they gave their agreement.

"As Frumentius now had the government of the country in his hand, his understanding and faith, under the guidance of God, began to inquire whether there might not be Christians among the Roman traders so that he might be able to secure for them the greatest possible freedom and at the same time encourage them to hold meetings at which they might hear sermons in the Roman manner. This he even began to do himself, and he exhorted and emboldened the others with approbation and favours to do good, to find suitable places for the building of churches and other necessary things.

"But when the king's son came to the age when he was capable of governing the country himself, they gave its entire control to him and faithfully handed over all the things they had been put in charge of and returned to our world, even though the queen and her son repeatedly tried to keep them there and begged them to stay. Aedesius made all haste to Tyre to meet once more with his parents and friends, but Frumentius journeyed to Alexandria, for he did not find it right to conceal the Word of God. He therefore related all his experiences to the archbishop there and exhorted him to appoint a worthy person who, as bishop, might be sent to the already numerous Christians, and to the churches which were already built in the land of the barbarians. Then Athanasius, who was at that time Archbishop of Alexandria, spoke to the assembled priests while carefully considering Frumentius' words and deeds, and said: 'Whom else could we find to do this other than you, who are so possessed by the Spirit of God?' — And he appointed him bishop and charged him, with the aid of the Lord, to return to the place whence he had come . . .

"I have not fetched the narrative of these events from tales which are told on the streets but have heard it from the mouth of the same Aedesius of Tyre who later was to become a servant of God himself, who previously had been Frumentius' companion."

Rufinus does not say where the land of the barbarians lay, but the tale is told by others who locate the country geographically as "the nearer regions of India which are turned towards us". We know that Frumentius went back there, and by Abyssinian church historians he is called Fremenatos and is officially referred to as Abba Salama— the Father of Salvation. Archbishop Athanasius of Alexandria was one of the foremost opponents of Arianism, and when the conflict within the Church was at its height

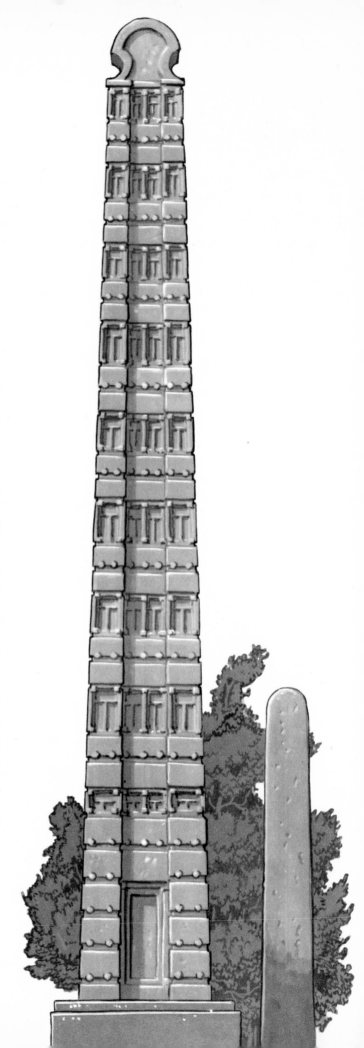

62

In the ancient capital of Axum there are many strange "obelisks". They are from the pre-Christian era and were presumably erected as memorials to kings and other prominent persons.

he was several times removed from office and reinstated. Soon after he had sent Frumentius to Axum, George of Laodicea, the Arian, was appointed archbishop in his place, and about the year 357 the Emperor Constantius wrote a letter to the kings in Axum in which, among other things, we find the following:

"... Therefore send Bishop Frumentius to Egypt immediately, to the Lord Archbishop George and the other Egyptian bishops who have the authority to ordain him in his office and to make decisions in such matters ... It is known to us and we remember, however, that Frumentius was appointed to his office by Athanasius who is weighed down with a multitude of sins. Since the latter has not been able to disprove even one of the accusations which have been made against him, he has been relieved from his office and, now that he has lost his means of livelihood, he wanders from one country to the other as if he might in this way avoid the censure befitting a lost soul ... Should he [Frumentius] delay and seek to evade judgement, however, then it will be clear that he himself has been perverted by the teachings of the offender Athanasius, that he sins against the Deity and is most certainly to be considered as a heretic just as that offender has been found to be a heretic. It is thus to be feared that he now, since his return to Axum, corrupts you with insidious and ungodly speech and not only throws the churches into confusion and blasphemes before God but may also thereby become the cause of corruption and destruction among the whole of your people."

This was the spirit in which church politics were managed in those days. But Frumentius did not return to Alexandria. Athanasius was reinstated as archbishop, Arianism was denounced by the Emperor, and, in Axum, Christianity was soon to become the state religion.

Axumite priests singing and dancing to the accompaniment of drum and sistrum.

63

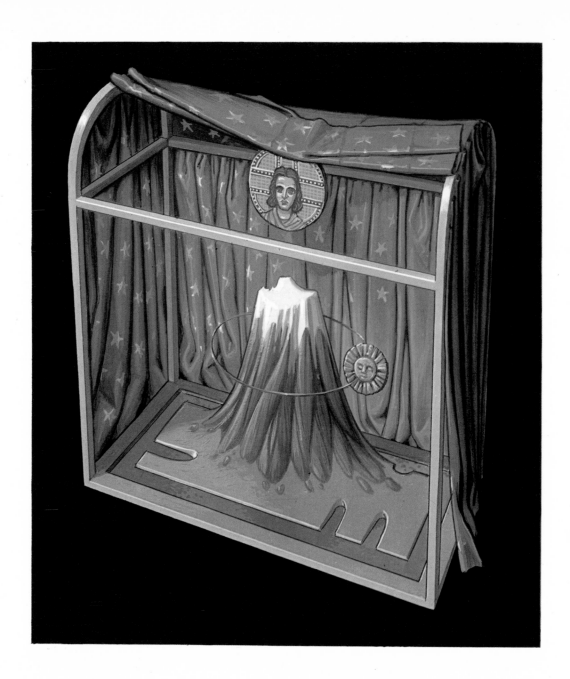

The Tabernacle World of Cosmas Indicopleustes

The world picture which the heathen philosophers, astronomers and geographers of the classical period had gradually drawn up was an abomination to the leading men in the Church. Although it is true that their main interests were in a kingdom outside this world, even the Christians needed some conception of the world of reality in which they were, after all, forced to live; and this they managed to obtain for themselves with the guidance of the Bible.

God had once explained to Moses on Mount Sinai exactly how the Tabernacle was to be built, and when it was found in the writings of St. Paul that there was a passage which could be interpreted to mean that the Tabernacle was a picture of the world, it was quite natural for the world to be looked on as a vast tabernacle-tent with rectangular base, twice as long as it was broad, and with an arched roof supported by four pillars. Then came the belief that the world was divided into three storeys. The first contained the land, the sea and the inhabitants of the world, with angels hovering close to the roof, holding the sun and the moon and the stars. In the second storey were the angels and the saints, and at the very top sat Christ surrounded by the greatest saints of all. At the north of the disc-shaped earth rose the high World Mountain which was there so that the sun would have somewhere to go at night.

There were of course those who opposed this theory, who wished to defend the classical conception of the earth as a sphere, but they were jeered at and told to consider the truths of the Bible. Even St. Augustine intervened and wrote: "Regarding the idea of Antipodes, that is to say people on the opposite side of the earth where the sun rises when it sets with us, where men walk with the soles of their feet turned towards us, the man of common sense will not see any truth whatsoever in this."

The new Christian picture of the world received its greatest support from a man called Cosmas, with the honorary title of Indicopleustes, i.e. the India-sailor, who was a travelling merchant and, later, a monk. As a merchant at the beginning of the 6th century, he had made long journeys, but it has been questioned whether they reached as far as India itself—many believe that he only sailed the waters around Arabia. However, he tells of both India and Ceylon with such exactitude that I for one think that he had really been there.

Since he seems to have been a keen and intelligent observer it is surprising that the world picture which he later put forward is wholly based on the tabernacle idea. But in order to do him justice let me quote from his own topographical description: "He who travels from Tzinitza [China] to Persia by land will thereby shorten his journey considerably. This is the reason why one finds such great quantities of silk in Persia. Beyond Tzinitza there is no seafaring and no land of human habitation... On the island of Ceylon in India proper there is in the Indian Sea a Christian Church with priests and believers—as on the Coast of Male [the Malabar Coast] where pepper also grows, and in the place called Calliana. There is even a bishop there, ordained in Persia. The same is also true of the island called Dioscorides [Socotra] in the Indian Sea. Living on this island are people who speak Greek, descendants of the Ptolemies who held sway here after Alexander the Macedonian, together with priests who were ordained in Persia and sent to this people, and a Christian community. I have only sailed past this island and have not been on land there. But I have spoken with its Greek-speaking inhabitants who came to Ethiopia. Furthermore there are innumerable monks and bishops in Bactria, in the land of the Huns, in Persia, in Indo-China, among the Perso-Armenians, among the Medes, the Elamites and in the entire country of Persia, and, added to this, many Christians, many martyrs and hermits... Since the island of Ceylon does in fact lie in a central position, it is visited by ships from all parts of India, Persia and Ethiopia, and, in the same manner,

sends out many ships of its own. Ceylon obtains silk, aloes, cloves, sandalwood and other products from the most distant lands, such as Tzinitza and other places of trade. These goods are then transported to trading stations on our side, for example to Male where the pepper grows, and to Calliana which produces copper, sesame and material which is used for the making of clothes... and on to Sindu [at the mouth of the Indus] where musk and lavender oil are made, to Persia, to the land of the Homerites [Yemen] and Adulis [Zula on the Red Sea]."

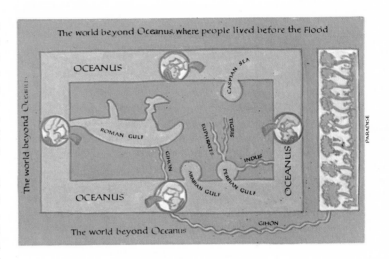

The land mass on Cosmas Indicopleustes' map is a rectangle. This is surrounded by a likewise rectangular Oceanus which in turn is surrounded by a border of land "where men lived before the Flood". In the eastern side of this "borderland" there is a large rectangular lake, and from this the Nile—or the Gihon as it is called in the Bible—runs through the south side of the borderland and then through, or under, Oceanus to the inhabited world and the Mediterranean. Cosmas shows Asia Minor, the Black Sea and the Adriatic, but of the western part of the Mediterranean he does not seem to have known more than that it narrowed to a strait towards Oceanus. The Euphrates and the Indus are comparatively correctly drawn, but the Indus, like a canal, cuts off a corner of the inner rectangle, and the Caspian has once again become a bay of Oceanus. The figures blowing horns are the four winds.

The Silk-Worm Comes to Europe

The trade in silk was just as important for the Sassanids in the restored Persian Empire as it had been earlier for the Parthians. It is true that a certain amount of silk was still being imported to Europe by the southern sea routes—Cosmas writes of merchants who "have no fear of journeying to the very ends of the world to fetch silk"—but this means of importation was insufficient, and, as a result of the Persian monopoly in silk, the prices rose catastrophically. Furthermore, the many wars between the Byzantine Empire and the Sassanids had at times put a stop to all such trade.

In order to circumvent this dependence on Persia, and in the interests of Christianity, the Emperor Justinian sent an ambassador to Axum in 535 to try to persuade the Axumites, and with them the Himyarites of southern Arabia, to intensify their seafaring and with it their silk trade with Ceylon. But the Persians had come to learn of Justinian's plans, and made haste to buy up all the silk that was to be had in Ceylon, with the result that the Himyarite ships had to return home with empty holds, or at any rate without silk. Then Axum, too, soon lost its power over the Himyarites and declined politically as well as economically, and not only the trade in silk but also all other kinds of trade with India and Ceylon almost came to a standstill. One of the reasons for this was that Justinian no longer needed to seek his silk along such troublesome routes. The silk-worm had come to Europe.

The Byzantine historian Procopius writes at about the middle of the 6th century: "At the same time there came several monks from India. Since they had learned that the Emperor Justinian was most desirous that the Romans should not buy silk from the Persians, they came before the Emperor and promised so to settle the silk question that the Romans would no longer need to do business with their enemies the Persians, or any other peoples. For they had spent much time in a weil-populated district in India which they called Serinda, and there they had carefully learned how the people of the Roman Empire would be able to produce silk for themselves. After repeated questions concerning these things, the monks finally told the inquiring Emperor that it was certain worms, which are continually kept at work by the art of Nature, that made the silk. It was not possible to transport the worms hither in the living state, but they could easily be engendered since the eggs of the individual generations were innumerable. As soon as these are laid, people cover them with manure, and when they have become warm enough the animals creep out of them.

"Having been given this information, the Emperor, with liberal promises, persuaded them to confirm their account in action. They therefore returned to India. When they again came back to Constantinople with the eggs, they, in the manner described, caused them to be transformed into worms, which they fed on the leaves of the mulberry tree. — Silk has been produced in the Roman Empire since that time."

Theophanes the Confessor, another Byzantine historian, sheds further light on the scene: "The production of silk is the work of worms, as shown by a Persian during the reign of the Emperor Justinian. The Romans knew nothing of this art before that time. This Persian had left the land of the Seres, taken the eggs of the silk-worms with him in a hollow stick and come safely with them to Constantinople. In the spring he transferred the worms to the mulberry leaves they lived on, and when they thus were fed with leaves they grew wings. Then he also treated the other parts [i.e. the cocoon] whose genesis and further

preparation the Emperor Justinian showed to the amazed Turks.

"At that time the trading stations and ports of the Seres belonged to the Turks. Previously they had belonged to the Persians. But when Ephthalinus, the king of the Eph-thalites who had given his name to the people, had defe-ated Peroz and the Persians, the Persians lost control of their property and the Ephthalites became masters. Short-ly afterwards, the Turks defeated the Ephthalites in a battle and took them [the trading stations of the Seres] from them again."

We are able from all this to understand that one or more Persian monks, who presumably were opposed to Persian Nestorianism, smuggled the eggs of the silk-worm past the Persian customs to the Emperor Justinian in Constantinople at about the middle of the 6th century. This silk country of Serinda, which had successively come under the sway of Persians, Ephthalites and Turks, was in all probability Sogdiana, between the rivers of the Amu Darya and the Syr Darya, for we know of no other region better fitting the context. The kingdom of China had extended as far as this during the 2nd century, and, in order to reduce transportation to the European market, silk began to be cultured as far west as this.

But of course a few silk-worms in Constantinople could not fill Europe's demand for silk all at once. The countries in the West were still to depend on the importation of silk from the East for a long time. And then, quite unexpec-tedly, Justinian found a new source, for this is when the aforesaid Turks suddenly appeared on the stage of history and made their large kingdom to the north of Persia, even though it was not to exist for more than a hundred years. Dissabulus, king of these Turks, was naturally keen to obtain an outlet for the silk which was produced in his kingdom, and, after inconclusive negotiations in Persia,

The long transport on camelback across Asia made silk extremely expensive in Europe.

he sent a delegation to Justinian, who was of course more than happy over the new possibility of circumventing the Persians.

A Byzantine embassy, led by a certain Zemarchus, was sent to the Turks in 569. Dissabulus was residing in Aktag beside the "white mountain"—probably the Altai range. He received Zemarchus in a tent which inside was hung with silken draperies and decorated in rich colours, invited him to partake of a brew of mare's milk, and showed him his vast wealth of gold. Zemarchus and his followers then took part in the Turkish campaign against the Persians, but at the city of Talas they parted company, with assurances of friendship from Dissabulus, and set out on the journey home. They took the route north of the Caspian, crossed the Ural River and the Volga, passed down through the Caucasus to the Black Sea and then sailed to Trebizond. From there they were taken by the regular post horses along the northern coast of Asia Minor to Constantinople, where they were able to tell the Emperor of their journey.

Nestorians in China

Even though the Church preferred that people should concentrate their wanderlust on the Kingdom of Heaven, it came about that many of its most zealous servants were nevertheless to travel, in the service of God, to the outermost bounds of the known world—and even beyond. These were men who fled to deserts and lonely places from the pomps and vanities of this wicked world in order to await the rewards of the life to come in quiet contemplation or hard labour. And there were those who set out to persuade all the nations of the earth to become followers of Christ. Many, perhaps most, of these missionary expeditions met with little success, and it is only by pure chance that we have later come to know of a few of them. Other such expeditions, on the other hand, obtained very tangible results: St. Willibrord preached

to the Frisians and the Danes, and was to rediscover Heligoland; Ansgar braved the waves all the way up to darkest Sweden and was able to supply Europe with information about the forgotten "island" of Scandia.

Cosmas Indicopleustes had reported on the existence of Christian churches around the Indian Sea. When Jesuit missionaries came to Sian in China during the 16th century, they were shown a tall carved stone with a long inscription, and when they had interpreted this they understood that Nestorian missionaries had been there almost a thousand years before them. The stone is inscribed with 1,780 Chinese characters; at the bottom is an inscription in Syriac, giving the name of the patriarch and the priests who had helped raise the monument in the year 781. Let us read just a small part of the text:

"When the brilliant Emperor Tai Tsung was beginning his happy reign in glory and splendour, wisely ruling the people in an enlightened manner, one of high virtue called

大秦景教流行中國碑

Olopun the Nestorian was well received in China and was allowed to preach the Christian Faith there. — Left, the stone at Sian which tells of his missionary work.

Olopun, of the Kingdom of Great Chin [Syria], observed the bright clouds and took with him the true Scriptures, watched the harmony of the wind and faced the difficulties and dangers [of the journey]. In the ninth of the Cheng Kuan years [A.D. 635] he reached Chang-an. The Emperor sent his Minister of State, the lord Fang Hsüanling, with an escort to the west suburb to meet the visitor and bring him in. When the Scriptures had been translated in the Library, and the doctrine searched in his private apartment, [the Emperor] thoroughly understood their propriety and truth, and specially ordered their preaching and transmission."

69

St. Brendan

Ireland had already been converted during the 5th century, and since the island escaped the ravages of the Great Migrations, it came about that much of the ancient culture that was lost on the continent was preserved here. It is said that not one drop of blood was spilled for the sake of the True Faith on the Emerald Isle and that Irish monks, in their longings for the martyr's crown, invented something which they called "the white martyrdom". This was the hermit's life of self-denial brought to perfection. The hermits of Egypt had gone out into the desert and there had finally come to group themselves into small colonies which later developed into monasteries proper. Although there were no deserts in Ireland, the surrounding ocean did contain rocky islands, and this was where many of the men who wished to follow the example of the Egyptian monks went to live. When, in the course of time, all the neighbouring islands had come to be overcrowded, such men sought islands further away from the mainland, even islands beyond the horizon.

Norsemen reached the Faeroes towards the end of the

8th century, but the monks of Ireland had already arrived before them. About thirty years after this the Irish monk Dicuil was to write in his work *De Mensura Orbis Terrae*: "There are many further islands in the ocean north of Britain which may be reached from the British Isles in two days and a night when winds are favourable. A holy man, whose word was to be trusted, told me that he had sailed for two summer days and the intervening night in a little boat with two rower's thwarts and reached land on one of these islands. They are for the most part small, and nearly all are separated from one another by narrow straits, and the settlers on them, men who have sailed there from our Ireland, have been living there for about a hundred years. But since they have been forgotten by the world from the very beginning, so are they now, because of the Norse plunderers, without priests, but they do have innumerable sheep and many different species of sea birds. We have not found these islands mentioned in the works of scholars."

This was written after the Vikings had begun to harass the coasts of Europe. The Norwegian Vikings first reached Iceland in about 860, but there too the Irish were before them. Dicuil writes: "Thirty years have passed

since certain holy men, who had been on this island from the first of February to the first of August, told me that the sun had, as it were, merely hidden itself behind a little hill so that it was not dark for one moment, not only at the summer solstice but also on the days before and after. One was able to do whatever work one wished, just as if the sun had been in the sky, were the work as demanding as the picking of lice from shirts. Had they been on the highest spot on the island, it is probable that the sun would not have been hidden from their sight at all."

St. Brendan, who according to tradition was a great seafarer and is also considered by many to have been an explorer of importance, was born on the Dingle Peninsula in south-west Ireland. Stone huts dating from his days are still to be found there, and there are also ruins of churches which—as tradition has it—he built with his own hands, such as the one at Inishtooskert, the northernmost of the Blasket Islands (to the right in the picture).

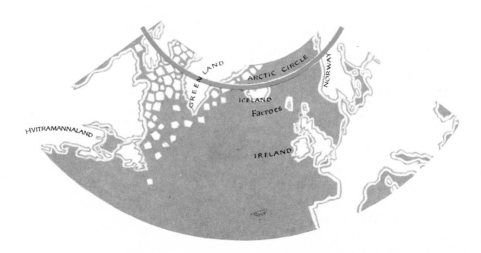

No one knows what the highly educated Irish monks of those days believed about the shape of the world and the universe, but a hundred years earlier, during the first half of the 8th century, the Irish monk Virgilius, who for a time was a missionary bishop in Salzburg, had attempted to prove the sphericity of the earth and the existence of Antipodes—to the horror of the other bishops.

The legend of St. Brendan and his ocean voyages became highly popular in Europe during the Middle Ages, and Brendan himself became perhaps the most popular patron saint of seafaring. The legend is preserved in various different versions and in various different languages, in prose as well as verse, and tells in the main the following story: St. Brendan, in conversation with one of his brother monks, had once heard of a promised land beyond the sea and was immediately possessed with an irresistible desire to visit the place. He set out on this journey in a large hide boat in the company of several other monks, and when, well out to sea, they were becalmed for so long that the monks began to feel anxious, he untied the rudder of the craft and put himself and the others completely into the hands of Divine Providence.

After forty days adrift, they came to an island where a table with wheaten bread and fish stood waiting for them. They then continued their voyage and came to the Isle of Sheep and further again to a completely bare island where they went ashore to offer the Paschal Lamb. No sooner had they made their fire, however, than the

No one knows when Irishmen first reached the Faeroes, but when the Norsemen arrived in the 8th century Irish monks were already there. If St. Brendan visited the islands himself, he probably did so in the early 6th century.

island began to move, and it appeared then that it was a great whale they had landed on, and the name of the whale was Iasconius—a Latinizing of the Irish *iasc* which means "fish". The men saved themselves by hurriedly clambering back on board. — They found the time to visit many islands on their long voyage, which took seven years to complete. Finally, after a bad storm and after having been becalmed for a considerable time in a fog, they came to an island where the trees were bowed down with the weight of their fruit and the beach was strewn with precious stones. After forty days of trekking on the island, they came to a river where the Angel of the Lord appeared before them and called to them to return to their own country, for it was only when all the peoples of the earth had become converted that the Promised Land would be opened to the chosen of God. And Brendan and his monks sailed home.

Brendan is a historical figure, born in 485, who founded many monasteries. He died in 577. He is still far better known in Ireland than is Sindbad the Sailor. Even so, it is probable that it is the same story with him as with Sindbad and Ulysses. For some unknown reason

it is these figures in particular who have become the points of crystallization of innumerable true, or not so true, sailor's stories which in their time flourished in the ports around the Indian Ocean, the Mediterranean and the waters that surround Ireland.

Many have wished to see the discoverer of America in Brendan. I prefer to look on him as a symbol of the early medieval Irish seafarer, and I think that one or more of them did in fact reach the mainland of North America. Before the Vikings. — As we shall see from what is to follow, the Norsemen came to a land which they called Vinland or Wineland, a land which has been identified as a part of North America. Eric the Red's Saga—like all the Icelandic sagas, a reproduction of an oral tradition—was written down during the 13th century. In it we can read the following about the voyage home from Vinland: "When they sailed from Vinland they were given a southerly wind. It was thus they reached Markland where they came across five Skraelings [Indians or Eskimos], one bearded man, two women, and two children. They captured the boys, but the others escaped and sank down into the ground [vanished into caves?]. They took the two boys with them, taught them the language and had them baptized. They said their mother's name was Vaetilldi and their father's Uvaegi; that the Skraelings were ruled by two kings called Avalldamon and Valldidida; and also that there were no houses there—the people lived in caves and hollows. They said that there was a land on the other side, immediately opposite their

According to legend, Brendan came to an island of the purest crystal, which could well be interpreted as an iceberg. Later, he and his men saw the terrible apparition of Judas Iscariot on a rock in the sea— Judas was supposed to be given respite from the fires of Hell for one day each year. It has been suggested that this apparition was really a walrus.

own, which was inhabited by people who wore white clothes, carried poles with flags before them and bellowed loudly. And it is believed that this was Hvitramannaland [Whitemanland or Land of the White Men] or Great Ireland."

In the Icelandic *Landnámabók,* also from the 13th century, there are the following lines: "Ari was driven out to sea to Hvitramannaland which many call Great Ireland. It lies to the west in the sea near Vinland the Good."

Hvitramannaland has been interpreted in many different ways, but it appears to be most probable that the men in this Whitemanland were white-garbed monks who held their Mass with plainsong. In the sea to the west there is no island larger than Ireland, but the seafarers coming to a large mainland with many very deep inlets would naturally think at first that they had come to large islands. It should not be forgotten that Scandinavia, lying as it does so close to the rest of Europe, was portrayed as an island on many maps from later times than this.

73

Iceland, Greenland and Vinland

Iceland was discovered by unknown Irish monks about 795 A.D. It is uncertain who first reached Iceland from Norway, but two sagas tell that a Swede called Gardar sailed round the island, spent the winter there and then sailed to Norway, where he spoke highly of the new land which to begin with was called Gardarsholm after him. This happened about the year 860. At that time King Harald Fairhair had begun to obtain control over the whole of Norway for himself, and since the landowners, originally independent, had no wish to submit to the new order of things they began to emigrate, to Iceland among other places. As early as 930 the whole island was occupied and its various parts were organized into a national federation.

At the time when the first Norwegians began to emigrate, one of them had been taken too far west into the waters past Iceland and there had sighted a number of islands which were called Gunnbjorn's Skerries after him. About the middle of the 10th century there came to

Iceland an exile from Norway, the berserk and man-killer Thorvald, and his son Eric, called the Red. The father died shortly afterwards, but his son had inherited his temperament, and, when he was outlawed for three years after a killing, he fled the island like many of his outlaw kinsmen.

His story is told in the *Landnámabók*: "Eric the Red said that he wished to find the country sighted by Gunnbjorn, Ulf Krake's son, when he drifted west of Iceland and discovered Gunnbjarnarsker, Gunnbjorn's Skerries. He gave his assurance that he would be returning to his friends when he had found the country. Eric sailed past Snefellsness and out into the sea. He came to the country at Midjokul which is now called Blaserk, Blacksark. From there he sailed south along the coast of the country to see if it was habitable."

We understand from the continuation that he rounded Cape Farewell, probed to the north-west and came to the deep fjords and the land which was later to be called Eystribygd (the East Community). The book tells of how he explored the south-west coast of the country for three years, in summer penetrating deep into the fjords, in winter living nearer the coast. The tale goes on in the following manner: "He spent that winter with Ingolf at

The Icelandic "Flateyjarbók" tells of how the man-killer Thorvald Osvaldson sailed from Norway with his son Eric the Red and the people of his household and landed in northern Iceland at Hornestrandene.

Holmlat. In the spring he fought with Thorgest. Eric was defeated, and thus they came to terms. Eric sailed away that very same summer to colonize the country he had found. He called it Greenland, for he felt that people would be more willing to go there if the country had an attractive name . . . Twenty-five ships sailed from Breidar-fjord and Borgarfjord to Greenland that same summer, but only fourteen of them arrived, a number of them having turned homewards and others being lost. This occurred fifteen winters before the Christian faith became law in Iceland [985]."

In the *Groenlendinga Saga* of the *Flateyjarbók*, written towards the end of the 14th century, we are told the story of Bjarni Herjolfsson who sailed to Iceland the same spring his father had sailed with Eric the Red and the other emigrants to Greenland. He made inquiries as to where Greenland lay and roughly what it looked like, whereupon his men began to ask what he had in mind. The saga goes on: "He replied: 'If you are prepared to go with me, my wish is to sail to Greenland.' All said that they were willing to sail with him. Bjarni then said: 'Our voyage will seem foolhardy to all, since none of us has been in the Greenland Sea before.' Nevertheless they sailed away as soon as they were equipped, and they

sailed for three days until they had lost sight of land. Then the favourable wind fell off, and they were beset with a northerly wind and fog so that they did not know where they were, and this lasted for many days. After this they were once again able to see the sun and decide where the eight cardinal points lay. They set the sail and journeyed on that day and a further night until they came in sight of land.

"They discussed among themselves which country this could be, but Bjarni said that it was not Greenland. They asked him whether he wanted to sail to this country or not, and he replied: 'It is my intention to sail close in to land.' This they did, and they were soon able to see that the country was low and wooded, and that there were small hills there. They left this country to port and turned the stern towards land. Then they sailed for two days and once again sighted land. They asked Bjarni if he thought that this was Greenland. He replied that this country could not be Greenland either, for it is said that Greenland has great glaciers. They soon came close to the country and saw that it was low and covered with trees. The favouring wind fell off, and the men on board said that they thought it most advisable to go ashore here, but this Bjarni would not do. They said that they

75

needed firewood and drinking water. 'You have all you want', Bjarni replied. Although the men protested at this, he ordered them to hoist the sail, which was done. They steered away from the country, sailed for three days with a south-westerly wind and then sighted land for the third time. But this country was lofty and covered with glaciers. They asked Bjarni if he wished to go ashore here, but he replied: 'No, I do not wish to, for this country does not seem good to me.' They did not lower the sail but moved on along the coast of the country, discovering in this way that it was an island. Once more they turned their prow from land and sailed on with the same wind across the sea.

"But the wind grew very strong. Then Bjarni gave orders to reef the sail so that neither ship nor tackle would be endangered. They journeyed on for four days and then sighted land for the fourth time. They asked Bjarni if he throught that this was Greenland. Bjarni replied: 'This country appears to be like what people have told me of Greenland. We go ashore here.' This they did immediately, landing at a ness. A boat was there, and Bjarni's father Herjolf lived on the ness. The cape was named after him and has been known ever since as Herjolfsness."

The news of the country Bjarni had seen to the south-west of Greenland inspired other Greenlanders to make voyages of exploration. The testimony of the sagas differs,

but they seem to be in agreement that Eric the Red's son Leif, called the Lucky, was the first to set foot in the new country, and the man who found Vinland. Leif sailed from Greenland to Norway during the summer of 999 and stayed for a time with King Olaf Tryggvason, who had adopted Christianity as the State religion. Both Leif and his men allowed themselves to be baptized, and the King urged Leif to return to Greenland so that he might spread the Christian Faith there. After some protests, Leif agreed to do this, and in the spring of 1000 he sailed away with thirty-five men, among them a priest, and probably several monks.

The voyage is best described in the *Groenlendinga*

It was not warlike Vikings in chain-mail and shining helmets sailing in shield-studded "sea-dragons" who discovered Markland and Vinland the Good, but simple farmers and merchants sailing in short, high-boarded, prosaic trading vessels.

Saga: "They prepared their ship, and when they were ready they sailed out to sea and came first to the country which Bjarni had seen last. They sailed to land, anchored, put out the boat and rowed ashore. From the shore to the glaciers was as one flat slab of stone, and the country did not appear attractive to them. Then Leif spoke,

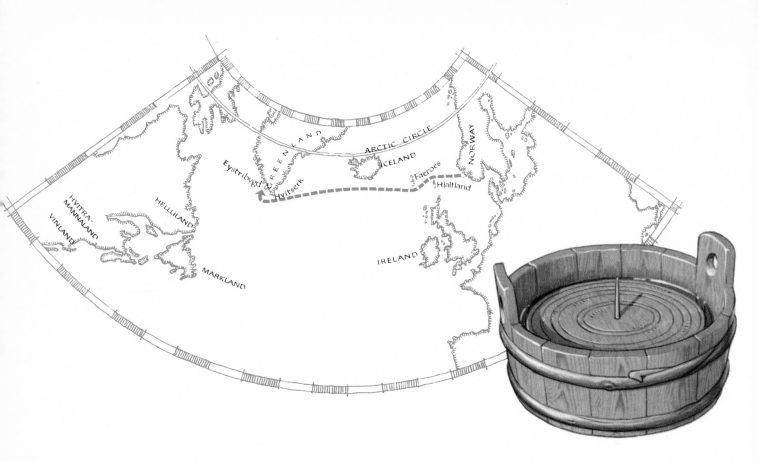

In a collection of sailing instructions for the route from Norway to Eystribygd in Greenland we read the following: "From Hernum [islands off Bergen] west to Hvarf in Greenland: by going so far north of Hjaltland [the Shetlands] that it can hardly be seen, then so far south of the Faeroes so that only half of their mountains are seen—south of Iceland so that it is possible to see its sea birds and whales, whereafter one reaches the high parts of Greenland called Hvarf."

saying: 'Things have not gone for us as they did for Bjarni regarding this country, for we have been ashore here. I shall now give the country a name and call it Helluland, Flatstone Land.' After which they returned to the ship. They sailed on and found another land. They went in to land, anchored, put out the boat and went ashore. This country was low and wooded. Stretches of white sand spread out before them, and the coastline did not fall off sharply into the sea. Leif said: 'We shall give this country a name fitting its appearance and call it Markland, Wood Land.' Then they rowed straightway back to the ship.

"They sailed on over the sea for two days with a north-easterly wind and again came to a country and an island which lay north of the country . . . They then returned to

Like other seafarers, the Norsemen navigated by the stars when they were out of sight of land. The Pole Star showed them where the north lay, but during the short light nights of summer it was of little use to them. They probably came to know the Greek scaphe (see p. 43) at an early period and developed it during the early Middle Ages into an instrument which they called a "solskuggafjol". This was a wooden disc floating in a tub of water. A short stick projected from the centre of the disc, and around it were drawn concentric circles representing the position of various places in the north-south direction. The length of the stick's shadow at midday had been marked at the various places, and it was known that the shadow became longer or shorter if one sailed north or south. As the length of the shadow also depended on the time of year, the stick was so constructed that its length could be regulated each week according to values marked on the instrument. If one wanted to sail from one place to another out of sight of land, the vessel was steered so that the stick's shadow at midday gradually approached the circle of the place of destination. When the shadow and the circle coincided, all that had to be done was to sail, if possible, along the same latitude until one arrived at the intended place.

the ship and sailed into a sound between the island and the ness which projected from the country to the north. They steered west past the ness. It was very shallow there at ebb tide. The ship went aground, and soon they had to look far to catch sight of the sea at all. But they were so eager to go ashore, and not wishing to wait until the sea once again lifted the ship, that they landed immediately. There was a river running from a lake there. When the sea again lifted the ship off, they entered their boat and rowed to it and took it up the river and then into the lake. There they anchored, carried their sleeping bags ashore and pitched tents.

"They decided to spend the winter there and built large huts. Neither the river nor the lake was lacking in salmon. They had never seen such large ones. The country was so good that it did not seem to them that they needed to procure fodder for the cattle for the coming winter. There was no frost there in wintertime, and the grass hardly withered at all. Day and night were not so different in length as in Greenland and Iceland. On the shortest day the sun rose in the *eyktarstadr* and set in the *dagmálastadr*. [The precise meaning of these directions is very uncertain and much debated].

"When they had finished building their quarters, Leif said to his followers: 'I now wish to divide our group into two and explore the country. The one half is to remain here and the other half to reconnoitre the land, but not too far to get back before nightfall, and not to become split up.' This was done for some time to come ... One evening it happened that one of their company was missing, and this was Tyrkir the German. Leif worried himself greatly over this, for Tyrkir had been with him and his father for many years and had loved him much in his childhood. Leif called to his men and went out to look for him. Twelve men were with him. They had gone only a short distance when Tyrkir came towards them. They greeted him with much joy.

"Leif immediately saw that his foster-father was not himself. He asked him: 'Why are you so late, foster-father, and why did you separate from your companions?' Tyrkir then spoke for a long while in German, rolled his eyes and twisted his mouth. No one understood what it was he said. After a while he began to speak in Norse, saying: 'I was not so very far ahead of you others, and yet I am able to tell of a new discovery—I have found vines and grapes.' 'Is this the truth, foster-father?' Leif inquired. 'It is indeed true,' Tyrkir replied. 'After all I come from a region where there is no lack either of grapes or of vines.'

"They slept overnight. In the morning Leif spoke to his men: 'There are now two things we shall do: one day we shall spend picking grapes, and the next we shall cut vines and fell timber so that we can load our ship.' And thus it was decided. It is told that the boat was soon filled with grapes. Then trees were felled. At the approach of spring they prepared to leave. Leif gave the country a name in accordance with its nature and called it Vinland, Wineland."

Most scholars seem to agree that Leif reached the mainland of North America, but differences have arisen about the exact position of Vinland. Some have wished to place it as far south as Florida. The most usual opinion today is that Vinland was the region round Cape Cod. Markland would seem to correspond most closely to Newfoundland, and Helluland to Labrador. Yet many of the sources do not mention Helluland or Markland in connection with Leif Ericsson. The *Kristni Saga*, which tells of the coming of Christianity to Iceland, says briefly: "So he [Olaf Tryggvason] also sent Leif Ericsson to Greenland to preach the Faith there. This was when Leif found Vinland the Good. He also found people on a wreck in the ocean. This is why he is called Leif the Lucky." — Snorri Sturluson says very briefly in his *Heimskringla:* "Leif also found Vinland the Good."

Several years after this, Thorfinn Karlsefne, Leif's brother-in-law, set sail with a large expedition and tried to settle the country, but after skirmishes with the natives the colonists were forced to return to Greenland. On the way home they came across the two Skraeling children who were later to tell of the white-garbed, bellowing men in Hvitramannaland (see the previous chapter). Other settlers probably had better luck than Thorfinn, and it seems as if there was still a Norse colony in North America during the 12th century, since the Icelandic annals from 1121 state that Bishop Eric Gnupsson from Greenland made a journey to Vinland. — And even as late as 1347 the following was noted down in the annals of the Icelandic Diocese of Skálholt: "A boat came from Greenland, smaller than the small vessels coming to Iceland. It arrived in the lower stretches of Straum Fjord and was without an anchor. There were seventeen men on board, and they had been on the way to Markland but had drifted hither off their course."

Then no more is heard of the countries which Leif discovered, and it is not likely that Norse expeditions became known in southern Europe before modern times. Vinland, like so many other previously discovered lands, had to be discovered all over again.

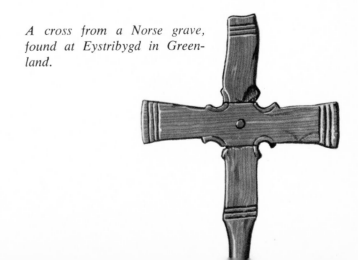

A cross from a Norse grave, found at Eystribygd in Greenland.

The World Empire of the Arabs

While the Vikings were raiding the coasts of western Europe and colonizing previously unknown islands in the north-west, things were happening in the south which threatened all that was still left of European culture. During the 7th century, the previously free and independent Bedouin tribes in Arabia were brought to unity by the Prophet Mohammed and his teaching. Like a fire they spread in all directions and drew other peoples along with them into vast armies whose aim was to conquer the world in the name of Allah. The Byzantine Empire and Persia had long expended their energies in protracted wars with each other, and in 642, only ten years after the great campaign had begun, the Arabs had seized the Byzantine possessions of Syria, Palestine, Mesopotamia and Egypt, and furthermore the whole of Sassanid Persia.

Then they conquered the Mediterranean coast of Africa, crossed the straits at the Pillars of Hercules in the year 711, and took Visigoth Spain, which was by that time weakened by internal strife. They crossed the Pyrenees and burst into the kingdom of the Franks, crossed the Garonne and the Dordogne, and in 732 were pushing on towards the Loire when they were met by the Frankish army under Charles Martel and were decisively defeated at Poitiers. In 759 they were forced back over the Pyrenees by Pippin. But the Battle of Poitiers would not have been able to save Europe if Byzantium had not held out.

It was not the seafaring southern Arabians who were doing all the fighting but the forceful Bedouins, and these put most unwillingly to sea. Yet for the war against Byzantium they needed a fleet, and this they probably built and manned with a great deal of help from the subjugated Phoenicians and Syrians. Then they took Cyprus, Rhodes, Cos, Chios and Cyzicus—stages on the way to Constantinople—and in 657 they forced their passage through the Dardanelles. They besieged the Byzantine imperial city for four years, and what finally turned the bitter sea fighting beneath the sea-wall of the city in the favour of the Byzantines was "Greek fire", an ignited mixture of naphtha, sulphur and saltpetre, which was discharged at the Arabian ships. The Arabs returned with a great offensive in 718, but were once again defeated.

The Arabs cut off European trade routes to India more effectively than the Persians. In the north-east they had pushed their way forward to the Caucasus, east of the Caspian to the Aral Sea and the Jaxartes, and apart from Persia they had also taken a part of India proper so that the mouth of the Indus was in their hands. All seafaring in the Indian Ocean was soon to fall under the control of the Arabs, and they were masters in the western Mediterranean. They also commanded the entire coast up to Asia Minor as well as many Greek islands, but the Byzantines were nevertheless able to save both Greece and Italy from Arabian invasion with their powerful navy. But the Mediterranean, which previously had been a connecting link between differing peoples and cultures, became the boundary between Christian Europe and Mohammedanism and remained so for many hundreds of years to come.

When the Arabs invaded Spain in 711, Tarik, their commander, built a fortress on the Spanish side of the Pillars of Hercules, called Jebel el Tarik (later Gibraltar). In 785 the Arabs began work on a building which was to become one of the most beautiful in the world—the Mosque at Cordova.

Ibn Wahab and the Emperor of China

The Arabs had built up their world empire with exceptional wisdom. Their wars were not religious wars, even though their religion had made them a united, strong and terrible people who fought in the name of Allah. Wherever they conquered they usually allowed those they had subjected to retain their own religion and their own temples (which did not hinder the majority within their empire soon going over to Mohammedanism, since conversion, to begin with at least, led to exemption from taxes). Then pilgrims set out from all Mohammedan countries to the holy places in Arabia, primarily to Mecca, as ordained in the Koran. The Koranic commandment that all true believers should show hospitality towards travellers and, when necessary, even provide them with funds to help them on their way, naturally encouraged the habit of travelling and created understanding between the peoples. Arabic, the language of the Koran, soon began to unite the various peoples of the Moslem world also, and the common language was to become of great value, especially for trade.

The Arabs did no sea trading of their own with Europe, and at first it was really the Jews alone who saw to the exchange of goods between Moslem and Christian. But by the beginning of the 9th century, ships started to come from Venice to Antioch in Syria and Alexandria in Egypt to trade with the Arabs, and this is why the little lagoon city gradually grew into a world commercial centre on which the routes from northern Europe, Byzantium and the Orient converged. To begin with, Venice suffered no competition from the other Italian trading cities. Italy was weak and in a state of discord for many hundreds of years, but a few of its cities managed to rise to power and glory through wise and cool-headed commercial policies. On the west coast, the most important were Amalfi, Pisa and Genoa, in that order. They fought against each other and badly injured each other, often to the advantage of Venice. Later, ships from Marseille and Barcelona also began to make appearances in Alexandria and other ports of the Arab world, and towards the end of the Middle Ages ships were coming all the way from Flanders, Britain and Denmark.

Arabian merchants made their way north from the Caucasus to the country of the Khazars and to the fur-trapping peoples at an early stage, and they also forged links with the peoples around the Baltic. In Africa they traded with the kingdoms near Senegal and the Niger and at the same time managed to spread Islam. The entire coast of East Africa as far as the golden city of Sofala came into their trading area and was won over to Islam early on. Most important of all, however, was the trade they carried on with India and China.

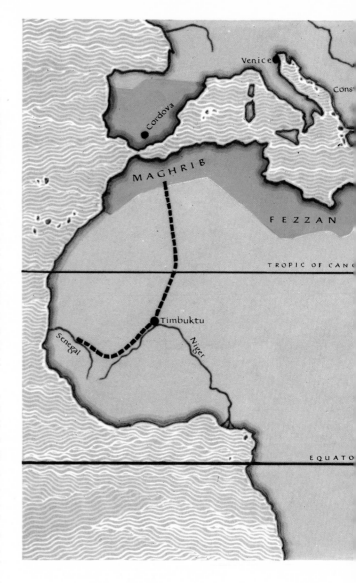

In order to lend support to this trade, they set up their own trading stations in India and Ceylon, the Malay Peninsula and Sumatra, and in a number of places in southern China. Chinese trading junks had begun to make appearances to the west of India even before the days of Mohammed, and when the Arabs gained control over the Indian Ocean and peaceful seafaring in these waters became safer, the traffic to and from China became more vigorous than ever before. We hear of Kia-Tan, a Chinese, who during the 9th century wrote a navigation guide to the passage from Canton to the Persian Gulf. And we know that there were so many Arabian, Persian and other foreign merchants in southern China that they once, in 763, were able to band themselves together to attack Canton and rob the city warehouse. This is doubtless one of the reasons why direct trade with China ended

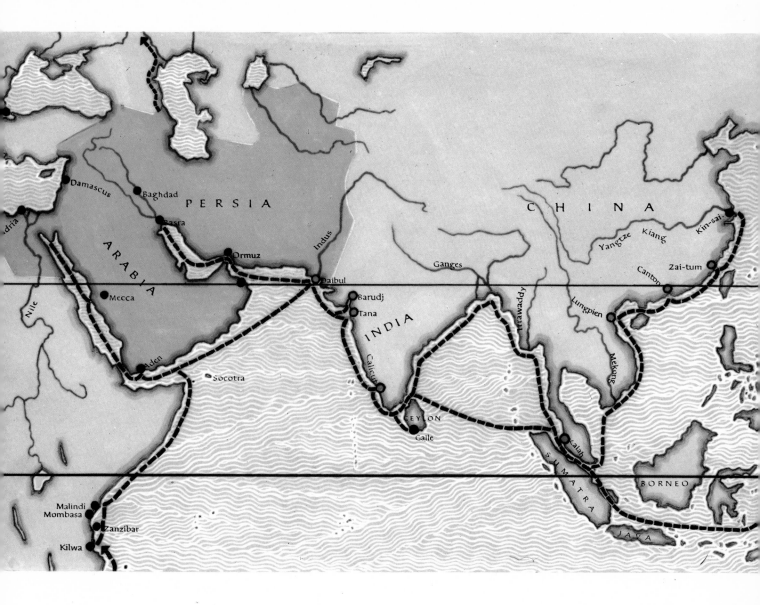

The map shows the world of the Arabs, their trading stations and most important trade routes.

so horribly. For during a civil war, the anger of the Chinese turned itself against the foreign merchants, and it is stated that 26,000 foreigners were put to death in the city of Hangchow alone during the troubles of 875.

After this massacre and other hostilities, the Arabian merchants ceased to sail beyond their trading station at Kalah on the Malay Peninsula which, together with Galle in Ceylon, was for a time the most important place of trade in the East. For Europe, India and the East became a closed world of which less and less was known. We know from Arabian authors that a few Jewish merchants were still able to travel the long road from the kingdom of the Franks and across the Red Sea or the Persian Gulf to China, but apart from this the merchants of the West could reach no further than to ports in Syria, Egypt and North Africa. Europe traded in wood, hemp

and tar, in copper, zinc, lead and iron, in furs and wool, in olive oil, almonds, honey and saffron, and, when the harvest in Egypt was bad, even in grain. Furthermore people soon began to export slaves, in particular children who had been kidnapped in southern Russia. When the price of Eastern goods rose to such an extent that Western exports were unable to cover them, people paid with silver and gold.

In return, the merchants received pepper which came from India, Sumatra and Java. They obtained cinnamon

and ginger and nutmeg, and the expensive cloves from the Moluccas. Also camphor, aloes, dyestuffs and incense, and, the most expensive of all, musk and ambergris. Musk is a strong-smelling substance secreted by a gland under the belly of the musk-deer, a substance which was used in perfumes and as a stimulant. Ambergris was to be found in clumps floating on the sea or washed up on the shore. (At that time it was not known that this substance is formed in the intestines of the spermaceti whale.) Ambergris was also used in the manufacture of perfume. — It was thus only luxury goods which were considered profitable enough to transport over the long route from the East. Europeans seemed able to pay the price of long and dangerous transport and the takings of many intermediaries for the wares of ostentation alone.

Of all the merchants and travellers who journeyed to China before the massacre, only two are known to us: the Andalusian Jew Suleiman and Ibn Wahab of Basra who is described as a traveller for curiosity alone. Both of them recorded their experiences, and we find them in a 10th-century anthology entitled *Akhbar al-Sin wa'l Hind*—Reports on China and India. The narratives are in part far too fantastic to be considered of much historical value. We learn that Ibn Wahab visited the Emperor in Nanking, and Suleiman seems to have visited the Nicobar and Andaman Islands. He tells of the "sea jumper", i.e. the flying fish, and of another fish that climbs up out of the sea to drink the milk of the coconut. We may presume by this that he meant the mudskipper. I should like to quote a few details which we find first mentioned by Suleiman. He writes of the Chinese: "They have excellent earth of which they make vases that are just as fine and transparent as glass." He had thus seen Chinese porcelain. And he tells of wine which is made from rice, and of another remarkable beverage which "is prepared from a herb or rush that has more branches than the pomegranate tree but is of more pleasant smell. The Chinese boil water and then pour it in the scalding state over the leaves. The beverage which is obtained in this manner possesses a somewhat bitter taste, but is exceptionally good for the health." Suleiman had tasted tea.

The oldest representation of a Chinese junk is a model from the 1st century A.D. The same type still exists today; the picture of it here shows it in the Gulf of Tonkin, and the earlier picture (on p. 56) off Cattigara.

Adventurers in the Atlantic

The Arabs had long been sailing with the reliable monsoons in the Indian Ocean, and they were used to patient waiting in the ports until the right season came. But the changeable winds of the Mediterranean alarmed them, and they considered the Atlantic Ocean a sea of terrors. They were convinced that it was the will of Allah that no one should sail on that sea, and even the great astronomer and geographer al-Biruni was to write in the beginning of the 11th century: "No seafaring is done on this sea, for the air is dark, the water is thick, the navigable channels in confusion, and here there are many ways of losing oneself; the only beneficial thing about it being the small profits that one might win on arrival home from such a voyage. This is the reason why people before us set up signs in this sea as a warning to all who wish to rush out into its hazards."

One hundred and fifty years later, the geographer al-Idrisi was to write the following words which no doubt came to influence the views of Europeans: "No seafarer dares to sail out into the Atlantic Sea and steer a course away from land. Men sail along the coastline and never leave it out of sight . . . What lies beyond the sea is known to no man. No one has yet been able to discover anything that is to be trusted with regard to the ocean, this by reason of the difficulties in the way of seafaring, the lack of light and the numerous storms." In order to illustrate his point, he describes a reckless voyage made by certain Arabs. It is in fact the only description we have of any Arabian voyage out in the open Atlantic.

Al-Idrisi writes: "It was from Lisbon that certain adventurers set sail on an expedition with the object of exploring the ocean and its bounds. Near the Hot Baths in Lisbon there is a street which is still called 'Street of the Adventurers'.

"It happened in this way. Eight closely related men entered into partnership with one another, built a trading vessel and loaded it with water and provisions in sufficient quantities for a voyage of several months. They steered out to sea when they felt the first breaths of the east wind. After a journey of about eleven days they came to a sea where thick waves gave off a rotten smell, where many almost invisible banks were to be met with. Since they feared that they might founder, they altered course and then sailed on for twelve days to the south and came to Goat Island where innumerable herds of goats were grazing, without drovers or other guards.

"When they came ashore they found a well with running water and, close to this, a wild fig-tree. They caught several goats and killed them, but the meat was so bitter that it could not be eaten. So they kept only the hides, sailed for another twelve days to the south and finally sighted an island which seemed to be inhabited and built

85

upon. They moved closer to investigate this matter. Soon afterwards they found themselves surrounded by boats, taken prisoner and removed to a city which lay close to the shore. They came to a house and there saw large red men who had little growth of beard and long hair, and also women of the greatest beauty. They were held cap-

diately there came some of the natives of this land to us, found us in our woeful state, freed us of our ropes and asked of us various questions which we answered by relating of our adventures. They were Berbers. One of them asked us: 'Do you know how far you are from home?' When we replied that we did not know, he went

The venturesome Arab youths probably reached the Canary Islands; their ship is shown here off the island which today is called Fuerteventura.

tive in a room in this house for three days. On the fourth day there came a man to them who asked in the Arabic tongue what sort of men they were, why they had come thither and from what country they had set out. They told him their entire story. He begged them to be of good courage and said that he was the king's interpreter.

"On the following day they were brought before the king who asked them the same questions, and they answered them in as faithful a manner as they had answered the interpreter: that they had braved the waters of the ocean in order to find out what features and remarkable things it contained, and to see where its outermost bounds lay.

"When the king had heard what they had to say, he burst out laughing and said to the interpreter: 'Tell these men that this was already done during the reign of my father. He ordered some of his slaves to explore this sea, and they sailed for a whole month on its waters until they found they had to give up this hopeless enterprise after they had lost sight of all land.' The king then bade the interpreter give them avowals of his friendship so that they might think well of him, and this was done. They returned to the house and had to stay there until the west wind began to blow.

"When the wind came at last, they were blindfolded and led on board their vessel, and for a time they drifted about in the sea: 'We sailed for about three days and nights,' they said, 'and then came to a land where we were left to our fates on a river bank with our hands tied behind our backs. We stayed there until sunrise, very troubled by the tight ropes and in a very pitiful condition. Finally we heard the voices of people and began to call. Imme-

on to say: 'Between your own land and the place where you now are there lies a journey of two months.' The leader of the party of adventurers then said: 'Wa asafi!' [The rough meaning of this is 'alas']. Which is the reason why this place is still called Asafi to this day'."

Nowadays the spot is known as Safi; it is in Morocco. The adventurous explorers had found some fellow-believers and were able to make the journey home without mishap. It seems likely to me that the stinking waters full of shallows were in the vicinity of the Azores where, for instance, there are the Formigas Banks far from the islands, and where the smell may have come from a volcanic eruption above or below the surface of the sea. Such eruptions are still quite common in our own times. The island with the goats was probably one of the northerly Canary Islands, and the island with the "red" men another in the same group. The description fits that of the Guanches who inhabited the islands when the Portuguese and the Spaniards arrived there in the 14th century. This tribe of "red" men were either exterminated in slow stages or partially incorporated into the Spanish population on the islands.

We are not told when this remarkable voyage was made, but it must have been before 1147 when the Moors had to abandon Lisbon to the new conquerors—those who later were to be called Portuguese.

The map on the left was drawn by Istakhri in the 10th century. The smaller picture is of al-Idrisi's circular silver map. The shape of the land mass in both is a legacy from Ptolemy.

Al-Idrisi's Map of the World

The Arabs came across many scientific works by classical authors, and it is surprising how quickly and discerningly they appreciated their value. Ptolemy's astronomical-mathematical work *Mathematikes Syntaxeos*, which the learned of classical times had called "Megiste", the greatest, was translated into Arabic by the 9th century and was thus preserved for Europe as well. The Arabs referred to it as Al Magesti, a title which was later shortened to *Almagest*, and it was under this name that it spread and became known throughout the entire scientific world. His great geographical work was also saved by the Arabs, and they tried to draw maps according to his system and their own enlarged knowledge of geography.

As a rule, however, the Arabs were not good cartographers. They were apt to use compass and ruler far too often, so that land contours became stereotyped and rather arbitrary. Yet it must be admitted here that we do not know that the Greeks were any better. We have only had descriptions on which to work, and it is probable that the reconstructions of our times are too much coloured by our greater geographical and technical knowledge.

Of the Arabian geographers, the best known in the West is al-Idrisi who, after studies in Cordova and extensive travelling, came to the Christian court of the Norman King Roger III at Palermo in Sicily. He spent fifteen years there about the middle of the 12th century compiling maps and writing commentaries on them, and we know that he made a seventy-page Atlas of the world, as well as a smaller, circular, general map. A copy of his map of the world is said to have been engraved on a silver plate about 12 feet by 5, but this was destroyed by a plundering mob only a few years after it was made.

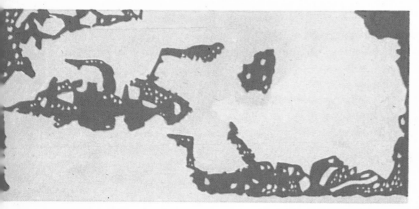

Al-Idrisi's map in greatly simplified reconstruction. Compare it with the similarly simplified European maps at the bottom of the opposite page.

It is clear that the part of southern Africa which is extended far to the east is a legacy from Ptolemy, but Arabian seafarers had taught al-Idrisi that the sea was open in the east, and in his own commentaries he writes: "The Sea of Sin [China] is an arm of the ocean which is called the Dark Sea [the Atlantic]." Otherwise the map is not so very much better than might have been drawn according to Ptolemy's description during classical times, apart from the fact that al-Idrisi is able to name several islands in the Indian Ocean. He was not able to put the countries around the Baltic into any proper shape, even though his notes show him to have been familiar with a great many places there, as in the rest of Europe.

He had no doubt met travellers and merchants from Scandinavia at the court of King Roger and received important information from them, but we know that the Arabs too had connections with the Baltic peoples and the peoples in Russia at that time. He knows of Danu (the Danube), Arin (the Rhine) and Alba (the Elbe). He mentions Denmark and Snislua (Schleswig), and describes Norway as if it were an island. Furthermore al-Idrisi notes that in the Baltic there is an Isle of Amazons.

Medieval European Maps

Contemporary Europe was of course unable to produce anything comparable. Although the classical tradition was not quite dead, Europeans still had no access to Ptolemy, and furthermore, since the educated were to be found only among monks and the clergy, any possible individual view was always bound to be checked against relevant passages from the Bible and the pronouncements of the Church Fathers.

And yet the tabernacle world of Cosmas Indicopleustes seems to have been put aside at an early stage: the "four corners" of the rectangular earth gradually came to be rounded off until it was a perfect disc. It has been thought that these circular European maps from the Middle Ages reflected a conception of the earth as a flat disc, but I believe that many of the cartographers knew that it was a sphere. The accepted view of the Church as to the shape of the world began to be questioned by many Christian geographers, especially since the Crusades had given men the opportunity of coming into contact with the world of Islam. But how would one have portrayed a sphere in those days if one had dared or wished to? Even al-Idrisi and other Arabs drew circular maps, though they knew quite well that the world was spherical.

The Arabs drew their maps with the south at the top, whereas the Christians had the east at the top. The 8th-century "Merovingian" map of the world is still partly influenced by Cosmas, but the proportions, with the inordinately large Mediterranean, are worse than in its precursor. I find it difficult to believe that the "O-T" maps from the 9th and 10th centuries represent the artist's real idea of the world; as I see it they are only to be regarded as a simple symbol in which the Cross of Christ is inscribed within the circle of the ocean. The upright is the Mediterranean, dividing Europe from Africa, and the cross-piece is the Tanais (i.e. the Don) and the Nile—the rivers separating Europe from Asia.

The 10th-century Anglo-Saxon map of the world has little convention left. The British Isles, in particular, are portrayed so that we are able to recognize them, and in the Mediterranean it is possible to make out the boot of Italy, the Peloponnese and the Greek archipelago. Later, it seems to have been the rule that Jerusalem was placed in the centre of the world, and the maps came to be richly decorated with churches and fortresses, people and animals and fabulous monsters. It seems as if a map became more of a pretext for the artist to show off his abilities than a cartographic attempt to draw the world as accurately as possible. The Ebstorf map of the world was made a hundred years after al-Idrisi's map: a deplorable indication of the difference between Christian and Mohammedan geographical knowledge.

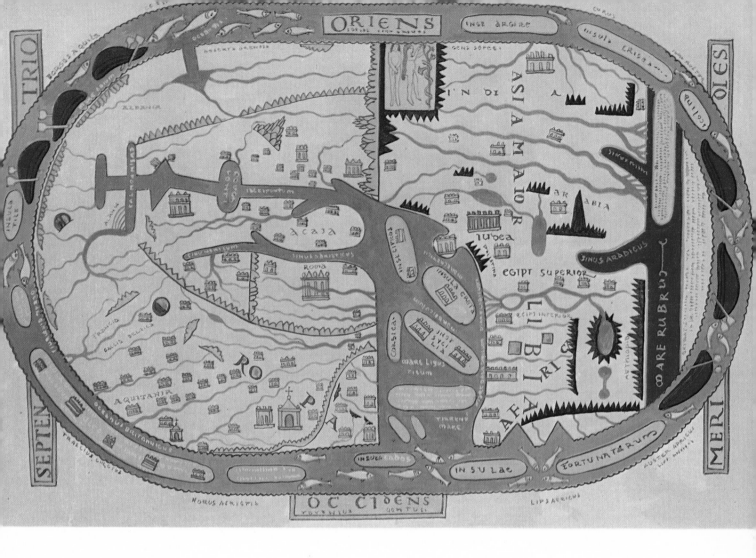

The map above was drawn by the Spanish friar Beatus in the 8th century. Left: the "Merovingian" map, 8th century, and below it the Anglo-Saxon map, 10th century. The "O-T" map is from the 9th century, and the Ebstorf map of the world, below, from the 12th.

Prester John and the Crusades

Christians had been making pilgrimages to Palestine and Jerusalem ever since the time of Constantine the Great, and when the Arabs conquered the Holy Land in 637 they allowed the pilgrim traffic to continue just as before. Diplomatic contact between Charlemagne and Harun al-Raschid at the end of the 8th century resulted in the grant to Charlemagne of a protectorate over the Christians in Palestine; for practical reasons this was later transferred to the Byzantine emperors. To begin with, the attitude of the Arabs towards the Christians was not in the least hostile. They allowed missionaries to pass through Syria and Persia on their way to the Christians of India, and we even hear of an English bishop who visited India about 884 at the wish of King Alfred. The journey is described during the 13th century by William of Malmesbury, a monk, who among other things has this to say: "Bishop Sigelmus Scriburnensis [of Sherborne], the man appointed for this task, arrived safely in India, this being a thing to be much wondered at in our age. When he returned from that country, he brought with him foreign splendour in the form of precious stones and fragrant oils which are to be found there. Furthermore he brought a gift more precious than all gold, namely a piece of the Cross of Our Lord, which Pope Marinus sent to the King."

For some reason or other, Caliph Hakim had the Church of the Holy Sepulchre pulled down in 1010. This naturally caused great astonishment and anger in the West, and it is said that the Pope called for a crusade even then. But it was only later, when the Seljuks—a Turkish people who had been converted to Islam and had won control of Syria, Mesopotamia and Palestine—began to threaten Byzantium and the Emperor called for aid from the Christian world at a synod, that the Crusades really got under way.

Pope Urban II saw in this a chance to strengthen the Papacy, and encouraged war against the infidels. And kings and knights-at-arms from almost every country in Europe marched east with their armies under the sign of the Cross, to liberate the Holy Land. Nicaea was the first Mohammedan city to fall to the crusading armies; yet it was not to the barbarians of western Europe that it opened its gates, but to the army of the Byzantine emperor Alexius. Jerusalem fell in 1099, after three years of campaigning, and a Christian kingdom was founded with Jerusalem as its capital.

In order to facilitate the expedition, the Crusaders had turned to Venice, Pisa and Genoa for aid in the shape of transport ships for their troops. Pisa and Genoa immediately sent fleets which helped to capture cities on the coasts of Palestine and Syria, but the Venetians, heedful of their trade interests in the Arab world, calmly waited to see what would happen; it was not till Jerusalem had fallen that they sent a fleet to Joppa. The Crusades turned out to be highly profitable for the three trading cities, which apart from the very remunerative transport of troops, munitions and supplies, obtained trading stations in the conquered regions and many kinds of privileges; at the same time they continued to trade with the Infidels in Egypt and the rest of Africa.

Enthusiasm over the initial successes in Palestine spread all over Europe. New Crusaders gathered to fight for the Faith, but many of them died of disease and hardship before reaching the Holy Land, and only a few found their way to Jerusalem. The Seljuks had not been defeated, moreover; they made continual thrusts against Byzantium and the defenders of the Holy Land, and when in 1144 they took Edessa, Pope Eugenius III found the time ripe to exhort his flock to a new crusade. Two great armies moved down through Constantinople to Asia Minor, but later they were to suffer much from hunger and unabated harassing attacks, with the result that only a small part of them reached Jerusalem.

In Syria a strange rumour had sprung up about a Christian king who lived beyond the Mohammedan Empire, and in 1145, while the Second Crusade was assembling, the rumour reached Europe. Otto of Freising, the histo-

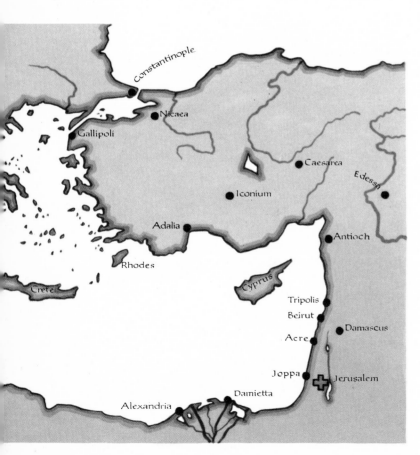

rian who had been called to a meeting in Viterbo in Italy by the Pope, met a Syrian bishop there who informed him and the others of the good news; he writes: "The bishop told of a certain John, a king and priest, reigning over a Christian people—Nestorian Christians, it is true —who lived beyond Persia and Armenia in the remote

East; that a few years ago he had defeated two brothers, the kings of the Medes and the Persians, called Samiards, and taken their residence in Egbattana [Ecbatana], which we mentioned above ... After the victory, this same John had moved on with his army to lend support to the Church in Jerusalem. But on coming to the Tigris and being unable to find any vessels in which to cross it, he had marched north, for he had heard that there the river freezes over in winter. After having waited in vain there for the cold of winter for several years, and not being able to reach his destination on account of the mild air, he found that he must return to his homeland, especially since he had lost many men in his army because of the unhealthy climate ... It is also said that he is one of the old race of Magi."

This news caused a great sensation among the rulers of Europe, who saw in Prester John a new and entirely unexpected ally. But the Second Crusade failed utterly, no help came from the east, and it was long before any more was heard of the mysterious monarch. At last, in 1165, a letter suddenly came to the Emperor Manuel Comnenus in Constantinople, the Emperor Frederick Barbarossa, and the Pope—the three great rulers in the West. The sender described himself as "Johannes, Presbyter, by the Might of God and the Power of Our Lord Jesus Christ, Lord of Lords."

The letter was no more than a communication as to the existence of Prester John and to the importance of his kingdom and himself. Among other things it contained the following: "I, Johannes the Presbyter, Lord of Lords, am superior in virtue, riches and power to all who walk under Heaven. Seventy-two kings pay tribute to Us. Our might prevails in the three Indies, and Our lands extend all the way to the Farthest Indies where the body of St. Thomas the Apostle lies ... Our country is the home and dwelling-place of elephants, dromedaries, camels, meta collinarum [?], cametennus [?], tinserete [?], panthers, forest asses, red and white lions, white bears, white merles, cicadas, mute gryphons, tigers, hyenas, wild horses, wild asses, wild oxen and wild men, horned men, one-eyed men, men with eyes to the fore and to the rear, centaurs, fauns, satyrs, pygmies, giants forty cubits tall, cyclops both male and female, the bird called Phoenix

This 12th-century gravestone shows a Crusader's homecoming. It is to be found in the Franciscan chapel at Nancy in France, and is said to represent the Duke of Vaudemont and his faithful wife Anne of Lorraine.

and nearly all the various kinds of animals that live under the sun ... 30,000 people eat at Our table each day, apart from casual guests, and all receive gifts from Our stores, sometimes horses, sometimes other things. This table is of the richest emerald and is supported by four pillars of amethyst ... Your wisdom must not be surprised that Our Eminence does not permit Himself to be called by a worthier name than that of presbyter. At Our court there are many servants who hold high spiritual offices and honours. Our steward is a primate and king; Our cupbearer a king and archbishop; Our chamberlain a bishop and king; Our marshal a king and archimandrite; and Our head cook a king and abbot ... In the one direction Our kingdom reaches for four months' journey; but how far it reaches in the other direction no one knows."

We do not know what the reaction of the two emperors was to this letter, but in 1177 Pope Alexander III sent his physician, Master Philippus, with a letter addressed to "the most excellent in Christ, the wondrous and magnificent King of the Indies, the most holy Presbyter Johannes". In respectful wording he explained that there was only one successor to Peter, namely the Pope in Rome, and that it was only if Prester John recognized this that he would be able to count on co-operation from the West. Master Philippus set off east to find the priest-king, but he was never to return, and nothing more was heard of him. Nor did any further letters come from the "Lord of Lords".

Today we believe that we know the secret of Prester John. In the beginning of the 12th century, an Asian tribe, which was called the Kara-Kitai and was presumably Nestorian Christian in its belief, reached great power for a short period under its chieftain Yeliutashi. In 1141 this Yeliutashi defeated a Seljuk army near Samarkand and conquered the whole of Turkestan, intending to press further west with his army, as the Huns had done before him and as the Mongols were to do after him. But Yeliutashi died in 1144, and his empire fell with him. By the time the myth of the priest-king reached Europe, its prototype was thus already in his

This is what Prester John's standard was believed to be like.

grave. The explanation put forward for the name John is that Yeliutashi must have called himself Uang Khan, which means "king of the people". Uang and Jean sound alike, and on the way from Turkestan to Italy the name would have passed through many mouths. "Khan" means "king" and "kham" means "priest", and so gradually this became "Priest-King John". The explanation is questionable, but I have been unable to find any better. The letter written in his name is of course a forgery, compiled by a lunatic or a humorist, and the fact that the Pope himself took it seriously shows how superstitious and imaginative the times were.

When Saladin, already Sultan of Egypt, had added Syria to his dominions, he took the Holy City in 1187. Then the Pope called for another crusade. This time the Christians managed to take the city of Acre, and, by agreement with the Sultan, they were allowed to keep the stretch of coastline between Tyre and Joppa. But they were not able to take Jerusalem; all they were able to obtain was permission to make pilgrimages to it unarmed. The undertaking profited nobody outside the trading cities of Italy.

The Fourth Crusade, which began in 1202, was directed at Egypt. As Pisa and Genoa were at war with each other at the time. Venice was the only city asked to give the Crusaders transport. But the Venetians saw no reason to spoil their good Egyptian market, and their old ruler, Doge Enrico Dandolo, succeeded in steering the Crusaders in a completely different direction. He promised to make a certain reduction in the heavy transport charges if the would first help Venice to take Zara in Dalmatia, and most of them agreed to this in spite of the Pope's veto. On the pretext of intervening in a Byzantine war of succession, Dandolo then got the Crusaders to take Constantinople, and it all ended by the Byzantine Empire becoming what is known as the Latin Empire under Baldwin of Flanders. The Empire was divided up into small vassal states, and Venice's share was three-eighths. Only a few Crusaders reached the Holy Land, and there they were unable to accomplish anything of importance.

During the mad Children's Crusade in 1212, on which many children, mainly from France and Germany, were sent off to fight in Palestine, most of them to die on the way and many of them to be sold as slaves to the Arabs, a number of Crusaders managed to take Damietta in Egypt, but were unable to hold the city for more than a few years. Then came fresh news of Prester John.

In April 1221 the Bishop of Acre wrote to the Pope of a King David, by the people called Prester John: "King David has three armies. One of them he has sent to the country belonging to Colaph, a brother of the Sultan of Egypt, the other against Baghdad and the third against Mosul, which in the Old Testament is called Nineveh.

And now he is not more than fifteen days' march from Antioch, and he makes all speed to reach the Promised Land to see the Sepulchre of Our Lord and to rebuild the Holy City. But before he does this, it is his intention, God willing, to subdue the land of the Sultan of Iconium, Calaphia and Damascus, and all the regions lying between, so that he will not leave one enemy behind him."

There were also other reports about King David and about great armies which threatened the Infidel Empire from the east. There was in actual fact a King David, a Georgian who had defeated a large Mohammedan army, but the armies that approached from the east and awakened such hope in the Christian world were led, not by Prester John, but by Jenghiz Khan.

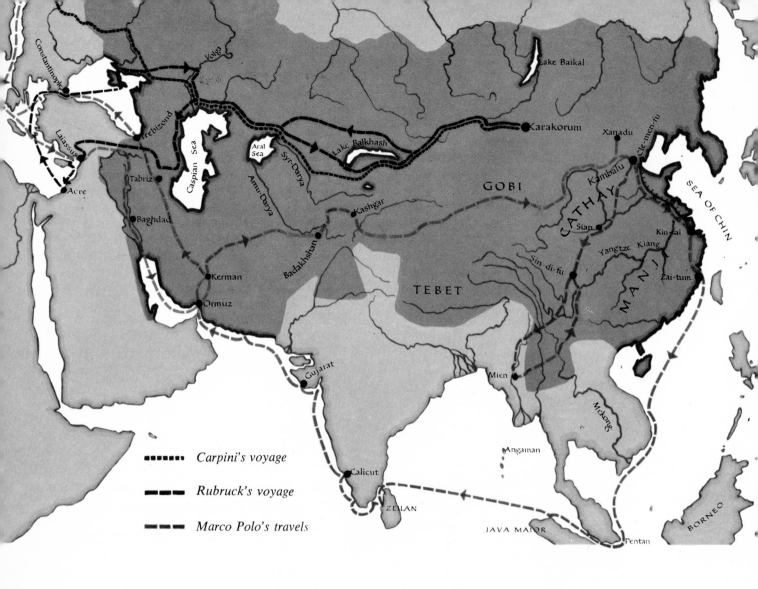

- ▪▪▪▪▪▪▪ *Carpini's voyage*
- ▬▬▬ *Rubruck's voyage*
- ▬ ▬ ▬ *Marco Polo's travels*

The World Empire of the Mongols

Temujin, who was the son of a relatively unimportant tribal chieftain, succeeded in the 13th century in uniting the nomadic Mongol tribes south and east of Lake Baikal and, with their aid, in suppressing neighbouring tribes. Later he took the name Jenghiz Khan and became known as one of the greatest and most vicious conquerors in history. With his armies he first took northern China, and then he turned towards the West. In 1219 he and his hordes forced their way into Mohammedan Turkestan, plundered and sacked Samarkand, Bokhara and other cities, and made further raids in Persia and northern India. One division of his army pushed its way up into southern Russia as far as the Dnieper, crushed the hastily organized Russian defence forces, and tortured their leaders to death. After plundering the prosperous Crimea,

and other places, it rejoined the main army and returned with it to Mongolia. Jenghiz Khan died after a campaign in western China in 1227.

The Mongol Empire then reached from the Volga in the west to Korea in the east, from Siberia in the north to the Caucasus, Afghanistan and central China in the south. On the instructions of Jenghiz Khan, it was divided into four sections to be governed by his three sons, Jagatai, Ogotai and Tului, and his grandson Batu. Ogotai, who inherited the title of Grand Khan, was no warrior, but he was a wise statesman, and during his reign his minister Yeliu Chutsai organized the giant empire according to Chinese patterns. A fixed system of taxation was introduced so that the empire could be financed, if need be, without foreign tribute; communication within the empire was maintained by a network of mounted couriers; and the nomadic chieftains were forced into accepting Karakorum as a fixed capital.

Jenghiz Khan's policy of annexations and indemnities was carried on by Jagatai and Tului, and especially by his energetic grandson Batu, who led the great invasion of Europe. The Mongols crossed the Volga and forced the Russian princes into subjection. Then the army split up so that one section moved through Poland into Germany, crossed the Oder and defeated an army of German knights at Wahlstatt in 1241. It then turned south towards Hungary and joined up with the other part, whereupon they crossed the Danube together and forced their way into Serbia and Bosnia. Smaller forces pushed right to the Adriatic. Europe was in the gravest danger, and it is likely that a far more extensive area would have been pillaged if the news of Ogotai's death had not induced Batu to return in order to look after his interests in the succession.

After much intrigue, Batu's cousin and enemy Kuyuk, son of Ogotai's favourite wife, was elected Grand Khan, but he died in 1248 and was succeeded by Tului's son Mangu. Mangu was perhaps the best of the Mongol rulers, and he further extended the boundaries of the empire by letting his brother Kublai wage a war of conquest in southern China, while his youngest brother Hulagu led an expedition in the south-west which resulted among other things in the taking of Baghdad and the crushing of the Abbassid Caliphate. After Hulagu had taken Aleppo and turned south towards Jerusalem, he received news of Mangu Khan's death and returned to Karakorum.

Mangu was succeeded in 1259 by Kublai, who moved his court to Peking, and it was during his reign that the Mongol Empire became the largest which has ever existed in the world.

There are a few fairly contemporary likenesses of Jenghiz Khan; this is a copy of one of them.

Carpini's Journey to Mongolia

Europe had learned only too clearly that the Mongol armies were not headed by any well-disposed priest-king, yet in spite of everything it was rumoured that the khans were not malevolently inclined towards Christianity, and that there were many Christians in their empire in the east. Therefore when Batu retired with his army from the ravaged countries of Europe on the death of Ogotai, and furthermore when the momentarily free Jerusalem once more had fallen into Mohammedan hands, the Pope tried to make contact with the Mongols in the hope of converting them to Christianity. He sent out two expeditions, led by the Franciscan monks Johannes de Plano Carpini and Laurentius of Portugal, which were to make separate attempts to reach the Grand Khan. Laurentius did not succeed in reaching his destination, and turned back, but Carpini completed his mission and wrote a report of the journey which is still in existence.

Johannes de Plano Carpini was a pupil and follower of St. Francis of Assisi, and on behalf of his Order he had already made long journeys—to Spain in the south and to Scandinavia in the north. When he started on his protracted journey to the Far East he was already sixty-two years old. Pope Innocent IV, who shortly before had fled to Lyons from his enemy the Emperor Frederick II, had given him complete liberty of action and provided him with letters of introduction, including one addressed to "the King and Peoples of the Tartars", for no one in Europe then knew the name of the man who ruled over the Mongols—or the Tartars, as they were called by Europeans in those days.

Among other things the papal letter contained the following: "Not only men, but also the animals of little understanding, indeed, even the material elements of which the world is made are united to each other as if by a natural association, according to the example of the heavenly spirits . . . We are therefore greatly surprised that you, as We have learned, have attacked and cruelly destroyed many countries belonging to Christian and other peoples . . . We now wish that all shall live in peace and in the fear of God, according to the example of the Prince of Peace. We therefore pray and call to you with all earnestness that you should relinquish all such undertakings and above all your persecution of Christians, and, by suitable penance, appease the wrath of God which you have most certainly brought upon yourselves by reason of your many great deeds of outrage . . . Lo, I find it proper to send to you My beloved son, Brother Johannes, and his companions as carriers of this letter, for they are known by their great spiritual responsibility and righteous habits, and they are well acquainted with the Scriptures. Receive them as friends, out of reverence to God; yea, in the same manner as if you were receiving Ourself in person. Treat them honourably and accept with trust and assurance all that they have to tell you of Us."

Carpini and his followers left Lyons in April 1246, and, having inquired in Prague about the most suitable route, they journeyed on to Poland so that they could have the company and escort of a Russian prince who was on his way to Batu's camp somewhere near the Volga. Early in the following year they arrived at the almost completely destroyed city of Kiev; there they met some Mongols who gave them a mounted escort to Batu. Carpini writes: "We rode as fast as our horses could manage, and, since we were able to change horses three or four times nearly every day, we were in the saddle from the early morning to the night, indeed, very often during the night as well. In spite of this we did not find it possible to reach him until the Wednesday in Holy Week . . . On Easter Eve we were called into his yurt where we were met by Batu's chancellor, who had been instructed to tell us that we must go on to the Emperor Kuyuk, who lives in the land of the Mongols. A few of our company were held there, however . . . We rode on with two Tartars, feeling so exhausted that we were hardly able to keep in the saddle. For during the whole of the forty days' fasting of Lent our only nourishment had consisted of millet boiled in salt and water, this also being the case during other days of fasting. We had nothing else to drink but snow, which we first had to melt in a pot."

Their route passed north of the Caspian and the Aral

Sea along the courier roads, the horses being changed up to seven times a day. In May they came to the Syr Darya; at the end of June they had to ride through the bitter cold of a snowstorm in the land of the Naimans. Carpini writes: "We rode for many days through this country. Then we passed into the true land of the Mongols or the Tartars. We crossed this with all speed in three

An army encamped somewhere in Mongolia; yurts, palisades and tents according to a Chinese drawing. Left: an obo, a place of cult worship, marked by stones, branches and brightly coloured bands.

96

weeks, as far as we now remember, and reached Kuyuk, who is now emperor there, on Mary Magdalene's Day [22nd July]. This stage of the journey was made with all possible speed, for our Tartars had been ordered to bring us to the long-announced festal assembly for the election of the emperor with the utmost speed so that we could attend it . . . When we came to Kuyuk, we were given a yurt and gratuitous fare at his command, as is the custom among the Tartars. We were better taken care of than the other ambassadors, however . . . Prince Yaroslav of Suzdal in Russia was there, together with many princes of the Kitai and the Solangs, and also two of the King of Georgia's sons. Furthermore there was a Sultan who had been sent as ambassador by the Caliph of Bagh-

dad and more than ten other Saracen Sultans, as we thought. And, according to what was told us by the Imperial Recorder, there were more than four thousand ambassadors there."

Later, when Kuyuk had been installed as Grand Khan, he received the papal legates and their message, and had an answer drawn up. On the 13th of November, Carpini and his men were allowed to return to their home country. Carpini writes: "We immediately set off on the journey home and travelled right through the winter. We often had to lie in snow in the wilderness . . . For there were no trees there, only flat plains. When we awoke in the morning, we often found ourselves completely covered with snow which the wind had blown over us. Then, towards Ascension Day [9th May 1247], we came to Batu and asked him what answer he wished to give. He replied that he had nothing to add to what the emperor had already written."

In November, after an absence of two and a half years, Carpini and his followers returned to the Pope at Lyons and delivered Kuyuk Khan's letter, which contained among other things the following: "It was also expressed in your letter that the killing of people, above all Christians and chiefly Hungarians, Poles and Moravians, had caused you distress and perplexity. Our answer to this is brief: that We are not able to understand it. So that it may not appear that We wish to be silent on this point, We believe that We must answer you as follows: God gave them into Our hands because they did not comply with the commandments of God and Jenghiz Khan, but rather, in their infamy, deliberately murdered Our ambassadors. How can anyone do other than make use of the power of God to kill and to plunder except at the com-mand of God? But you inhabitants of the West pray to God and presume yourselves alone to be Christians, while you despise others. But how is it then that you can know who is worthy in the eyes of God to receive His grace? We pray to God, and by His power We shall lay waste the whole earth from east to west. If a man did not have the power of God, how could he have done such things? When you say: I am a Christian, I praise God and hate all others, how is it that you know who it is that is considered to be in the right before God, and to whose advantage He shows His grace? . . . Today you shall say from the depths of your heart: we wish to be Your subjects and give You some of our power. You must therefore come to Us, on behalf of all kings, and offer your services and your homage. Only then will We recognize your servitude. If you disregard this Divine Commandment and pay no heed to Our wishes, We shall consider you as Our enemies."

But the Pope was not to be put off by this letter. He carried on a great correspondence and was an avid missionary; he had also sent letters of exhortation to the King of the Bulgars and to the Sultan of Morocco, and presumably to many other princes who in his eyes were lacking in piety. So he sent out new missionaries, this time Dominican friars, and these were joined by Andrew of Longjumeau, who had been sent to negotiate with the Grand Khan by St. Louis. But the missionaries failed miserably, and, when Andrew of Longjumeau reached Karakorum, Kuyuk Khan had died, and his grasping widow received St. Louis' gifts as a tribute and sent Andrew back with the message that, if he wanted peace, the King should send her all the silver and gold he had in his kingdom.

A Mongol field emblem.

Seal portraying St. Louis.

William of Rubruck among the Mongols

While St. Louis was waiting at Caesarea in Palestine for reinforcements from France so that he could continue the unsuccessful crusade he had been making against Egypt, Andrew of Longjumeau came directly to him there from Mongolia to report on his fruitless mission and to bring him the insulting reply from Kuyuk's widow. Also in Caesarea at that time was a Franciscan friar whose name was William of Rubruck. Like many of his Brotherhood he was an educated man with a good knowledge of languages, and he immediately offered to go with a new embassy to the ruler of the Mongols. However, as Louis did not wish it to appear as if he were deferring to the ruling widow, Rubruck suggested that he might travel as a private individual and missionary, to which the King was quite ready to agree provided that Rubruck made it clear to the Mongols and others that he did not come as an ambassador.

Rubruck's journey was not more remarkable than Carpini's, but he was a very shrewd observer and a good writer—he was the first to make a detailed description of conditions in Asia, and he was also to make important geographical observations. Because of this, I do not want to quote so much of the description of the journey itself, but more of his descriptions of peoples and customs and other things he saw. He was accompanied by another Franciscan friar, one Bartholomew of Cremona, an assistant called Gosset, an interpreter with the strange name of Homo Dei, and also a slave boy, Nicolaus by name, whom he had bought in Constantinople.

They left the imperial city in May 1253 and sailed across the Black Sea to Soldaia in the Crimea. Even at this early stage of their journey they met Mongols who gave them oxcarts and horses for the next stage of their journey to Batu's son Sartach, who was encamped somewhere between the Don and the Volga. According to rumours in Palestine, this Sartach was supposed to be a Christian sympathizer. They went from the Volga to Batu's camp by boat. Gosset and Nicolaus were not allowed to continue further, but the others left under escort, and just before the new year they reached Mangu Khan's camp, a six days' journey from Karakorum. They remained close to the Khan right up until 10th April. Then Rubruck set off on the journey home, but Brother Bartholomew, who had been ill for a considerable time, had to remain behind—no one knows what happened to him. On 19th April 1255 Rubruck was in Iconium in Asia Minor, and then he went on to Cyprus in order to discover where he might find King Louis. He was told that the King had sailed home the year before. He then wished to travel to France to report of his journey to the King, but at the request of his Order he had to remain preaching in Acre for a time. There he wrote a long description of his journey and sent this to St. Louis instead of appearing before him in person. — Let me quote a few passages:

"To the most illustrious and Christian Lord Louis, by the Grace of God renowned King of the French, from William of Rubruck, the meanest in the order of Minor Friars: greetings, and may he always triumph in Christ!... It is written in the Book of Ecclesiasticus that the wise man shall journey to foreign lands, and that he shall experience the good and the bad in all things ... This I have done, most Royal Lord; may it be as a wise man and not as a fool."

About the Crimea he says: "All the way from Kherson to the mouth of the Tanais there are high mountain peaks

Mangu Khan, after a Chinese woodcut.

along the coast, and there are forty villages between Kherson and Soldaia, of which almost every one has its own language. Dwelling here were many Goths, whose language is German . . . In the remotest region of this province there are many large lakes with salt wells along the shores. When their waters enter the lake they are immediately turned to salt, as hard as ice. Batu and Sartach derive great revenues from this salt, since people from the whole of Russia come here to fetch their salt, and each waggonload they purchase with a piece of cotton cloth worth half an yppera. Many ships cross the seas to fetch salt also, and all pay tribute in proportion to their load. On the third day after leaving Soldaia, we met the Tartars, and when I was among them, it seemed to me as if I had been transported into another world, whose life and customs I shall describe for you as best I can.

"Nowhere do they have fixed dwelling-places, nor do they know where they will live next. They have divided

Rubruck tells of how the yurts were transported on carriages. Over longer distances it was usual for them to be dismantled and carried on camelback.

Scythia, which stretches from the Danube to the eastern extremity of the world, and each commander, according to whether he has a greater or a lesser number of men under him, knows the bounds of his grazing-lands and where he is to graze his animals during the summer and the winter, during the spring and the autumn. For in the winter they move down to warmer climes in the south, and in the summer they move north to cooler. They use the less well-watered lands during the winter when there is snow, for they use the snow as water. The tent which they sleep in is set up over a circle of interwoven branches. The sides are also of branches, these joining together at the top in a smaller circle from which a sort of chimney rises. They cover it with white felt and often rub chalk or white clay or bonemeal into this so that it may be the whiter, and sometimes they colour it black ... They make these tents so large that they are often 30 feet across. I once measured the width between the tracks left by a cart; it was 20 feet, and when the tent was on the cart it projected at least five feet over the wheels on either side. I counted 22 oxen drawing a cart with a tent on it, eleven abreast in front of the cart and the other eleven in front of them. The shaft of the vehicle was as long as a mast, and in the entrance to the tent stood a man guiding the oxen ...

"So we journeyed east, seeing nothing but sky and earth and now and again on the right hand the sea, which is called the Don Sea [Sea of Azov], and also the graves of the Cumans, which were visible at a distance of a mile, for they are accustomed to bury their entire family in one spot. As long as we travelled in the desert regions we fared well, but the vexations I had to put up with when we came to their camps I am unable to describe. Our guide wanted us to call upon each chieftain with a gift, but our stores were not sufficient for this, since there were eight mouths which ate of our bread each day, apart from chance visitors, all of whom wished to eat with us ... Even when we were sitting under our carts to obtain a little shade, for the heat was great at this season, they forced themselves on us unashamedly and almost trampled us down out of curiosity to see all our things. When they needed to empty their bellies, they did not go further away from us than the distance a man can throw a bean; indeed, they defecated right beside us in the middle of a conversation and did many other things that appalled us. But more than anything else it troubled me that I was unable to teach a word of the Scripture to them, for my interpreter said: 'You cannot force me to preach when I do not know the right words.' And he was right. Later, when I had begun to understand a little of their language, it was so that when I said one thing, I heard him say something quite different, just as it occurred to him. I then understood the danger of speaking through him and decided that it would be preferable to keep silent."

Of his impressions after the meeting with Batu's son Sartach, the supposed Christian convert, Rubruck writes: "I do not know whether Sartach believes in Christ or not, but I do know that he does not wish to be called a Christian; to be honest, it seems to me as if he simply makes fun of the Christians ... Also in his company he has Nestorian priests who beat drums and sing their Masses."

He was the first European who could ever firmly assert that the Caspian was an inland sea: "Thus we came to the Etilia [the Volga], a very large river. It is four times as wide as the Seine and very deep, comes from Greater Bulgaria far in the north, flows south and runs out into

The framework of a yurt with smoke-hole ring, roof struts and collapsible walls.

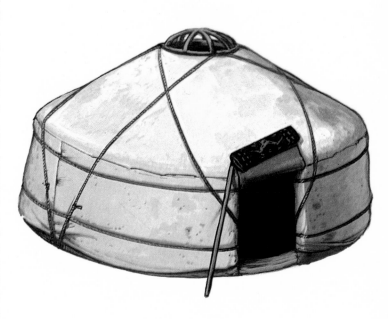

The frame was covered with felt and the yurt secured with ropes. A carpet hung across the entrance.

a lake or a sea, which is called Lake Sirsan after a city which lies on its shores in Persia. But Isidorus calls it the Caspian Sea ... Brother Andrew [of Longjumeau] travelled along two of its shores, the south and the east. I travelled along the other two, the north when journeying from Batu to Mangu Khan and again on the way back, and the west when returning from Batu to Syria. It is possible to travel round the sea in four months, and what Isidorus says of it, that it is an arm of the ocean, is not true. For it is never in contact with the ocean, and is surrounded everywhere by the mainland . . ."

The Isidorus whom Rubruck corrects is the Spanish bishop Isidore of Seville who, in the 7th century, attempted to write a book containing all that his contemporaries knew about the world; this shows that he was still an important authority six hundred years later. Rubruck goes on: "When I caught sight of Batu's *ordu* [residence], I was astonished, for the camp he lived in looked like a great city with an overabundance of people in an area of one and a half to two miles in circumference. And, as among the people of Israel, who each of them knew on which side of the Tabernacle he was to set up his tent, so do also these men know on which side they may erect their dwellings."

They were taken to an audience in Batu's tent: "We stood there barefooted and bareheaded in our attire, doubtlessly proving to be a strange sight in their eyes. Brother Johannes de Plano Carpini had indeed been there before us, but he had changed his robes so that he might not suffer derision, for he was the Papal Ambassador. Then we were led forth to the centre of the tent, but they did not demand of us that we should kneel in obeisance as is usually done by ambassadors. We stood before him for as long a time as it takes to read the *Miserere mei, Deus*, all the while in the gravest silence. He himself was sitting on a couch which was as long and as broad as a bed and gilded all over. Three steps led up to it. His wife sat beside him. The men sat here and there, both to the right and to the left of his wife, and the places that were not taken by the women on their side—for only Batu's wives were present—were occupied by the men. At the entrance stood a table laid with *cosmos* [koumiss, a drink made from fermented mare's milk] and large silver and gold cups, set with jewels.

"Batu observed us closely, and we him. His build seemed to be like that of John of Beaumont, may his soul rest in peace. At that time, his face was quite covered with red blotches. Finally he commanded that I should speak. Our guide then indicated to us that we should kneel. I knelt on one knee, as is customary before a human being, but he made a sign that I should fall on both, which I did, since I was not inclined to dispute the matter. He then commanded that I should speak, and I, thinking, as I was on both knees, that I was praying to God, began in the following manner with a prayer: 'Sire, we pray God, from Whom all good things come and Who has given you these worldly joys, that He hereafter may give you the joys of heaven, without which all this is vanity.' He was listening attentively, and I continued: 'Be it known to you that you will never experience the joys of heaven if you do not become a Christian. For the Lord has said: He that believeth and is baptized shall be saved; but he that believeth not shall be damned.' At these words he

smiled a little, and the other personages began to clap their hands in mockery of us. My interpreter became so afraid that he was unable to speak, and I had to persuade him not to be dismayed. When all was once again quiet, I continued: 'I came to your son, for we heard that he was a Christian, bringing a letter from my master, the King of France. And he [the son] sent me here to you, and you yourself must know the reason why.'

"He then allowed me to rise and asked your name, and mine, and those of my companions and my interpreter, and had them all written down. He also asked against whom you were waging war, for he had understood that you had left your country with an army. I answered: 'Against the Saracens, who are violating Jerusalem, the home of the Lord.' He asked moreover whether you had ever sent ambassadors to him, and I replied: 'Never to you.' Then he allowed us to sit and gave us some of his milk to drink. That someone be asked to drink cosmos with him in his own house is considered by them to be a great honour . . .

"Finally, at the time of the Mass of the Cross [14th September] there came a rich Moal [Mongol] to us. His father was in command of 1,000 men, which is a high rank among them. And he said: 'I will take you to Mangu Khan. It is a journey of four months, and the cold there is so bitter that it cracks both stones and trees. Consider whether you are able to endure this.' I answered him: 'I hope that we, by the Grace of God, will be able to endure what others can.' He said: 'If you are not able, I shall leave you by the wayside.' Then I replied: 'That would not be right, for we do not travel of our own free will, but at the command of your master. And since we are thus in your care, you should not abandon us.' In reply to this he said: 'All will be well', whereupon he asked us to show him all our clothing, and those things which seemed less necessary to him he let us leave with our host. On the next day, each of us was given a sheepskin coat and sheepskin trousers, boots such as they themselves wear, and felt stockings and fur caps that are used by them. And on the second day after the Mass of the Cross, the three of us set out with two pack-horses."

Their journey was full of hardships and adversities, and the horses were not of the best, but Rubruck says: "They always gave me a strong animal on account of my great weight . . . There was no end to hunger and thirst, cold and exhaustion. For they gave us to eat only in the evening. In the morning we were given something to drink, perhaps a little millet porridge. But in the evening they gave us meat, a shoulder of mutton with the spare-ribs, and also a measure of soup to drink. Having drunk our fill of this meat-juice we felt much revived, and I thought it was a fine and nourishing drink."

After three and a half months of hardship, they reached Mangu Khan's camp, and, after a week of waiting, they were at last given audience by the Grand Khan. Rubruck relates: "On the 3rd of January we were taken to his Court. Then came some Nestorian priests, whom I did not recognize as Christians, and asked us in which direction we prayed. I answered: 'To the east.' They therefore asked whether it was on the advice of our guides that we had shaved our beards before our audience with the Khan, as was the custom in our country. This was why they took us to be Tuins, that is idolaters [Buddhist priests]. They also made us explain things from the Bible. They then asked us what signs of respect we intended to show the Khan, those according to our own usage or according to theirs. I answered: 'We are priests, the servants of the Lord. Great men in our country do not permit priests to kneel before them, out of respect for God. But for the sake of Our Lord we are prepared to humble ourselves before all men. We have come from afar, and therefore, if it so pleases you, we should like to sing praise to God Who has brought us this great distance unharmed. Then we shall do all that you desire before your master, provided you do not wish us to perform things that are dishonourable towards God or contrary to His commandments.'

"They went into the house and related what I had said. My words pleased the Khan, and they brought us before the entrance and lifted up the felt hanging of the door, and, as it was Christmastide, we began to sing:

> A solis ortus cardine
> et usque terrae limitem
> Christum canamus principem
> natum Maria virgine.

When we had sung this hymn, they searched about our arms and bodies and legs to see whether we had knives on us. After this they searched the interpreter and made him leave his belt and knife outside with the guard. And so we went in, and at the entrance stood a table with cosmos, beside which the interpreter was made to stand. We were allowed to seat ourselves on a couch in front of the women. Inside, the house was completely hung with cloth of gold, and burning there was a fire of wormwood, which grows to a great size in that country, and thorns and cow-dung in a fireplace in the centre of the room. The Khan himself was seated on a bed covered with a smooth spotted fur, something like sealskin. He is a flat-nosed man, forty-five years old, of middling height. At his side sat a young wife. One of his daughters named Cirina, fully-grown and horribly ugly, sat with some babies on a bed behind them. This house had belonged to a Christian woman whom he had greatly loved and by whom he had this daughter. Then he had taken the young wife, but the girl was nevertheless mistress over the whole of this ordu, which had been her mother's.

"The Khan let it be asked what we wished to drink, whether wine or terracina [rice wine] or caracosmos [clear mare's milk] or bal [mead]. For these are the four beverages they drink during the winter. I then answered: 'Sire, we are not such as seek their joy in the cup. Whatever you yourself may choose will suit us well.' Then he let us be given of the rice drink, which was clear and aromatic, like white wine, and I tasted of it out of respect for him. But to our misfortune the interpreter stood close to the cup-bearers, and they gave him so much to drink that he immediately became drunk . . . I then spoke the following words: 'Sire, we heard tell that Sartach was a Christian', and we Christians that heard this rejoiced at it, in particular my master, the King of France. We therefore journeyed to him, and my master the King sent him letters with us which contained words of peace, giving

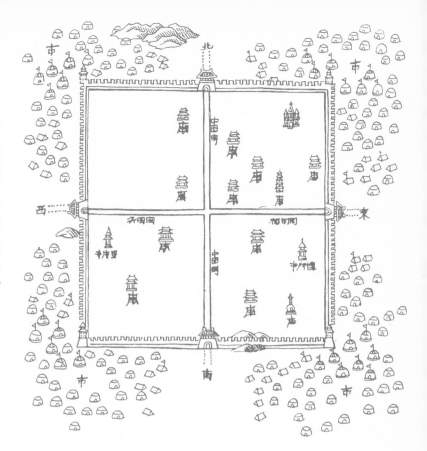

Karakorum, the Mongol capital, was founded in 1235 by Ogotai Khan and was presumably built on the instructions of the minister Yeliu Chutsai according to the Chinese model — square, with four gateways and two main streets which crossed one another. The city was later destroyed and levelled to the ground by the Chinese, but a Chinese drawing (right) gives us an idea of what it looked like. Rubruck spoke of its insignificance, and we must presume that apart from the temples, palaces and houses for the most prominent foreigners, the living quarters were mostly yurts, many of which, as will be seen in the drawing, were located outside the walls, or, more properly, the earthworks. The picture to the left shows what one of the city gates probably looked like.

him at the same time testimonials as to ourselves and who we were, and asking him to allow us to stay in his country. But he sent us to his father Batu, and Batu sent us to you. You are one to whom God has given great power on earth. We therefore pray that you, by your authority, will allow us to remain in your country in order that we may serve God for you, your wives and your children. We cannot offer you gold or silver or precious stones, but only ourselves, whom we beg you to receive that we may serve God and pray to the Lord for you. We trust that you will at least give us permission to remain here until the winter is past, for my companion is so weak that he will be unable to endure the difficult ride again without risk for his life' . . .

"He then began to reply himself: 'As the sun lets his rays fall on all things, so has the Empire which belongs to me and Batu spread everywhere. We therefore need neither silver nor gold.' Thus far I was able to understand my interpreter, but after this I could not grasp any sentences perfectly, and that is when I found that he was drunk. Nor did Mangu Khan himself seem to me to be sober. But his speech, as far as I could understand, ended by his saying that he was not pleased that we had first visited Sartach and not him . . .

"A woman from Metz in Lorraine, Paquette by name, who had been captured in Hungary, sought us out and

provided for us to the best of her ability . . . Furthermore, she told us that in Caracora [Karakorum] there was a goldsmith, William Buchier by name, who was born in Paris. His father's name was Laurence Buchier . . .

"Cathay [China] lies by the ocean, and Master William told me that he had seen ambassadors from peoples called the Caules and the Manses, who live on islands in a sea which freezes over during the winter so that the Tartars can attack them . . . The regular currency in Cathay is cotton paper, a handsbreadth square, on which they print lines which are like those on Mangu's seal. They write with a brush, such as artists use, and in one sign they combine letters which form a whole word. The Tibetans write as we do and have letters which are very like ours . . . Nor is there any city to the north, but there is a people whom the herdsmen call Kerkis [the Kirghiz]. Also living there are the Orengai, who bind polished slats of bone beneath their feet and glide over frozen snow and ice . . .

"Concerning the city of Karakorum, may you know that with the exception of the Khan's palace it is not as large as the village of Saint-Denis, and the monastery of Saint-Denis is ten times as large as the palace. It is divided into two districts. The one is the Saracens', where the market lies, and numbers of merchants gather there since the Court is always close by, and for the sake of the many

105

ambassadors. The second is the Cathayans' district, where all are craftsmen. Outside these districts are large palaces belonging to the Court Secretaries. There are twelve temples for idol worship, belonging to various nations, two mosques where the teachings of Mohammed are spread, and one church in the outskirts of the city. The city is surrounded by an earth wall with four gates in it."

Rubruck was allowed to stay until the middle of June at the Grand Khan's Court and was treated well. When he departed with interpreter and escort, he carried with him a letter from Mangu Khan to St. Louis, in which Mangu explained that the letter which the King had earlier received from Kuyuk's wife through the hands of Andrew of Longjumeau was worthless. — "How could this miserable woman, more wretched than a bitch, possibly know anything of war or peace, of providing a great people with happiness and doing it good?" And he exhorts the King to send ambassadors so that he may know whether the French want peace or war.

At the final audience, Mangu Khan said to Rubruck: "We Mongols believe that there is only one God, by Whom we live and die, and before Him we are righteous of heart. But just as God has given the hand a variety of fingers, so has he given mankind a variety of ways. To you He has given the Scriptures, and you do not abide by them. There you do not find that the one shall find fault with the other—or do you? Nor do you find there that a man shall turn from righteousness for the sake of profit alone. Unto us He has given soothsayers, and we do what they say and live in peace."

Rubruck refused all gifts, but William Buchier, a former subject of King Louis, persuaded him to take the King a jewelled belt as a protection against thunder and lightning. The rigorous journey home took nearly a whole year, and when Rubruck had completed his narrative at Acre, he ended it with a prayer to the King that the local superior of his Order might be persuaded to give permission for Rubruck to go to France and visit the King. The King agreed, and we know that he reached Paris; but of his fate after this nothing is known.

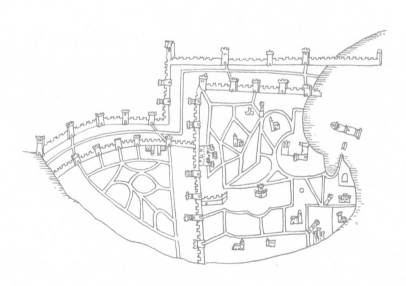

Acre at the end of the 13th century according to Marino Sanuto's map.

No authentic portrait of Marco Polo exists. This is a copy of a much-reproduced 17th-century portrait supposed to represent the great traveller. The landscape in the background is a Chinese painting from the middle of the 13th century.

Marco Polo

In 1296 the Genoese and the Venetians fought a minor naval battle which is remembered by us only because a wealthy Venetian merchant by the name of Marco Polo happened to fall into Genoese captivity. In Genoa he later shared a prison cell with the writer Rustichello, a prisoner from Pisa. In order to pass the time, Marco Polo began to tell of his adventures in Cathay (China) in the East, and it was not long before Rustichello became greatly interested, wanting to write a book about it all. Marco Polo sent for his notes from Venice, and with their help he narrated and dictated, Rustichello writing down the narrative in a peculiar Italian French which was the literary language of that period—in Pisa at least.

We must presume that even this original book contained a number of misunderstandings and orthographic errors, in particular as regards the names of people and places. Rustichello's valuable manuscript has been lost, and nor do any of the transcripts made directly from the manuscript appear to have been saved. However, these copies were the basis for the one hundred and twenty manuscripts still in existence, documents which all differ from each other in one respect or another. The reason for the differences was presumably the lack of skill or carelessness of the transcriber, lack of interest or a need to abbreviate, and perhaps the wish of the transcriber to correct and embroider a little himself. Scholars have since compared the material and have arrived at what they believe to be as close as possible to the original, and they have also reconstructed the Asian journey itself—a difficult task, for it sometimes happened that Marco Polo described places which he had never seen.

The introductory chapter describes the entire journey, or journeys, in summary, and the following two hundred and five chapters—certain editions have fewer—contain detailed descriptions of different places, of peoples and their customs and religions, of seafaring and wars, and of the riches that are to be found in the East. Marco Polo is not a particularly humorous storyteller, nor do we find many anecdotes in his book, but he is extraordinarily conscientious and a great lover of the truth—when he tells of demons and monsters and other things that we do not readily accept, he is simply relating what others have told him. Those who later called him a great liar made no objections to the fabulous monsters and other superstitions which he described, but they were quite unable to believe his descriptions of the magnificence and riches and plenty in the palaces and cities of China. It is said that the Venetians called him "Il Milione" as he always used such large figures when describing things in the East. But those coming after him, who have been able to check his statements critically, have found that he confined himself strictly to the truth for the most part, at least as far as a man living in those times could understand the truth.

I should like to quote the book's prologue and the introductory chapter up to the arrival of Marco Polo, his father and his uncle at the court of Kublai Khan, then to give a picture of the journey through Asia and finally, with quotations, to demonstrate a part of what Marco Polo saw and noted in the Far East.

"Ye emperors, kings, dukes, marquises, earls, and knights, and all other people desirous of knowing the diversities of the races of mankind, as well as the diversities of kingdoms, provinces, and regions of all parts of the East, read through this book, and ye will find in it the greatest and most marvellous characteristics of the peoples especially of Armenia, Persia, India, and Tartary, as they are severally related in the present work by Marco Polo, a wise and learned citizen of Venice, who states distinctly what things he saw and what things he heard from others. For this book will be a truthful one. It must be known, then, that from the creation of Adam to the present day, no man whether Pagan, or Saracen, or Christian, or other, of whatever progeny or generation he may have been, ever saw or inquired into so many and such great things as Marco Polo above mentioned. Who, wishing in his secret thoughts that the things he had seen and heard should be made public by the present work,

for the benefit of those who could not see them with their own eyes, he himself being in the year of our Lord 1298 in prison at Genoa, caused the things which are contained in the present work to be written by master Rustichello, a citizen of Pisa, who was with him in the same prison at Genoa; and he divided it into three parts.

"It should be known to the reader that, at the time when Baldwin II was Emperor of Constantinople, where a magistrate representing the Doge of Venice then resided, and in the year of our Lord 1259, Nicolo Polo, the father of the said Marco, and Maffeo, the brother of Nicolo, respectable and well-informed men, embarked in a ship of their own, with a rich and varied cargo of merchandise, and reached Constantinople in safety. After mature deliberation on the subject of their proceedings, it was determined, as the measure most likely to improve their trading capital, that they should prosecute their voyage into the Euxine or Black Sea. With this view they made purchases of many fine and costly jewels, and taking their departure from Constantinople, navigated that sea to a port named Soldaia, from whence they travelled on horseback many days until they reached the court of a powerful chief of the western Tartars, named Barka [he was a younger brother of Batu's, and had succeeded Sartach], who dwelt in the cities of Bolgara and Assara, and had the reputation of being one of the most liberal and civilized princes hitherto known amongst the tribes of Tartary. He expressed much satisfaction at the arrival of these travellers, and received them with marks of distinction. In return for which courtesy, when they had laid before him the jewels they brought with them, and perceived that their beauty pleased him, they presented them for his acceptance. The liberality of this conduct on the part of the two brothers struck him with admiration; and being unwilling that they should surpass him in generosity, he not only directed double the value of the jewels to be paid to them, but made them in addition several rich presents.

"The brothers, having resided a year in the dominions of this prince, then became desirous of revisiting their native country, but were impeded by the sudden breaking out of a war between him and another chief, named Alaù, who ruled over the eastern Tartars [Alaù = Hulagu, Mangu's and Kublai's brother]. In a fierce and very sanguinary battle that ensued between their respective armies, Alaù was victorious, in consequence of which, the roads being rendered unsafe for travellers, the brothers could not attempt to return by the way they came; and it was recommended to them, as the only practicable mode

The brothers Nicolo and Maffeo Polo leave Venice in 1259. The Basilica of St. Mark and the Doge's Palace in the background.

of reaching Constantinople, to proceed in an easterly direction, by an unfrequented route, so as to skirt the limits of Barka's territories. Accordingly they made their way to a town named Oukaka, situated on the confines of the kingdom of the western Tartars. Leaving that place, and advancing still further, they crossed the Tigris [this was actually the Volga], one of the four rivers of Paradise, and came to a desert, the extent of which was seventeen days' journey, wherein they found neither town, castle, nor any substantial building, but only Tartars with their herds, dwelling in tents on the plain. Having passed this tract they arrived at length at a well-built city called Bokhara, in a province of that name, belonging to the dominions of Persia, and the noblest city of that kingdom, but governed by a prince whose name was Barak. Here, from inability to proceed further, they remained three years.

"It happened while these brothers were in Bokhara, that a person of consequence and gifted with eminent talents made his appearance there. He was proceeding as ambassador from Alaù before mentioned, to the Grand Khan, supreme chief of all the Tartars, named Kublai, whose residence was at the extremity of the continent, in a direction between north-east and east. Not having ever before had an opportunity, although he wished it, of seeing any natives of Italy, he was gratified in a high degree at meeting and conversing with these brothers, who had now become proficient in the Tartar language; and after associating with them for several days, and finding their manners agreeable to him, he proposed to them that they should accompany him to the presence of the Grand Khan, who would be pleased by their appearance at his court, which had not hitherto been visited by any person from their country; adding assurances that they would be honourably received, and recompensed with many gifts. Convinced as they were that their endeavours to return homeward would expose them to the most imminent risks, they agreed to this proposal, and recommending themselves to the protection of the Almighty, they set out on their journey in the suite of the ambassador, attended by several Christian servants whom they had brought with them from Venice. The course they took at first was between the north-east and north, and an

Traditionally, the building of the Great Wall of China began in the 3rd century B.C., on the orders of the Emperor Ch'in Shi Huang Ti, who united the separate Chinese Kingdoms and hoped to introduce a new age. The wall did not stop the Mongols from invading the country. The Polo brothers and their nephew Marco must have seen it and passed through it on their way to Cambalu (Peking), although it is not mentioned in Marco Polo's Travels. — Opposite is a Chinese warrior.

entire year was consumed before they were enabled to reach the imperial residence, in consequence of the extraordinary delays occasioned by the snows and the swelling of the rivers, which obliged them to halt until the former had melted and the floods had subsided. Many things worthy of admiration were observed by them in the progress of their journey, but which are here omitted, as they will be described by Marco Polo, in the sequel of the book.

"Being introduced to the presence of the Grand Khan, Kublai, the travellers were received by him with the condescension and affability that belonged to his character, and as they were the first Latins who had made their appearance in that country, they were entertained with feasts and honoured with other marks of distinction. Entering graciously into conversation with them, he made earnest inquiries on the subject of the western parts of the world, of the emperor of the Romans, and of other Christian kings and princes. He wished to be informed of their relative consequence, the extent of their possessions, the manner in which justice was administered in their several kingdoms and principalities, how they conducted themselves in warfare, and above all he questioned them particularly respecting the Pope, the affairs of the Church, and the religious worship and doctrine of the Christians. Being well instructed and discreet men, they gave appropriate answers upon all these points, and as they were perfectly acquainted with the Tartar language, they expressed themselves always in becoming terms; in so much that the Grand Khan, holding them in high estimation, frequently commanded their attendance.

"When he had obtained all the information that the two brothers communicated with so much good sense, he expressed himself well satisfied, and having formed in his mind the design of employing them as his ambassadors to the Pope, after consulting with his ministers on the subject, he proposed to them, with many kind entreaties, that they should accompany one of his officers, named Khogatal, on a mission to the See of Rome. His object, he told them, was to make a request to His Holiness that he would send to him a hundred men of learning, thoroughly acquainted with the principles of the Christian religion, as well as with the seven arts, and qualified to prove to the learned of his dominions by just and fair argument, that the faith professed by Christians is superior to, and founded upon more evident truth than, any other; that the gods of the Tartars and the idols worshipped in their houses were only evil spirits, and that they and the people of the East in general were under an error in reverencing them as divinities. He moreover signified his pleasure that upon their return they should bring with them, from Jerusalem, some of the holy oil from the lamp which is kept burning over the sepulchre of our Lord Jesus Christ, Whom he professed to hold in veneration and to consider as the true God. Having heard

Buddhism reached China from India by the 2nd century A.D.*, and by the time the Mongols invaded the country it was the predominant religion. Neither Kublai Khan nor any other of the Grand Khans seems to have had any particular interest in religion, but the Church missed a great opportunity when it ignored his request for Christian priests and teachers. — Above is a Buddha from Kublai Khan's days. — Left: a gold tablet of the type given to the Polo Brothers on their departure from the Grand Khan.*

these commands addressed to them by the Grand Khan they humbly prostrated themselves before him, declaring their willingness and instant readiness to perform, to the utmost of their ability, whatever might be the royal will. Upon which he caused letters, in the Tartar language, to be written in his name to the Pope of Rome, and these he delivered into their hands. He likewise gave orders that they should be furnished with a golden tablet displaying the imperial cipher, according to the usage established by his majesty; in virtue of which the person bearing it, together with his whole suite, are safely conveyed and escorted from station to station by the governors of all places within the imperial dominions, and are entitled, during the time of their residing in any city, castle, town, or village, to a supply of provisions and everything necessary for their accommodation.

"Being thus honourably commissioned they took their leave of the Grand Khan, and set out on their journey, but had not proceeded more than twenty days when the officer, named Khogatal, their companion, fell dangerously ill, in the city named Alau. In this dilemma it was determined, upon consulting all who were present, and with the approbation of the man himself, that they should leave him behind. In the prosecution of their journey they derived essential benefit from being provided with the royal tablet, which procured them attention in every place through which they passed. Their expenses were defrayed, and escorts were furnished. But notwithstanding these advantages, so great were the natural difficulties they had to encounter, from the extreme cold, the snow, the ice, and the flooding of the rivers, that their progress was unavoidably tedious, and three years elapsed before they were enabled to reach a sea-port town in the lesser Armenia, named Laiassus [Ayash in modern Turkey]. Departing from thence by sea, they arrived at Acre in the month of April, 1269, and there learned, with extreme concern, that Pope Clement the Fourth was recently dead. A legate whom he had appointed, named M. Tebaldo de Vesconti di Piacenza, was at this time resident in Acre, and to him they gave an account of what they had in command from the Grand Khan of Tartary. He advised them by all means to await the election of another pope, and when that should take place, to proceed with the object of their embassy. Approving of this counsel, they determined upon employing the interval in a visit to their families in Venice. They accordingly embarked at Acre in a ship bound to Negropont, and from thence went on to Venice, where Nicolo Polo found that his wife, whom he had left with child at his departure, was dead, after having been delivered of a son, who received the name of Marco, and was now of the age of fifteen years. [We must therefore presume that Nicolo Polo had already left Venice several years before his arrival in Constantinople.] This is the Marco by whom the present work is composed, and who will give therein a relation of all those matters of which he has been an eye-witness.

"In the meantime the election of a Pope was retarded by so many obstacles, that they remained two years in Venice, continually expecting its accomplishment; when at length, becoming apprehensive that the Grand Khan might be displeased at their delay, or might suppose it was not their intention to revisit his country, they judged it expedient to return to Acre; and on this occasion they took with them young Marco Polo. Under the sanction of the legate, they made a visit to Jerusalem, and there provided themselves with some of the oil belonging to the Lamp of the Holy Sepulchre, conformably to the directions of the Grand Khan. As soon as they were furnished with his letters addressed to that Prince bearing testimony to the fidelity with which they had endeavoured to execute his commission, and explaining to him that the Pope of the Christian Church had not as yet been chosen, they proceeded to the before-mentioned port of Laiassus. Scarcely however had they taken their departure, when the legate received messengers from Italy, despatched by the College of Cardinals, announcing his own elevation to the Papal Chair; and he thereupon assumed the name of Gregory the Tenth. Considering that he was now in a situation that enabled him fully to satisfy the wishes of the Tartar sovereign, he hastened to transmit letters to the King of Armenia, communicating to him the event of his election and requesting, in case the two ambassadors who were on their way to the court of the Grand Khan

should not have already quitted his dominions, that he would give directions for their immediate return. These letters found them still in Armenia, and with great alacrity they obeyed the summons to repair once more to Acre; for which purpose the king furnished them with an armed galley; sending at the same time an ambassador from himself, to offer his congratulations to the sovereign pontiff.

"Upon their arrival, His Holiness received them in a distinguished manner, and immediately dispatched them with letters papal, accompanied by two friars of the Order of Preachers, who happened to be on the spot; men of letters and of science, as well as profound theologians. One of them was named Fra Nicolo da Vicenza, and the other, Fra Guielmo da Tripoli. To them he gave licence and authority to ordain priests, to consecrate bishops, and to grant absolution as fully as he could do in his own person. He also charged them with valuable presents, and among these, several handsome vases of crystal, to be delivered to the Grand Khan in his name, and along with his benediction. Having taken leave, they again steered their course to the port of Laiassus, where they landed, and from thence proceeded into the country of Armenia [probably at the end of 1271]. Here they received intelligence that the Sultan of Babylonia, named Bundokdari, had invaded the Armenian territory with a numerous army, and had overrun and laid waste the country to a great extent. Terrified at these accounts, and apprehensive for their lives, the two friars determined not to proceed further, and delivering over to the Venetians the letters and presents entrusted to them by the Pope, they placed themselves under the protection of the Master of the Knights Templars, and with him returned directly to the coast. Nicolo, Maffeo and Marco, however, undismayed by perils or difficulties (to which they had long been inured), passed the borders of Armenia, and prosecuted their journey. After crossing deserts of several days' march, and passing many dangerous defiles, they advanced so far, in a direction between north-east and north, that at length they gained information of the Grand Khan, who then had his residence in a large and magnificent city named Cle-men-fu [probably modern Kaiping]. Their whole journey to this place occupied no less than three years and a half; but during the winter months,

A crystal vase of the type which Pope Gregory X sent to Kublai Khan by the Polo brothers.

their progress had been inconsiderable. The Grand Khan having notice of their approach whilst still remote, and being aware how much they must have suffered from fatigue, sent forward to meet them at the distance of forty days' journey, and gave orders to prepare, in every place through which they were to pass, whatever might be requisite to their comfort."

Modern historians believe that they can recognize the route which the travellers took from Laiassus to the summer residence of Kublai Khan at Kaiping, even though opinions may differ on certain points (see the map on p. 94). Passing from Armenia they reached Arzingan, then turned towards the south-west and moved along the Tigris to Baghdad and Basra and still further to Ormuz, and it seems as if they had held hopes of sailing to China. But then they continued their journey from Ormuz by branching off directly north through the deserts of Kerman in Mongol-occupied Persia right up to the northern border of the country, and east from there to Badakhshan north of Kashmir where Marco Polo

lay ill for almost a whole year. From there they travelled along the River Pandj, over the Pamirs to Kashgar, through the most important towns in the Tarim Basin,

It was on the plateau of the Pamirs that Marco Polo saw the large Pamir sheep, which is called Ovis Poli after him. He says: "In this plain there are wild animals in great numbers, particularly sheep of a large size, having horns, three, four, and even six palms in length. Of these the shepherds form ladles and vessels for holding their victuals; and with the same materials they construct fences for enclosing their cattle, and securing them against the wolves, with which, they say, the country is infested, and which likewise destroy many of these wild sheep or goats."

across a part of the Gobi to Kanchow, and finally through the provinces of Shensi and Shansi to Kaiping.

Let us now return to the introductory chapter of the book: "Upon their arrival they were honourably and graciously received by the Grand Khan, in a full assembly of his principal officers. When they drew nigh to his person, they paid their respects by prostrating themselves on the floor. He immediately commanded them to rise, and to relate to him the circumstances of their travels,

with all that had taken place in their negotiation with His Holiness the Pope. To their narrative, which they gave in the regular order of events, and delivered in perspicuous language, he listened with attentive silence. The letters and the presents from Pope Gregory were then laid before him, and, upon hearing the former read, he bestowed much commendation on the fidelity, the zeal, and the diligence of his ambassadors; and receiving with due reverence the oil from the Holy Sepulchre, he gave directions that it should be preserved with religious care. Upon his observing Marco Polo, and inquiring who he was, Nicolo made answer: 'This is your servant, and my son'; upon which the Grand Khan replied: 'He is welcome, and it pleases me much', and he caused him to be enrolled amongst his attendants of honour. And on account of their return he made a great feast and rejoicing; and as long as the said brothers and Marco remained in the court of the Grand Khan, they were honoured even above his own courtiers. Marco was held in high estimation and respect by all belonging to the court. He learnt in a short time and adopted the manners of the Tartars, and acquired a proficiency in four different languages, which he became qualified to read and write. Finding

him thus accomplished, his master was desirous of putting his talents for business to the proof, and sent him on an important concern of state to a city named Karazan, situated at the distance of six months' journey from the imperial residence; on which occasion he conducted himself with so much wisdom and prudence in the management of the affairs entrusted to him, that his services became highly acceptable. On his part, perceiving that the Grand Khan took a pleasure in hearing accounts of whatever was new to him respecting the customs and manners of people, and the peculiar circumstances of distant countries, he endeavoured, wherever he went, to obtain correct information on these subjects, and made notes of all he saw and heard, in order to gratify the curiosity of his master. In short, during seventeen years that he continued in his service, he rendered himself so useful, that he was employed on confidential missions to every part of the empire and its dependencies; and sometimes also he travelled on his own private account, but always with the consent, and sanctioned by the authority, of the Grand Khan. Under such circumstances it was that Marco Polo had the opportunity of acquiring a knowledge, either by his own observation, or by what he learned

from others, of so many things, until his time unknown, respecting the eastern parts of the world, and which he diligently and regularly committed to writing, as in the sequel will appear. And by this means he obtained so much honour, that he provoked the jealousy of the other officers of the court."

I should now like to quote passages in an order which may appear as disconnected as the chapters of his book sometimes are themselves. First Marco Polo's impression of Kublai Khan:

"Kublai, who is styled Grand Khan, or Lord of Lords, is of the middle stature, that is, neither tall nor short; his limbs are well formed, and in his whole figure there is a just proportion. His complexion is fair, and occasionally suffused with red, like the bright tint of the rose, which adds much grace to his countenance. His eyes are black and handsome, his nose is well shaped and prominent. He has four wives of the first rank, who are esteemed legitimate, and the eldest born son of any one of these succeeds to the empire, upon the decease of the

Kublai Khan, from a contemporary Chinese portrait. Right: a huntsman with eagle.

Grand Khan. They bear equally the title of Empress, and have their separate courts. None of them have fewer than three hundred young female attendants of great beauty, together with a multitude of youths as pages, and other eunuchs, as well as ladies of the bedchamber; so that the number of persons belonging to each of their respective courts amounts to ten thousand . . .

"The Grand Khan has many leopards and lynxes kept for the purpose of chasing deer, and also many lions, which are larger than the Babylonian lions, have good skins and are of a handsome colour—being streaked lengthways, with white, black, and red stripes. They are active in seizing boars, wild oxen and asses, bears, stags, roebucks, and other beasts that are the objects of sport. It is an admirable sight, when the lion is let loose in pursuit of the animal, to observe the savage eagerness and speed with which he overtakes it. His Majesty has

them conveyed for this purpose, in cages placed upon cars, and along with them is confined a little dog, with which they become familiarized. The reason for thus shutting them up is, that they could otherwise be so keen and furious at the sight of the game that it would be impossible to keep them under the necessary constraint. It is proper that they should be led in a direction opposite to the wind, in order that they may not be scented by the game, which would immediately run off, and afford no chance of sport. His Majesty has eagles also, which are trained to swoop at wolves, and such is their size and strength that none, however large, can escape from their talons."

About paper money:

"In this city of Kanbalu [= Khanbalik = "City of the Khan" = modern Peking] is the mint of the Grand Khan, who may truly be said to possess the secret of the alchemists, as he has the art of producing money by the following process. He causes the bark to be stripped from those mulberry-trees the leaves of which are used for feeding silk-worms, and takes from it that thin inner rind which lies between the coarser bark and the wood of the tree. This being steeped, and afterwards pounded in a mortar, until reduced to a pulp, is made into paper, resembling that which is manufactured from cotton, but quite black. When ready for use, he has it cut into pieces of money of different sizes, nearly square, but somewhat longer than they are wide. Of these, the smallest pass for a denier tournois; the next size for a Venetian silver groat; others for two, five, and ten groats; others for one, two, three, and as far as ten besants of gold. The coinage of this paper money is authenticated with as much form and ceremony as if it were actually of pure gold or silver; for to each note a number of officers, specially appointed, not only subscribe their names, but affix their signets also; and when this has been regularly done by the whole of them, the principal officer, deputed by His Majesty, having dipped into vermilion the Royal Seal committed to his custody, stamps with it the piece of paper, so that the form of the seal tinged with the vermilion remains impressed upon it, by which it receives

full authenticity as current money, and the act of counter-
feiting is punished as a capital offence."

About communications:

"From the city of Kanbalu there are many roads leading
to the different provinces, and upon each of these, that
is to say, upon every great high road, at the distance of
twenty-five or thirty miles, accordingly as the towns
happen to be situated, there are stations, with houses of
accommodation for travellers, called *yamb* or post-
houses. These are large and handsome buildings, having
several well-furnished apartments, hung with silk, and
provided with everything suitable to persons of rank . . .
At each station four hundred good horses are kept in
constant readiness, in order that all messengers going and
coming upon the business of the Grand Khan, and all
ambassadors, may have relays, and, leaving their jaded
horses, be supplied with fresh ones . . . In his dominions
no fewer than two hundred thousand horses are thus
employed in the department of the post, and ten thousand
buildings, with suitable furniture, are kept up . . . In the
intermediate space between the post-houses, there are
small villages settled at the distance of every three miles,
which may contain, one with another, about forty cot-
tages. In these are stationed the foot messengers, likewise
employed in the service of His Majesty. They wear girdles

round their waists, to which several small bells are attached, in order that their coming may be perceived at a distance . . . and preparation is accordingly made by a fresh courier to proceed with the packet instantly upon the arrival of the former."

About coal:

"Throughout this province there is found a sort of black stone, which they dig out of the mountains, where it runs in veins. When lighted, it burns like charcoal, and retains the fire much better than wood; in so much that it may be preserved during the night, and in the morning be found still burning . . . Every man of rank or wealth has a bath in his house for his own use; and the stock of wood must soon prove inadequate to such consumption; whereas these stones may be had in the greatest abundance, and at a cheap rate."

About the Yangtze Kiang:

"Its width is in some places ten, in others eight, and in others six miles. Its length, to the place where it discharges itself into the sea, is upwards of one hundred days' journey. It is indebted for its great size to the vast number of other navigable rivers that empty their waters into it, which have their sources in distant countries. A great number of cities and large towns are situated

The Yangtze Kiang and Yin-shan, or Silver Isle.

upon its banks, and more than two hundred, with sixteen provinces, partake of the advantages of its navigation, by which the transport of merchandise is to an extent that might appear incredible to those who have not had an opportunity of witnessing it . . . On one occasion, when Marco Polo was at the city of Sin-gui, he saw there not fewer than fifteen thousand vessels; and yet there are other towns along the river where the number is still more considerable . . . Kayn-gui is a small town on the southern bank of the before-mentioned river, where annually is collected a very large quantity of corn and rice, the greatest part of which is conveyed from thence to the city of Kanbalu, for the supply of the establishment of the Grand Khan; for through this place is the line of communication with the province of Cathay, by means of rivers, lakes, and a wide and deep canal which the Grand Khan has caused to be dug, in order that vessels may pass from one great river to the other, and from the province of Manji, by water, as far as Kanbalu, without making any part of the voyage by sea. This magnificent work is deserving of admiration; and not so much from the manner in which it is conducted through the country, or its vast extent, as from its utility and the benefit it produces to those cities which lie in its course."

119

About the city of Kin-sai:

"At the end of three days you reach the noble and magnificent city of Kin-sai [Hangchow], a name that signifies 'the celestial city', and which it merits from its pre-eminence to all others in the world, in point of grandeur and beauty, as well as from its abundant delights, which might lead an inhabitant to imagine himself in paradise ... According to common estimation, this city is a hundred miles in circuit. Its streets and canals are extensive, and there are squares, or market-places, which, being necessarily proportioned in size to the prodigious concourse of people by whom they are frequented, are exceedingly spacious ... It is commonly said that the number of bridges, of all sizes, amounts to twelve thousand. Those which are thrown over the principal canals and are connected with the main streets, have arches so high, and built with so much skill, that vessels with their masts can pass under them, whilst, at the same time, carts and horses are passing over their heads ... The natural disposition of the native inhabitants of Kin-sai is pacific, and by the example of their former kings, who were themselves unwarlike, they have been accustomed to habits of tranquillity. The management of arms is unknown to them, nor do they keep any in their houses. Contentious broils are never heard among them. They conduct their mercantile and manufacturing concerns with perfect candour and probity. They are friendly to-

Marco Polo tells of Lake Si-hu at Kin-sai: "In addition to this, there are upon the lake a great number of pleasure vessels or barges, calculated for holding ten, fifteen, to twenty persons, being from fifteen to twenty paces in length, with a wide and flat flooring, and not liable to heel to either side in passing through the water. Such persons as take delight in the amusement, and mean to enjoy it, either in the company of their women or that of their male companions, engage one of these barges, which are always kept in the nicest order, with proper seats and tables, together with every other kind of furniture necessary for giving an entertainment."

wards each other, and persons who inhabit the same street, both men and women, from the mere circumstance of neighbourhood, appear like one family. In their domestic manners they are free from jealousy or suspicion of their wives, to whom great respect is shown, and any man would be accounted infamous who should presume to use indecent expressions to a married woman. To strangers also, who visit their city in the way of commerce, they give proofs of cordiality, inviting them freely to their houses, showing them hospitable attention, and furnishing them with the best advice and assistance in their mercantile transactions. On the other hand, they dislike the sight of soldiery, not excepting the guards of the Grand

Khan, as they preserve the recollection that by them they were deprived of the government of their native kings and rulers . . . The streets of Kin-sai are all paved with stones and bricks, and so likewise are all the principal roads extending from thence through the province of Manji, by means of which passengers can travel to every part without soiling their feet . . . Marco Polo, happening to be in the city of Kin-sai at the time of making the annual report to His Majesty's commissioners of the amount of revenue and the number of inhabitants, had an opportunity of observing that the latter were registered at one hundred and sixty *tomans* of fireplaces, that is to say, of families dwelling under the same roof; and as a *toman* is ten thousand, it follows that the whole city must have contained one million six hundred thousand families, amongst which multitude of people there was only one church of Nestorian Christians."

About the port of Zai-tum (modern Tsingkiang):
"The quantity of pepper imported there is so considerable, that what is carried to Alexandria, to supply the demand of the western parts of the world, is trifling in comparison, perhaps not more than the hundredth part. It is indeed impossible to convey an idea of the concourse of merchants and the accumulation of goods, in this which is held to be one of the largest and most commodious ports in the world. The Grand Khan derives a vast

Of the courtesans of Kin-sai: "These women are accomplished, and are perfect in the arts of blandishment and dalliance, which they accompany with expressions adapted to every description of person, in so much that strangers who have once tasted of their charms, remain in a state of fascination, and become so enchanted by their meretricious arts, that they can never divest themselves of the impression. Thus intoxicated with sensual pleasures, when they return to their homes they report that they have been in Kin-sai, or the Celestial City, and pant for the time when they might revisit that paradise."
— Below: Kin-sai in the 13th century.

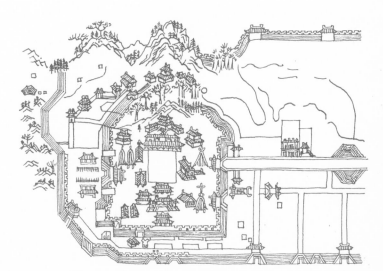

revenue from this place, as every merchant is obliged to pay ten per cent upon the amount of his investment. The ships are freighted by them at the rate of thirty per cent for fine goods, forty-four for pepper, and for lignum aloes, sandalwood, and other drugs, as well as articles of trade in general, forty per cent; so that it is computed by the merchants, that their charges, including customs and freight, amount to half the value of the cargo; and yet upon the half that remains to them their profit is so considerable, that they are always disposed to return to the same market with a further stock of merchandise."

About the porcelain city of Tin-gui:

"Of this place there is nothing further to be observed, than that cups or bowls and dishes of porcelain-ware are there manufactured. The process was explained to be as follows. They collect a certain kind of earth, as it were, from a mine, and laying it in a great heap, suffer it to be exposed to the wind, the rain, and the sun, for thirty or forty years, during which time it is never disturbed. By this it becomes refined and fit for being wrought into the vessels above mentioned. Such colours as may be thought proper are then laid on, and the ware is afterwards baked in ovens or furnaces. Those persons, therefore, who cause the earth to be dug, collect it for their children and grandchildren."

About merchant ships:

"We shall commence with a description of the ships employed by the merchants, which are built of fir-timber. They have a single deck, and below this the space is divided into about sixty small cabins, fewer or more, according to the size of the vessels, each of them affording accommodation for one merchant. They are provided with a good helm. They have four masts, with as many sails, and some of them have two masts which can be set up and lowered again, as may be found necessary. Some

ships of the larger class have, besides, to the number of thirteen, bulk-heads or divisions in the hold, formed of thick planks let into each other. The object of these is to guard against accidents which may occasion the vessel to spring a leak, such as striking on a rock or receiving a stroke from a whale, a circumstance that not unfrequently occurs; for, when sailing at night, the motion through the waves causes a white foam that attracts the notice of the hungry animal. In expectation of meeting with food, it rushes violently to the spot, strikes the ship, and often forces in some part of the bottom. The water, running in at the place where the injury has been sustained, makes its way to the well, which is always kept clear. The crew, upon discovering the situation of the leak, immediately remove the goods from the division affected by the water, which, in consequence of the boards being so well fitted, cannot pass from one division to another . . .

"Ships of the largest size require a crew of three hundred men; others, two hundred; and some, one hundred and fifty only, according to their greater or less bulk. They carry from five to six thousand baskets of pepper . . . The vessels are likewise moved with oars or sweeps, each of which requires four men to work it. Those of the larger class are accompanied by two or three large barks, capable of containing about one thousand baskets of pepper, and are manned with sixty, eighty, or one hundred sailors . . . The ships also carry with them as many as ten small boats, for the purpose of carrying out anchors, for fishing, and a variety of other services. They are slung over the sides, and lowered into the water when there is occasion to use them. The barks are in like manner provided with their small boats. When a ship, having been on a voyage for a year or more, stands in need of repair, the practice is to give her a course of sheathing over the original boarding, forming a third course, which is caulked and paid in the same manner as the others; and this, when she needs further repairs, is repeated, even

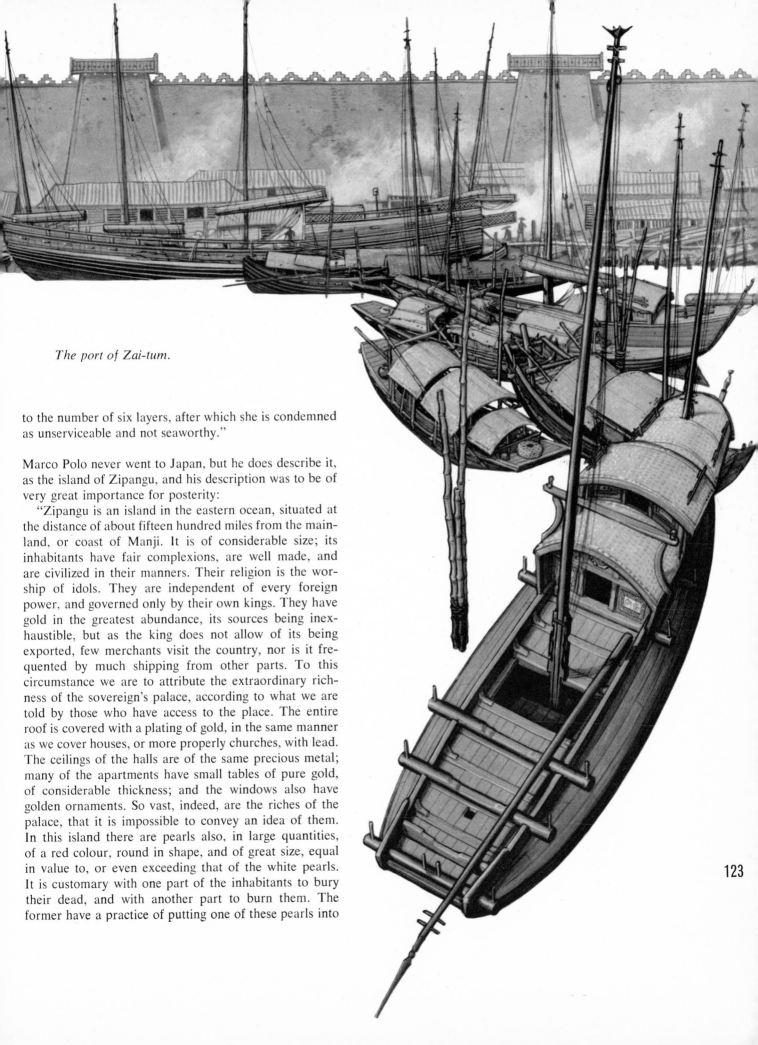

The port of Zai-tum.

to the number of six layers, after which she is condemned as unserviceable and not seaworthy."

Marco Polo never went to Japan, but he does describe it, as the island of Zipangu, and his description was to be of very great importance for posterity:

"Zipangu is an island in the eastern ocean, situated at the distance of about fifteen hundred miles from the mainland, or coast of Manji. It is of considerable size; its inhabitants have fair complexions, are well made, and are civilized in their manners. Their religion is the worship of idols. They are independent of every foreign power, and governed only by their own kings. They have gold in the greatest abundance, its sources being inexhaustible, but as the king does not allow of its being exported, few merchants visit the country, nor is it frequented by much shipping from other parts. To this circumstance we are to attribute the extraordinary richness of the sovereign's palace, according to what we are told by those who have access to the place. The entire roof is covered with a plating of gold, in the same manner as we cover houses, or more properly churches, with lead. The ceilings of the halls are of the same precious metal; many of the apartments have small tables of pure gold, of considerable thickness; and the windows also have golden ornaments. So vast, indeed, are the riches of the palace, that it is impossible to convey an idea of them. In this island there are pearls also, in large quantities, of a red colour, round in shape, and of great size, equal in value to, or even exceeding that of the white pearls. It is customary with one part of the inhabitants to bury their dead, and with another part to burn them. The former have a practice of putting one of these pearls into

123

A Japanese warrior.

the mouth of the corpse. There are also found there a number of precious stones.

"Of so great celebrity was the wealth of this island, that a desire was excited in the breast of the Grand Khan Kublai, now reigning, to make the conquest of it, and to annex it to his dominions. In order to effect this, he fitted out a numerous fleet, and embarked a large body of troops, under the command of two of his principal officers, one of whom was named Abbacatan, and the other Vonsancin. The expedition sailed from the ports of Zai-tum and Kin-sai, and, crossing the intermediate sea, reached the island in safety; but in consequence of a jealousy that arose between the two commanders, one of whom treated the plans of the other with contempt and resisted the execution of his orders, they were unable to gain possession of any city or fortified place, with the exception of one only, which was carried by assault, the garrison having refused to surrender. Directions were given for putting the whole to the sword, and in obedience thereto the heads of all were cut off, excepting of eight persons, who, by the efficacy of a diabolical charm, consisting of a jewel or amulet introduced into the right arm, between the skin and the flesh, were rendered secure from the effects of iron, either to kill or wound. Upon this discovery being made, they were beaten with a heavy wooden club, and presently died.

"It happened, after some time, that a north wind began to blow with great force, and the ships of the Tartars, which lay near the shore of the island, were driven foul of each other. It was determined thereupon, in a council of the officers on board, that they ought to disengage themselves from the land; and accordingly, as soon as the troops were re-embarked, they stood out to sea. The gale, however, increased to so violent a degree that a number of the vessels foundered. The people belonging to them, by floating upon pieces of the wreck, saved themselves upon an island lying about four miles from the coast of Zipangu. The other ships, which, not being so near to the land, did not suffer from the storm, and in which the two chiefs were embarked, together with the principal officers, or those whose rank entitled them to command a hundred thousand or ten thousand men, directed their course homewards, and returned to the Grand Khan."

About the Sea of Chin:

"It is to be understood that the sea in which the island of Zipangu is situated is called the Sea of Chin, which means 'the sea which lies close to Manji'. For Manji in the language of the island is called Chin. [Not only the Japanese but nearly all the peoples on the seaward side of the land of the Chinese call the country Chin—hence the name China. Marco Polo's 'Sea of Chin' includes more than what we call the China Sea: it seems to include

In 1277 Kublai Khan had conquered most of the region which we know as Burma, and in his service Marco Polo went all the way to the old capital of Pagan, which he called Amien (see the map on p. 94).

the whole Malay Archipelago.] So extensive is the eastern sea, that according to the report of experienced pilots and mariners who frequent it, and to whom the truth must be known, it contains no fewer than seven thousand four hundred and forty islands, mostly inhabited. It is said that of the trees which grow in them, there are none that do not yield a fragrant smell. They produce many spices and drugs, particularly lignum aloes and pepper, in great abundance, both white and black. It is impossible to estimate the value of the gold and other articles found in the islands; but their distance from the continent is so great, and the navigation attended with so much trouble and inconvenience, that the vessels engaged in the trade, from the ports of Zai-tum and Kin-sai, do not reap large profits, being obliged to consume a whole year in their voyage, sailing in the winter and returning in the summer. For in these regions only two winds prevail; one of them during the winter, and the other during the summer season; so that they must avail themselves of the one for the outward, and of the other for the homeward-bound voyage." (In the winter, the north-east monsoon blows across the China Sea, and this was the season for sailing to Java or Malaya. The south-west monsoon begins to blow in April or May, and with this the voyage home was made).

We now return to the introductory chapter of the book and read about the journey home and what occurred before it:

"Our Venetians having now resided many years at the imperial court, and in that time having realized considerable wealth, in jewels of value and in gold, felt a strong desire to revisit their native country, and, however honoured and caressed by the sovereign, this sentiment was ever predominant in their minds. It became the more decidedly their object, when they reflected on the very advanced age of the Grand Khan, whose death, if it should happen previously to their departure, might deprive them of that public assistance by which alone they could expect to surmount the innumerable difficulties of so long a journey, and reach their homes in safety; which on the contrary, in his lifetime, and through his favour, they might reasonably hope to accomplish. Nicolo Polo accordingly took an opportunity one day, when he observed him to be more than usually cheerful, of throwing himself at his feet, and soliciting on behalf of himself and his family to be indulged with His Majesty's gracious permission for their departure. But far from showing himself disposed to comply with the request, he appeared hurt at the application, and asked what motive they could have for wishing to expose themselves to all the inconveniences and hazards of a journey in which they might probably lose their lives. If gain, he said, was their object, he was ready to give them the double of whatever they possessed, and to gratify them with honours to the extent of their desires; but that, from the regard he bore to them, he must positively refuse their petition.

"It happened, about this period, that a queen named Bolgana, the wife of Arghun, sovereign of India [Persia], died, and as her last request (which she likewise left in a testamentary writing) conjured her husband that no one might succeed to her place on his throne and in his affections, who was not a descendant of her own family, now settled under the dominion of the Grand Khan, in the country of Cathay. Desirous of complying with this solemn entreaty, Arghun deputed three of his nobles, discreet men, whose names were Ulatai, Apusca, and Goza, attended by a numerous retinue, as his ambassadors to the Grand Khan, with a request that he might receive at his hands a maiden to wife, from among the relatives of his deceased queen. The application was taken in good part, and under the directions of His Majesty, choice was made of a damsel aged seventeen, extremely handsome and accomplished, whose name was Kogatin, and of whom the ambassadors, upon her being shown to them, highly approved. When everything was arranged for their departure, and a numerous suite of attendants appointed, to do honour to the future consort of King Arghun, they received from the Grand Khan a gracious dismissal, and set out on their return by the way they came. Having travelled for eight months, their further progress was obstructed and the roads shut up against them, by fresh wars that had broken out amongst the Tartar princes. Much against their inclinations, therefore, they were constrained to adopt the measure of returning to the court of the Grand Khan, to whom they stated the interruption they had met with.

"About the time of their reappearance, Marco Polo happened to arrive from a voyage he had made, with a few vessels under his orders, to some parts of the East Indies, and reported to the Grand Khan the intelligence he brought respecting the countries he had visited, with the circumstances of his own navigation, which, he said, was performed in those seas with the utmost safety. This latter observation having reached the ears of the three ambassadors [from King Arghun], who were extremely anxious to return to their own country, from whence they had now been absent three years, they presently sought a conference with our Venetians, whom they found equally desirous of revisiting their home; and it was settled between them that the former, accompanied by

their young queen, should obtain an audience of the Grand Khan, and represent to him with what convenience and security they might effect their return by sea, to the dominions of their master; whilst the voyage would be attended with less expense than the journey by land, and be performed in a shorter time, according to the experience of Marco Polo, who had lately sailed in those parts. Should His Majesty incline to give his consent to their adopting that mode of conveyance, they were then to urge him to suffer the three Europeans, as being persons well skilled in the practice of navigation, to accompany them until they should reach the territory of King Arghun.

"The Grand Khan upon receiving this application showed by his countenance that it was exceedingly displeasing to him, averse as he was to parting with the Venetians. Feeling nevertheless that he could not with propriety do otherwise than consent, he yielded to their entreaty. Had it not been that he found himself constrained by the importance and urgency of this peculiar case, they would never otherwise have obtained permission to withdraw themselves from his service. He sent for them, however, and addressed them with much kindness and condescension, assuring them of his regard, and requiring from them a promise that when they should have resided some time in Europe and with their own family, they would return to him once more. With this object in view he caused them to be furnished with a golden tablet which contained his order for their having free and safe conduct through every part of his dominions, with the needful supplies for themselves and their attendants. He likewise gave them authority to act in the capacity of his ambassadors to the Pope, the kings of France and Spain, and the other Christian princes.

"At the same time, preparations were made for the equipment of fourteen ships, each having four masts, and capable of being navigated with nine sails, the construction and rigging of which would admit of ample description; but, to avoid prolixity, it is for the present omitted. Among these vessels there were at least four or five that had crews of two hundred and fifty or two hundred and sixty men. On them were embarked the ambassadors, having the Queen under their protection, together with Nicolo, Maffeo, and Marco Polo, when they had first taken their leave of the Grand Khan, who presented them with many rubies and other handsome jewels of great value. He also gave directions that the ships should be furnished with stores and provisions for two years.

"After a navigation of about three months, they arrived at an island which lay in a southerly direction, named Java, where they saw various objects worthy of attention, of which notice shall be taken in the sequel of the work. Taking their departure from thence, they employed eighteen months in the Indian seas before they were enabled to reach the place of their destination in the

territory of King Arghun; and during this part of their voyage also they had an opportunity of observing many things, which shall, in like manner, be related hereafter. But here it may be proper to mention, that between the day of their sailing and that of their arrival, they lost by deaths, of the crews of the vessels and others who were embarked, about six hundred persons; and of the three ambassadors, only one, whose name was Goza, survived the voyage; whilst of all the ladies and female attendants only one died."

Their journey had begun in Zai-tum. From there they sailed across the Bay of Tonkin to a country which Marco Polo calls Ziamba. "The country abounds with elephants and with lignum aloes. There are also many forests of ebony of a fine black, which is worked into various handsome articles of furniture." — Ziamba was presumably the coastal region between Tonkin and Cambodia. The book goes on: "Departing from Ziamba, and steering between south and south-east, fifteen hundred miles, you reach an island of very great size, named Java, which, according to the reports of some well-informed navigators, is the largest in the world, being in circuit above three thousand miles. It is under the dominion of one king only, nor do the inhabitants pay tribute to any other

power. The people are worshippers of idols. The country abounds with rich commodities. Pepper, nutmegs, spikenard, galengal, cubebs, cloves, and all the other valuable spices and drugs, are the produce of the island; which occasion it to be visited by many ships laden with merchandise, that yields to the owners considerable profit. The quantity of gold collected there exceeds all calculation and belief. From thence it is that the merchants of Zai-tum and of Manji in general have imported, and to this day import, that metal to a great amount, and from thence also is obtained the greatest part of the spices that are distributed throughout the world."

A village near the northern extremity of Borneo. In the background is the mountain of Kinabalu, 13,455 feet high, and in the foreground a group of pandanus trees.

It is believed that this island which Marco Polo calls Java was modern Borneo, the largest island in the world, lying between south-east and south of the coastal land of "Ziamba". But his description is vague, and it is possible that he only heard tell of it, and that when dictating in the prison in Genoa he confused his data about Borneo and about the island of Java proper.

After having put in at islands off Cochin China and visited the kingdom of "Malaiur"—probably in the southern part of the Malay Peninsula—he came to "Java Minor", in all likelihood modern Sumatra. "In this island there are eight kingdoms, governed by so many kings, and each kingdom has its own proper language, distinct from those of all the others. The people are idolaters. It contains abundance of riches, and all sorts of spices, lignum aloes, sappan wood for dyeing, and various other kinds of drugs, which, on account of the length of the voyage and the danger of the navigation, are not imported into our country, but which find their way to the provinces of Manji and Cathay."

Marco Polo visited six of these kingdoms and describes them, telling among other things of the rhinoceros in the land of Basman: "In this country are many wild elephants and rhinoceroses, which latter are much inferior in size to the elephant, but their feet are similar. Their hide resembles that of the buffalo. In the middle of the forehead they have a single horn; but with this weapon they do not injure those whom they attack, employing only for this purpose their tongue, which is armed with long, sharp spines, and their knees or feet; their mode of assault being to trample upon the person, and then to lacerate him with the tongue. Their head is like that of a wild boar, and they carry it low towards the ground. They take delight in muddy pools, and are filthy in their habits. They are not of that description of animals which suffer themselves to be taken by maidens, as our people suppose, but are quite of a contrary nature."

According to popular medieval European tradition, the unicorn was a horse with one horn, which allowed itself to be captured by a pure virgin; the Virgin Mary was often portrayed together with one of these fabulous animals. If Marco Polo had really seen a rhinoceros at close quarters in Sumatra, he should have noticed that it does not have one but two horns, but it is possible that he was confused, and instead had seen the single-horned Indian rhinoceros.

About the kingdom of Lambri he says: "The country produces verzino [brazil or sappan wood] in great abundance, and also camphor, with a variety of other drugs. They sow a vegetable which resembles the sappan, and when it springs up and begins to throw out shoots, they transplant it to another spot, where it is suffered to remain for three years. It is then taken up by the roots, and used as a dye-stuff. Marco Polo brought some of the seeds of this plant with him to Venice, and sowed them there; but the climate not being sufficiently warm, none of them came up. In this kingdom are found men with tails, a span in length, like those of the dog, but not covered with hair. The greater number of them are formed in this manner, but they dwell in the mountains, and do not inhabit towns." — It is likely that Marco Polo formed this impression of ape-men by misunderstanding the Malayan word "orang-utan", which means "man of the woods". The orangutan does not have a tail.

The party were forced to spend five months in the waters off Sumatra while waiting for the right monsoon. Then they sailed past the Nicobar and Andaman Islands

130

to Ceylon. "Taking a departure from the island of Anga-man [the Andaman Islands], and steering a course something to the southward of west, for a thousand miles, the island of Zeilan presents itself. This, for its actual size, is better circumstanced than any other island in the world. It is in circuit two thousand four hundred miles, but in ancient times it was still larger, its circumference then measuring full three thousand six hundred miles, as the Mappa-Mundi says." — Ever since classical times, Ceylon had been drawn far too large on all maps, probably because of its great importance. But Marco Polo would not believe that the cartographers had been mistaken,

We do not know what places in Ceylon Marco Polo visited, but it is possible that he went to Polon-naruwa, one of the old capitals of the island. A hundred years before his arrival, a Buddhist temple had been carved out of a cliff face there. It was flanked by a sleeping and a meditating Buddha, and guarded by the disciple Ananda. — It must be taken for granted that the expedition put in at Galle, the port near the southern extremity of Ceylon which was already known to seafarers from the East and the West during the classical era.

Of the dancing-girls in the Indian temples Marco Polo has this to say: "Several times in the week they carry an offering of victuals to the idol to whose service they are devoted, and of this food they say the idol partakes. A table for the purpose is placed before it, and upon this the victuals are suffered to remain for the space of a full hour; during which the damsels never cease to sing, and play, and exhibit wanton gestures."

giving the following explanation: "But the northern gales, which blow with prodigious violence, have in a manner corroded the mountains, so that they have in some parts fallen and sunk in the sea, and the island, from that cause, no longer retains its original size."

They visited the Coromandel Coast and then sailed round Cape Comorin and along the Malabar Coast to

Ormuz in Persia, the country of King Arghun. It is true that Marco Polo has much to say about Aden and other places in Arabia, about East Africa, about "the second or middle India, named Abyssinia", about Madagascar —which he calls Magastar—and about other countries, but there is nothing to indicate that he actually visited these places himself; he just tells what he had heard from Chinese sailors or sailors in Ormuz.

"Upon landing they were informed that King Arghun had died some time before, and that the government of the country was then administered, on behalf of his son, who was still a youth, by a person of the name of Kiakato. From him they desired to receive instructions as to the manner in which they were to dispose of the princess, whom, by the orders of the late king, they had conducted thither. His answer was, that they ought to present the lady to Kasan, the son of Arghun, who was then at a place on the borders of Persia, which has its denomination from the *Arbor secco* [a tree], where an army of sixty thousand men was assembled for the purpose of guarding certain passes against the irruption of the enemy. This they proceeded to carry into execution, and having effected it, they returned to the residence of Ki-akato, because the road they were afterwards to take lay in that direction. Here [probably in Tabriz] they reposed themselves for the space of nine months. When they took their leave he furnished them with four golden tablets, each of them a cubit in length, five inches wide, and weighing three or four marks of gold. Their inscription began by invoking the blessing of the Almighty upon the Grand Khan, that his name might be held in reverence for many years, and denouncing the punishment of death and confiscation of goods to all who should refuse obedience to the mandate. It then proceeded to direct that the three ambassadors, as his representatives, should be treated throughout his dominions with due honour, that their expenses should be defrayed, and that they should

be provided with the necessary escorts. All this was fully complied with, and from many places they were protected by bodies of two hundred horse; nor could this have been dispensed with as the government of Ki-akato was unpopular, and the people were disposed to commit insults and proceed to outrages, which they would not have dared to attempt under the rule of their proper sovereign. In the course of their journey our travellers received intelligence that the Grand Khan had departed this life; which entirely put an end to all prospect of their revisiting those regions. Pursuing, therefore, their intended route, they at length reached the city of Trebizond, from whence they proceeded to Constantinople, then to Negropont, and finally to Venice, at which place, in the enjoyment of health and abundant riches, they safely arrived in the year 1295. On this occasion they offered up their thanks to God, Who had now been pleased to relieve them from such great fatigues, after having preserved them from innumerable perils."

A 13th-century relief from the door of the Basilica of St. Mark in Venice shows shipbuilders at work.

Missionaries and Merchants in China

We know that some of the Grand Khans had, like Alexander the Great, formed plans of world domination. In his letter to the Pope, Mangu Khan had written: "When, by the power of the everlasting God, the entire earth has become one in joy and peace from the rising of the sun even unto its setting, then will it be shown what we can do . . ." When they found that they could not achieve their aim—perhaps because of the almost pathological quarrelling among the Mongol chieftains—they endeavoured to maintain advantageous connections with Western traders and, sometimes at least, with Christian missionaries.

In particular, the Mongol rulers of Persia, who were almost always at war with the Arabs, were eager to arrive at an alliance with the Pope, and would have been only too happy to have been helped by Crusades. Hulagu, Mangu's and Kublai's brother, who had conquered Persia and sacked Baghdad, had already sent an embassy to the Pope; now his son and successor Aboga asked the Pope to send him missionaries, intimating that Kublai Khan had wanted to become a Christian. In reply to this, the Pope immediately sent him five Franciscan friars. They reached his court in 1282, but in the meantime Aboga had died and had been succeeded by his brother, Tigudar Ahmed, who was a fervent Mohammedan, and so the missionaries had little success.

Two years later, however, Tigudar Ahmed was murdered. His successor was Aboga's son Arghun (of whom Marco Polo tells) who planned to conquer Syria and Palestine, and to give Jerusalem to the Christians. In his turn he, too, asked the Pope for missionaries, and on this occasion there came, among others, a Franciscan friar called John of Montecorvino, one of the most devout missionaries of the Middle Ages. After spending some time in Persia and paying a short visit to Rome, he journeyed across India (where he pursued his missionary work for a time) to China, and we know that he reached Peking in 1293—one year after Marco Polo's party had gone with the Princess and the ambassadors to King Arghun. He was allowed to appear before the now ageing and tired Kublai Khan, who was certainly not converted—perhaps he was no longer as interested in Christianity as the West had hoped.

John of Montecorvino then lived in China for thirty-five years, and his letters to the dignitaries of the Franciscan Order show that he was forgotten for long periods, but nevertheless speak of his untiring work for the dissemination of Christianity. At times he was persecuted by the Nestorian Christians of Peking, but he managed to defend himself and found such favour with the new Grand Khan that he was even allowed to build a church beside the entrance to the Khan's palace. After having worked alone for eleven years, he was given help by a certain Brother Arnold, a German from near Cologne. He bought the sons of impoverished Chinese families, taught them Latin and Greek and employed them as choirboys. By 1306 he had baptized 6,000 souls, and he writes that he would have converted ten times as many if he had not been obstructed by the Nestorians. He translated both the New Testament and the Book of Psalms into "the speech and writing of the Tartars" (Chinese?), and he even painted pictures of scenes from the Old and New Testaments in order to make his lessons easier. The Pope realized his great merits, appointed him archbishop over the whole of China in 1307, and sent him nine Franciscan friars to act as bishops. Three of them died on the way, but the rest arrived safely. In 1311 the new archbishop was allowed to baptize the Grand Khan, Wu Tsung, but the period of success was not to be a long one, for that khan died a few months later, and his successor, Yen Tsung, was not so amiably disposed towards Christianity. John of Montecorvino died in China in July, 1328, at the age of eighty-one.

Another Franciscan friar, Odoric of Pordenone, returned to Padua in Italy in 1330 after a twelve-year missionary expedition to China and Tibet. Although only forty-three years old, he was weak and exhausted, and before he died in the following year he dictated from his sick-bed a narrative of his journey which partly contained fantastic stories and conjectures and partly information of much value. Like John of Montecorvino before him, he travelled via Constantinople, Trebizond and Erzerum to Baghdad and Basra, and then by sea round India to Sumatra and Java, and from there to China. Thus the Christians were able to pass directly into Mongol territory from the Black Sea in comparative safety.

Let me quote a few lines from his description: "I came to the most renowned city of Cartan or Catan [Marco Polo's Zai-tum = Tsingkiang]. It abounds in all things needful to man . . . It is twice the size of Rome, and it has monasteries in which all the monks are idolaters [Buddhists] . . . I came to a city called Catusay [Kin-sai = Hangchow] which means 'heavenly city'. Catusay is the greatest city in the entire world. It is one hundred miles in circumference, and in this vast area there is not a single spot that is not inhabited . . . The city has twelve main gates, and on either side of these gates there are great cities, each larger than Venice . . . I travelled to another very large province called Tiboth [Tibet] which lies on the way to India . . . The inhabitants of this country live in tents made of black felt. Their capital is very beautiful: it is built of white stone and its streets are well paved. It is called Gota [Lhasa]. No one in this

Odoric of Pordenone was probably the first European to visit the holy city of Lhasa in Tibet.

city dares to spill the blood of man or animal, out of veneration for an idol which they worship. Living in this city is Obassi [the Dalai Lama]—for such is the name of their Pope in their language."

It seems as if this Odoric had been granted permission to visit Lhasa, the capital of Tibet. He is also the first to tell us of the long nails of the Chinese aristocrats, of the girls whose feet are bound so that they will not grow, and of fishermen who fish with cormorants. And he says that he had met many men in Venice who had been to China, and could therefore corroborate his statements about all the things his contemporaries would not believe, especially the size and magnificence of the cities.

We do not know how many travellers of various kinds—missionaries, merchants, craftsmen and adventurers—journeyed from Europe to China during the Mongol supremacy, but there may have been hundreds, even thousands of them. At the beginning of the 14th century, one Francesco Balducci Pegolotti, a Florentine who had undoubtedly been to China, wrote a manual for other merchants. He describes the overland route from the Sea of Azov north of the Caspian to Peking, mentions the number of day-stages between various places, recommends the most suitable means of transport and the best places to do business.

In July 1336, the Grand Khan Shun-ti sent the following letter to the Pope: "In the power of Almighty God, it is thus ordained by the Emperor of Emperors. We send Our ambassador, Andrew the Frank, with fifteen followers across seven seas to the Pope, the Christian Lord in the land of the Franks, where the sun sets, in order to make a way, so that We may be able to send embassies to the Pope and the Pope send embassies to Us more often than before, so that the Pope's blessing may be over Us, and so that he may commend Us and Our servants the Alans, his own Christian sons, in his prayers. Also from the setting sun let there be sent to Us horses and other things of value. — Written at Cambaluc [Peking] on the third day after the new moon in the seventh month of the year of Rati."

Together with this there also came a letter from the Christian Alans telling that John of Montecorvino had died eight years before and that a new archbishop was wanted in his place. They also expressed the wish that the Pope would reply to the Grand Khan in friendly terms and send him ambassadors, for it had been long since any had come from the West.

The Pope granted the wishes of both the Grand Khan and the Alans. John of Marignola, a Franciscan friar who led the embassy, took a war horse with him as a gift; its size created such an impression that the court artist, Chou-lang, painted a portrait of it. It is possible that John of Marignola left some priests in China, but he himself did not stay there long, spending all the more time in India on his journey home. He wrote a long description of his experiences, but it is of no very great value.

John of Marignola was the last priest to visit China for many hundreds of years, and the Grand Khan Shun-ti, or Togan Timur, was the last Mongol emperor of China. The grand khans that had succeeded Kublai Khan had been weak—many of them completely incompetent—and a long series of disturbances culminated in an extensive revolt in the south. Its leader was Chu-yang-chang, who in 1368 conquered Peking and took the title of Emperor. He then assumed the name of Tai-tsu, and it is he who was to become the powerful and long-lived founder of the Ming Dynasty. The Grand Khan fled to Mongolia and died two years later. One of his successors tried to attack China in 1388, but he was easily repulsed; after that the Mongol Khanate declined and soon fell under the control of China. At the same time, another Mongol, Tamerlane by name, began to create a new world-empire, sweeping away all that Jenghiz Khan and his successors had built up, but not replacing it with anything comparable. He prepared an expedition against China, but died before it was set in motion. The direct route between the Far East and the West was closed.

But this did not mean that the ports on the Black Sea lost their importance: Indian goods still came along the caravan routes through Persia and Bokhara to Trebizond, which was Christian, to Tana at the mouth of the Don, which was under the control of the Venetians, and to Genoese Kaffa in the Crimea.

The Vivaldo Brothers

The last Crusade ended in 1272 and was followed by ten years of peace. For the trading cities on the Mediterranean, at least, it continued to be a happy time with many opportunities for profit. The Mongol Empire with its safe roads was still strong, and to the ports on the Black Sea came goods along the two main routes, from China by land right across Asia, and from China and India by sea to Basra, up the Tigris to Baghdad and then along the caravan routes to Trebizond and other cities. Trade with Syria was mainly carried on through the strongly fortified Christian city of Acre, and, as before, trade with Egypt continued to be done primarily through Alexandria and Damietta. The predominant European trading cities were Venice, Genoa, Barcelona, Marseille and Palma de Mallorca. In a sea-battle against Genoa in 1284, Pisa had suffered a crushing defeat and from then on was out of the game. A great change came when Acre, the last stronghold of the Christians in Palestine, fell to the Sultan of Egypt in 1291. In order to weaken Egypt and thus pave the way for a new crusade, the Pope forbade all trade with the Infidels, but, as before, the trading cities disobeyed the injunction.

The same year that Acre fell, an expedition left Genoa with the object of reaching India by sea. This we find described in *Jacobi Aurie Annales* for the year 1291: "That very same year, Thedisio Doria, Ugolino de Vivaldo and his brothers, and several other citizens of Genoa began to make preparations for a journey which no one before them had attempted to make. They equipped two galleys with victuals, drinking-water and other necessities as best they could, and sent them out in the month of May in the direction of Ceuta, so that they might

sail over the ocean to the Indian lands and there purchase useful goods. In their company were the two Vivaldo brothers and two young friars. This appeared marvellous not only to those that saw it but also to those that heard of it. Since they sailed past the point which is called Gozora [Cape Juby], nothing definite has been heard of them. But may God protect them and bring them safely and in good health back to the homeland."

Nothing more was ever heard of them. In order to try to find out something of the fate of the expedition, Sorleone, Ugolino de Vivaldo's son, journeyed to East Africa (!) in 1315, reaching as far south as Mogadishu. And we hear of another Vivaldo, perhaps a brother of Sorleone's—or even Sorleone himself—who was to have reached India proper and died there in 1321.

It must have been Moors who saw and reported the Vivaldo brothers' galleys on their southward journey past Cape Gozora to an unknown fate.

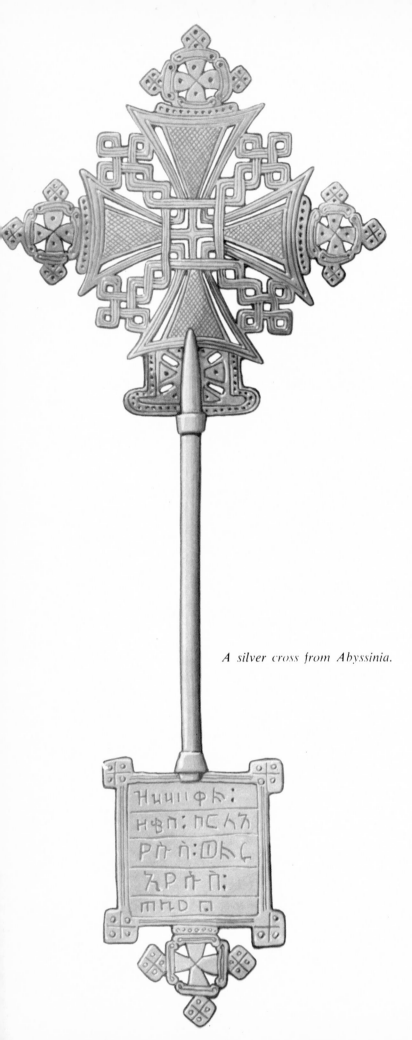

A silver cross from Abyssinia.

Prester John in Abyssinia

Marco Polo and other travellers had made inquiries in Asia about Prester John, and since they were unable to find any clear evidence of his existence, they put forward strange theories and conjectures which, however, do not seem to have satisfied Europe. Thus arose the 14th-century belief that the priest-king was not in the part of India where he had been sought at all, but was to be found in what Marco Polo calls "the other or Middle India, also called Abyssinia". By the Arab conquest of Egypt, the Christian kingdom of Axum, or Abyssinia, had become quite cut off from the Christian world, and its religion had gradually taken on features which differentiated it from Rome. Europeans were aware of the existence of Abyssinia, and the Church regarded its Coptic form of Christianity as heretical. A Papal Bull from 1267 did in fact exhort the leaders of the Dominican Order to send missionaries to Tartars, Ethiopians and Indians so that they might be dissuaded from their false doctrines.

During the Middle Ages, it was widely, though erroneously, held that St. Thomas the Apostle was buried in southern India where, on the Malabar Coast, there was in fact a group of "Thomas Christians"; but now, in the general confusion, the belief arose that St. Thomas' shrine was to be found in the other India, i.e. Abyssinia. In a medieval itinerary for travellers to Abyssinia we read: "Route for those travelling from Venice to India, where the body of St. Thomas lies. From Venice one reaches Rhodes in twenty days . . ." Then comes a description of the entire route from Rhodes via Ramallah, Jerusalem and Gaza to the Nile, across deserts and over mountains to Asmara in modern Eritrea, the residence of the first of Prester John's subject kings. From there it is not long before one is in the city of Achaxum (Axum) where there is a basilica, the most beautiful in the whole world, which is covered all over with tablets of gold. The description takes us all the way to the city of Sciahua where Prester John is said to reside. It is believed that Sciahua is the province of Shoa, where Addis Ababa lies today.

We do not know how many missionaries reached Abyssinia or to what extent they were allowed to work there; be that as it may, they were never able to redeem the heretical Coptic Church from its errors. However, not only the Pope but also many other Christian princes in Europe hoped that they would soon find Prester John a powerful ally against the Infidels.

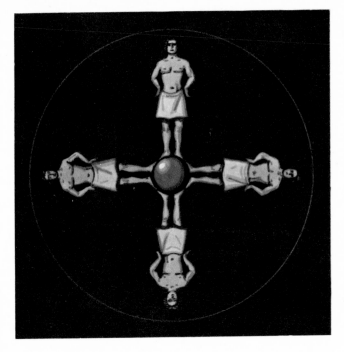

A picture of the kind commonly used during the Middle Ages to ridicule those who believed in the Antipodes.

The Southern Cross begins to appear over the horizon at about 30° north of the Equator, and can be seen in its entirety at about 15° N.

The Antipodes and the Southern Cross

Guillaume Adam, a Dominican friar, did much missionary work in Asia and Africa, and in a report which he sent to Philip VI of France in 1332 he propounded his view of the world. In the course of his travels he had crossed over into the Southern Hemisphere—in East Africa—and he proved this by noting the position of the sun and the stars above the horizon. He had come to the following conclusions, which he wrote down in the report: "Firstly, that between the east and the south, outside the Temperate Zone, a greater space is inhabited than the whole area between the lower and upper latitudes of the Temperate Zone; secondly, that Asia must be allowed to cover a greater area than is usually supposed; thirdly, that the belief in the Antipodes is not a blasphemous delusion; and fourthly, as rather supports my earlier belief, that we true Christians do not amount to one tenth, or even to one twentieth, of the world population."

We may observe that he does not mention the sphericity of the earth at all, presuming that the King knows of and accepts this view.

In Dante's *Divine Comedy,* Purgatory, Canto I, we read:

> Jo nu volsi a man destra, e posi mente
> All' altro polo, e vidi quattro stelle
> Non viste mai fuor ch'alla prima gente,
> Goder pareva il ciel di lor fiamelle,
> O settentrional vedovo sito
> Poi che privato se' di mirar quelle!

In Miss Dorothy Sayers' translation this runs:

> Right-hand I turned, and, setting me to spy
> That alien pole, beheld four stars, the same
> The first men saw, and since, no living eye;
> Me seemed the heavens exulted in their flame —
> Oh widowed world beneath the northern Plough,
> For ever famished of the sight of them!

Dante wrote this about 1318, and there is no doubt that he is describing the Southern Cross. There has been much speculation as to how he could have known about it, since it is not visible, in its entirety, above the latitude of 15° N. Guillaume Adam's report shows that many Christian missionaries had travelled far enough south to be able to tell of this and other constellations of the Southern Hemisphere when they returned to Europe.

139

Ibn Batuta, World Traveller

"I left Tangier, my city of birth, one Thursday, the second day in the month of God, Rajab the Unparalleled, in the year seven hundred and twenty-five [13th June 1325], with the intention of making a pilgrimage to the Holy House [in Mecca] and of visiting the tomb of the Prophet [in Medina], on Whom be God's richest blessing and peace. I left on my own and had neither companion to delight in nor caravan to accompany, my sole inspiration coming from an uncontrollable desire and long-cradled fancy in my breast to visit these glorious holy places."

So begins the narrative of Ibn Batuta's travels.

During his twenty-six years of travel, he visited nearly the whole of the known non-Christian world. He was a fanatically orthodox Moslem, and the only Christian places he happened to pass through were Constantinople and Sardinia. Yet his observations were to be of certain importance for later Christian travellers, among other things in the form of information on maps. It is probable that the picture of the African interior in Abraham Cresques' "Catalan Atlas" (see page 159) was mainly inspired by Ibn Batuta. When he returned to Morocco from his last great journey in 1353, the Sultan of Fez commanded him to dictate his experiences to Ibn Juzayy, the court secretary, and this description, which has been preserved for us in good copies, helps us to understand that Ibn Batuta was incomparably the greatest traveller of the Middle Ages. It is generally agreed that, after Ferdinand Magellan, the first man to circumnavigate the earth, he was the greatest explorer of all times.

The Holy Kaaba at Mecca is a temple shaped like a cube (the Arabic "ka'ba" = cube), and in its wall is "the black stone", according to legend a ruby which had fallen from heaven and turned black on account of the sins of man. It was an object of worship even before the time of Mohammed, but he included it in his teachings and made it into the central point of worship in the Islamic faith, exhorting all true believers to make pilgrimages to it. In pre-Mohammedan times it was many-coloured, in the days of Mohammed and the first Caliphs it was white, but ever since the time of the Abbasids, in the 8th century, it has been black.

He was born in 1304, the son of a kadi, or judge, and we may presume that he was already well educated and widely read when, at the age of twenty-one, he set off for Mecca. He passed through North Africa, along the Mediterranean, to Alexandria and Cairo, thence by boat up the Nile to Aswan and on to the port of Aidhab on the Red Sea, where he had hoped to obtain a passage across to Arabia. There was a war on there at the time, however, and no vessels were leaving for Jidda, and so he had to return to Cairo. After a thorough tour of Syria, he went down to Mecca and Medina. It is possible, as he intimates in his narrative, that he had already decided to visit all the countries in the world (except the Christian) while still in Egypt. And so, after only a short stay in the Holy Cities, he journeyed through northern Arabia to Basra at the mouth of the Euphrates, to Baghdad, along

*Arab travellers drawn from a
13th-century miniature.*

the Tigris to Mosul and Diarbekr, and then back again
to Mecca, where he studied for almost three years.

By the time he made his journey to East Africa in 1330,
his undertaking had taken on the dimensions of a large
expedition, and he was probably accompanied by wives,
children, slaves and other servants. They sailed down the
Red Sea to Yemen where they met with the rains and
storms of the south-west monsoon. When the friendly
north-west monsoon began to blow, the expedition left
Aden and sailed round Cape Guardafui. Ibn Batuta says:
"We came to Manbasa [Mombasa], a large island two
days distant from the country of Sanahil. We spent one
night there. Then we put to sea again in order to sail to
Kulua [Kilwa], a large coastal city whose inhabitants are
for the most part very dark-skinned Africans. — A merchant said that the city of Sofala is a fortnight's march
from Kulua, and between Sofala and Yufi in the land
of the Limiin is a further march of a month. — Gold-dust
is brought from Yufi to Sofala. Kulua is one of the most

beautiful and well-built of all cities. It is built entirely of
timber."

They returned from Kulua to southern Arabia and
sailed east along the coast to Zofar. Ibn Batuta says:
"Zofar lies in the outermost part of Yemen on the Indian
Sea, and horses are transported from there by sea to
India. When the wind is favourable, the voyage takes a
whole month. I have myself completed the voyage from
Calicut to Zofar in 28 days." — They then sailed round
Oman into the Persian Gulf, and from there Ibn Batuta
set out on his third pilgrimage to Mecca.

After this, he decided to sail to India to pay a visit to
Sultan Mohammed bin Tughlak who was famous, among
other things, for the hospitality he showed towards learned travellers from foreign countries. But he could find
no ship at Jidda to take him there, and so he chose the
northern route instead. With his retinue, he first crossed
over into Egypt, sailed along the Nile to Cairo and went
on by land to Syria, where he boarded ship at Latakia

for the voyage to the "land of the Turks", Asia Minor. Having thoroughly toured the country and visited its many sultans, he journeyed from Sinope to the Crimea, was given audience by the Khan of the Golden Horde in the Caucasus, went up the frozen Volga to Sarai, made a detour to Constantinople and then travelled once more on the ice of the Volga to Sarai and right the way to Bulghar. There he entertained plans for making a trading expedition to the fur-trapping district around the Pechora, but in some way he was prevented from doing this and instead he led the expedition north of the Caspian and the Aral Sea through Bokhara, Samarkand and Balkh, and then on by a rather obscure route through Khorasan and Afghanistan, finally reaching the border of India at the Indus with his entire retinue on September 12, 1333. After sailing down the Indus to the ocean, he turned once again inland until he reached Delhi, which he described as being the largest Mohammedan city in the East—if also the least populated, for Sultan Mohammed bin Tughlak, who resided there, was renowned not only for his hospitality but also, and above all, for his cruelty, and his reign of terror had caused a large proportion of Delhi's inhabitants to flee to safer places.

Ibn Batuta, however, had not been wrong about the hospitality of the Sultan, and he was soon appointed kadi over the city and was given robes of honour, a horse and saddle, 12,000 dinars for his immediate needs, an annual salary of 12,000 dinars and finally an estate which was calculated to bring in the same sum each year.

Ibn Batuta performed the duties of judge in Delhi for almost nine years, but since he had connections with a sheik who conspired against the Sultan, things might have come to a terrible end there and then. The Sultan caught wind of the conspiracy and arrested the sheik. Ibn Batuta writes: "When the Sultan had imprisoned him, he ordered his sons to be asked who had visited him. They named a number of people, among them myself. Then the Sultan commanded that four slaves were to watch over me in the audience hall and not to move from my side. Such an order usually means that the person under guard does not escape with his life. The first day I was watched in this way was a Friday. It then pleased God on High to allow me to say these words: 'God is our help and Sovereign Lord!' [From the Koran, III, 167.] On that day, I pronounced these words 33,000 times, spent the night in the audience hall and then fasted continually for five days. I read the Koran each day from beginning to end, and broke my fast only by drinking a little water. On the seventh day, I took food, and then fasted for another four days. When the sheik was dead, I was released. Praise be to God on High for this!"

Ibn Batuta was shown mercy and was reinstated in office, and shortly afterwards the Sultan instructed him to lead an embassy to the Emperor of China. The expedition left Delhi in July 1342, but it was soon attacked by

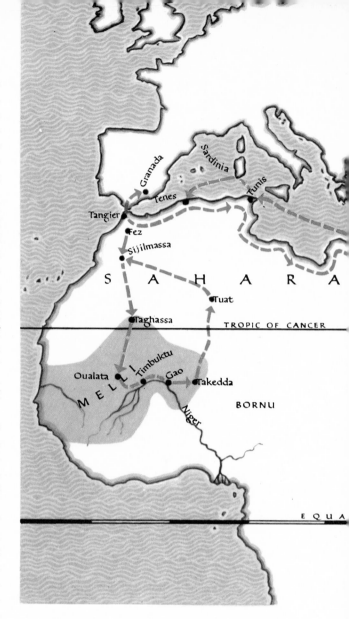

infidel (i.e. Buddhist) Indians and stripped of everything; it was only after great hardship that Ibn Batuta managed to return to Delhi. The gracious Sultan recompensed him with a large sum of money and equipped a new expedition. This time they journeyed down to the Gulf of Cambay and sailed from there via Goa, Onore and Malabar to Calicut, where they awaited the right season for the voyage to China. Just before the appointed day of departure, a storm raged over the coast, sinking most of the ships in the harbour at Calicut. Ibn Batuta happened to be ashore at the time, praying in the mosque for the success of the voyage, and he was the sole survivor of the expedition.

He now chose not to return to Delhi, and, after a series of ticklish encounters with the minor sultans on the Malabar Coast, he sailed across to the Maldive Islands, where

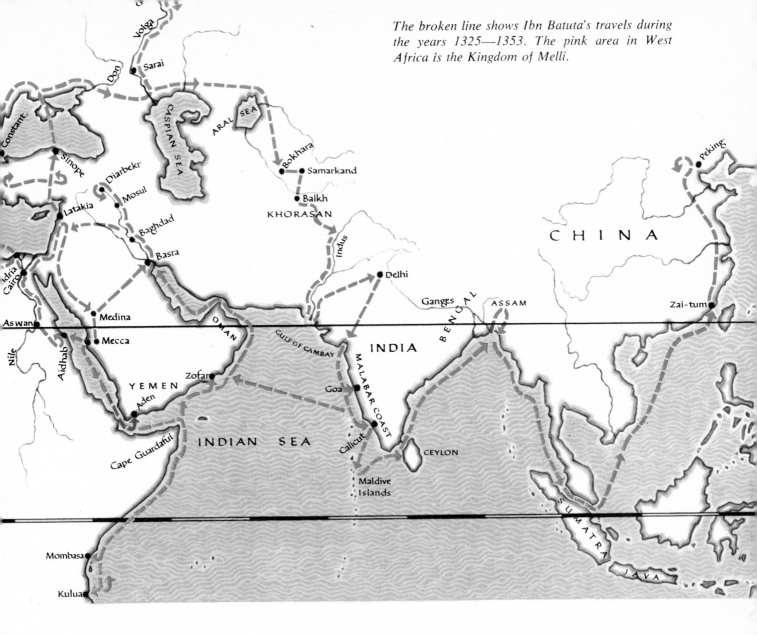

The broken line shows Ibn Batuta's travels during the years 1325—1353. The pink area in West Africa is the Kingdom of Melli.

he worked in his judicial capacity for eighteen months. He has strange things to tell of: "By their nourishment, which consists of honey, coconut milk and a kind of fish, the inhabitants possess a remarkable and unparalleled ability to perform the sexual act. The performance of the islanders in this respect is quite amazing. I myself had four legitimate wives there, apart from concubines. I found that I was potent for them all each day, and furthermore spent the night together with the one whose actual turn it was. I lived in this manner for one year and a half."

At last, he found he had had enough of the life on the islands, took one of his wives with him and sailed away in order to reach the mainland of India, but was driven off course and came instead to Ceylon. Among other things, he says: "The entire coast of the land of Ceylon [in reality only the regions around Puttalam] is littered with the trunks of the cinnamon-tree, which come floating down the rivers from the mountains. The inhabitants of Maabar and Malabar come and take away these trunks without paying anything for them, but they give the Sultan cloth in exchange ... On the forehead of the white elephant I saw seven rubies which were larger than hen's eggs, and at the palace of the Sultan Airi Sakarvati I saw a spoon of precious stone which was as large as the palm of a hand and filled with oil of aloes. I wondered at this, but he said: 'We have others which are far larger.' ... Mount Serendib [Adam's Peak, 7,365 ft.] is one of the highest mountains in the world. We were able to see it when at sea even though the distance between us and it was a nine-days' voyage. Long ago, a kind of stairway was cut into the mountain so that people could climb it, and iron

143

posts and chains have been affixed there to help the climbers. There are ten such chains. — A footprint of our venerable father Adam is to be found up there on a high black rock in an out-of-the-way place. His foot penetrated the rock. The print is 11 spans long. The Chinese have gone there on pilgrimage since time immemorial."

From Ceylon Ibn Batuta returned to Malabar, where he was shipwrecked and robbed; then he came back to Calicut and thence to the Maldive Islands. There he decided to carry out his journey to China as originally planned, but as the wind was not yet in the right quarter, he first sailed across the sea for forty-three days to Bengal and Assam, and from there down to Sumatra. The Mohammedan ruler of the island received him well and equipped a junk for him, and after a voyage of seventy-one days across a calm sea that was "stirred neither by wind nor wave", he finally reached Zai-tum in China.

Like Marco Polo, he had much to say about this and other cities, about paper money and other remarkable things to be found in China, making one reservation, however: "I did not like the land of China, in spite of the many beautiful things it may have possessed. On the contrary, I was greatly troubled at the idolatry that prevailed there ... When I happened to meet believers in China, it was as if I were meeting with my kith and kin." — He visited Peking, but his information is obscure and often uninteresting, and it seems as if he wanted to leave the place as soon as he could so that he might come back to the countries of the faithful.

Of the return journey to Sumatra he says: "In Zai-tum I found some junks ready for departure to India, among them one which belonged to King Es-Zahir, the ruler of Java [Sumatra]. The entire crew of this vessel were of the Faith. — We did not see the sun for ten days, and then we sailed into unknown waters. The crew of the junk were afraid and wanted to return to China, but this they could not do. Thus we spent forty-two days, not knowing in which part of the ocean we were. At dawn on the forty-third day, we discerned a mountain rising out of the sea about twenty miles away, and the wind carried us straight towards it. The sailors were amazed and said: 'We are nowhere near land, and there is not supposed to be a mountain in the sea here. We shall be lost if the wind carries us there.' All aboard now resorted to humble prayer and promises of penance, and the sailors repeated confessions of their sins again and again. We prayed in humility to God and to His Prophets so that they would speak for us. The merchants gave promises of generous almsgiving, which I put down in a list for them. The wind fell off a little, and now we saw in the early morning sun how the mountain rose high in the air, and we saw the daylight between the sea and the mountain. We were much amazed at this. I saw the sailors cry and take their leave one of another, and I asked: 'What is the matter with you?' They replied: 'What we thought was a mountain is the bird called the Roc. When it sees us it will put a miserable end to us all.' The distance between us and the bird was now no more than ten miles.

144

Then God had mercy upon us and sent a favourable wind, which carried us away from that place. We saw the bird no longer, and had never seen its true shape. Two months from that day we came to Java."

From Sumatra, Ibn Batuta sailed to Calicut and then to Zofar in Arabia. Via Persia and Syria, he came by degrees to Egypt and made yet another pilgrimage to Mecca. He then sailed from Alexandria in a Catalan ship to Sardinia, and from there to Tenes in Algeria, entering Morocco by an overland route and reaching Fez in November 1349. He was now 45 years old and had been travelling for twenty-four years.

But he was still not prepared to settle down. In the following year he sailed across to Spain and visited Moorish Granada, which was still powerful, and in 1352 he went to the interior of Africa at the wish of his Sultan.

It was not long after the Arabs had conquered Mauritania in the 8th century that they heard of the golden land of Ghana somewhere in the south. We know today that Ghana was a large empire north and west of the upper Niger, an empire that had used weapons of iron to subjugate its less well-armed neighbours. It possessed rich gold mines and controlled the trade routes to the north and to the important salt district of Taghassa. An Arab historian relates that a gold-mining people living south of Ghana were willing to buy salt with an equal weight of gold. And Ghana made full use of its position. The Almoravides, an Arab sect and dynasty which controlled north-west Africa and Spain from the middle of

Tradition has it that Mansa Kankan Musa the Great built the first flat-roofed buildings in Melli, including the Great Mosque at Timbuktu. In his days the country around the city was not the barren desert it is now; the annual Niger floods reached the small lakes near the city.

the 11th century, soon came into possession of Taghassa. They traded with Ghana to begin with, but they wanted to get at the source of the gold, and after fourteen years of fighting they managed to subdue the country. Later, they were not strong enough to prevent the neighbouring land of Soso from conquering Ghana and enslaving its people.

According to tradition, King Allakoi Keita founded the state of Madingo in 1213. This was to become known in history as the Empire of Mali or Melli. Twenty-five years later, his successor drove the Soso rulers out of Ghana, and from that time on Melli ruled the whole of the western Sudan. The rulers of Melli were Mohammedans, and Mansa Kankan Musa, the greatest of them, took Taghassa, and gained control of all the salt and the gold. During his reign, Djenne, Gao, and, above all, Timbuktu grew into important trading cities, and he built large palaces and mosques within their gates. As one of the faithful, he too made a pilgrimage to Mecca, and he caused a considerable stir when he appeared in Cairo

145

in 1324 at the head of a vast caravan, accompanied by his wives, and his court, bringing rich gifts to other sultans—all escorted by well-armed cavalry.

It was to know more of Melli and its ruler that the Sultan of Morocco sent Ibn Batuta on his long journey through the desert.

He left Fez with a caravan, and, arriving at Sijilmassa, set out on his journey through the desert. After twenty-five days the party came to Taghassa, and after a further thirty to Oualata, "the first city in the land of the negroes." Ibn Batuta was not satisfied with the reception he was given: "Since they were badly behaved and showed *white* people such little respect, I regretted that I had ever set out for the land of the blacks." He goes on in this way: "As I was determined to make the journey to Melli [by this he presumably means Timbuktu], a city which lies a fast march of twenty-four days from Djua-laten [Oualata], I hired a guide from the Messufah tribe. There is no need whatever to travel in large groups, since the route is very safe. I departed with three men, and all along the road we found great, hundred-year-old trees. One of them alone affords enough shade for a whole caravan. — In these parts a traveller needs neither provisions, ducats nor drachmas. It suffices if he has a piece of salt, glass beads or ornaments which are called nazhm. — No sooner does a traveller reach a village than negresses come with millet, sour milk, hens, lotus meal,

Mansa Kankan Musa is said to have brought back from Mecca an Arabian architect called Es Saheli, who designed mosques and other public buildings in Melli. No mosques of that date survive there in their original form, and we do not know how far the old west Sudanese style was influenced by Es Saheli. Some 13th-century ruins in the old Ghana capital of Koumbi-Saleh show details (1) which survive unchanged in modern houses. The Great Mosque at Timbuktu may have been of the same type as the old mosque in Djenne (2), in a style still common in western Sudan, found also in this mud palace in Ashanti (3), in northern Ghana.

rice, funi [?]—a seed like mustardseed which is made into dumplings—and also thick porridge and bean flour. A traveller may buy any of these things that he wants."

Ten days after leaving Oualata they came to Zaghari, where Ibn Batuta met white people, presumably Arabs. "We left Zaghari and came to a large river, which is the Nile or the Niger, lying near Carsakhu. From here the river flows to Cabara, then to Zaghah—and from Zaghah to Timbuktu and Kaukau [Gao?]. — The Nile flows into Nubia, whose inhabitants are Christians, and to Dongola,

146

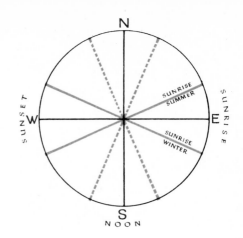

its capital [in Abyssinia]." Like Herodotus and other classical authors, Ibn Batuta believed that the Nile rose in West Africa. Since the upper Niger flows towards the east, his mistake is easily understandable.

He stayed seven months in Timbuktu and one month in Gao. From there he accompanied a large caravan to Takedda. He says: "Takedda exports copper to the city of Kuber, which lies in the land of the infidel blacks, and also to Zaghai and to the land of Bernu [Bornu]. It is a forty-days' journey from Bernu to Takedda, and the inhabitants of the country are Mohammedans. They have a ruler named Idris who never shows himself to his people, but speaks to his subjects only from behind a curtain. From Bernu are exported beautiful slaves, eunuchs and saffron-coloured cloth."

On the sixty-two-days' journey from Takedda to the oasis of Tuat, they passed through the country of Haggar (the Ahaggar Plateau), and Ibn Batuta relates that the inhabitants (the Touaregs) wore veils and were, incidentally, a lot of good-for-nothings. After a journey of three and a half months from Takedda, he found himself in December 1353 back at his starting-point in Sijilmassa, where he was met by a violent snowstorm. He sums up his last journey in the following words: "I have seen much snow on my travels, in Bokhara, in Samarkand, in Khorasan and in the land of the Turks, but I have never known a more unpleasant route than this."

The Plumb, the Compass, the Chart and the Astrolabe

Everywhere in the world where people have sailed the seas, they have given names to the winds, and the sailor's horizon has been gradually divided into quarters of wind and weather. For those who sailed in the Indian Ocean and other seas where there were regular seasonal winds, this division of the horizon was less necessary than for the Mediterraneans and other people who mostly sailed in waters where the winds varied. Most important for these people were the points where the sun rose and set, and these were later supplemented by the line of direction to the point where the sun was highest in the heavens. In this way they had four cardinal points of the compass.

However, in the Mediterranean the sun only rises exactly in the east and sets exactly in the west at the spring and autumn equinoxes, and in order to supplement the division of the horizon, the Greeks made use of the points where the sun rose and set at the summer and winter solstices, which lay roughly 30° north and south

of the east-west line. Later it was quite natural that people should define a further four points lying equidistant from each other on either side of the north-south line. The Romans also made use of this division of the horizon, and the twelve points of their compass were given the following names:

$$
\begin{array}{rl}
N = & Boreas \\
N\ 30°\ E = & Aquilo \\
E\ 30°\ N = & Caecias \\
E = & Subsolanus = Apeliotes \\
E\ 30°\ S = & Eurus \\
S\ 30°\ E = & Euronotus = Phoenicias \\
S = & Auster = Notus \\
S\ 30°\ W = & Austro-Africus = Libonotus \\
W\ 30°\ S = & Africus = Libs \\
W = & Favonius = Zephyrus \\
W\ 30°\ N = & Caurus \\
N\ 30°\ W = & Thrascias
\end{array}
$$

Early on, however, this division was simplified into eight points, and during the Middle Ages the Mediterraneans referred to the eight winds as:

$$
\begin{array}{rl}
N = & Tramontana \\
NE = & Greco \\
E = & Levante \\
SE = & Syroco \\
S = & Ostro = Mezzodi \\
SW = & Africa = Garbino = Libeccio \\
W = & Ponente \\
NW = & Maestro
\end{array}
$$

During the classical period and the beginning of the Middle Ages, when there were neither maps nor compasses to sail by, mariners steered by the direction of the winds, by the sun and the stars, and by the descriptions which had been handed down orally or on paper from generation to generation of navigators. The only real navigational instrument on board was the plumb, a piece

147

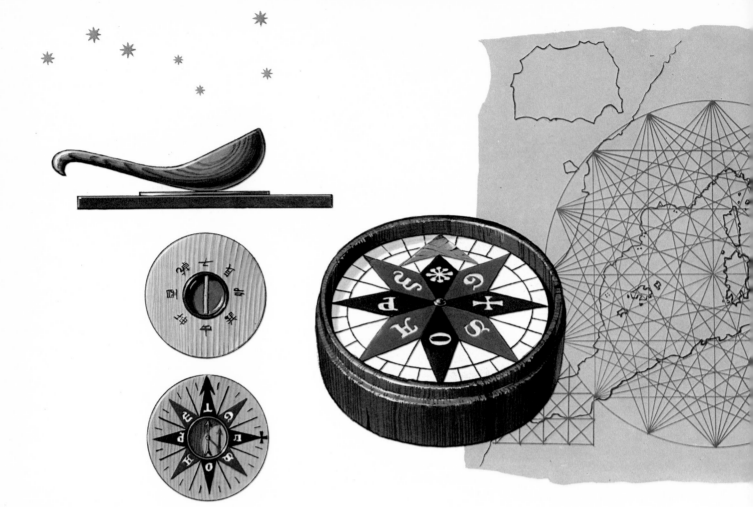

of lead attached to a long line. The bottom of the plumb had a depression which could be filled with wax so that particles of mud could be brought up from the sea bed. The depth together with the colour or smell of the mud was able to tell an experienced pilot how far he was from a particular spot on the coast.

We do not know when the compass was first used by Europeans. Before the Christian era, Chinese geomancers (fortune-tellers of a kind) had what was virtually a compass. A wooden spoon representing the Great Bear was fitted with a small magnet at the end of the bowl so that when it was balanced the handle pointed south. Several hundreds of years later, the Chinese learned how to magnetize iron needles, and when they inserted one into a straw and floated it in a small bowl, it served as a compass. A Chinese document from the early 12th century describes the magnetic needle as an instrument for navigation, but we may presume that it was used much earlier.

The first mention of the compass in Europe was in 1187. Here too a floating needle was used to begin with, but it did not take long before it could be balanced on a pin. According to tradition, Flavio Gioja of Amalfi discovered the compass in 1302. It is possible that it was Gioja who improved the compass by attaching the needle

to the "rose" (a card on which the compass points were set out in the shape of a flower or a star) so that the entire rose turned with the needle.

We do not know when and through what countries the compass came from China to the West. It could have come overland along the silk-routes during the early Middle Ages; it could have come by sea and then through the Persians and the Arabs in the 9th century when Chinese junks sailed to the Persian Gulf; and it is not absolutely impossible that the compass may have been invented in Europe quite independently of China.

The 15th-century Italian traveller Nicolo Conti says that mariners in the Indian Ocean did not use the compass. And an Arabic manuscript from 1282 informs us that neither did the world of Islam know of the compass at that time. Among other things the manuscript says: "When the night is dark and it is not possible to see the stars which show the four quarters, Syrian sailors use a bowl of water which they protect from the wind by going below deck. They take a needle which they push through a piece of acacia wood or a straw so that they form a cross. This they float on the water. They then take a lodestone, large enough to fill the hand, or smaller. This they hold just over the bowl of water and move their

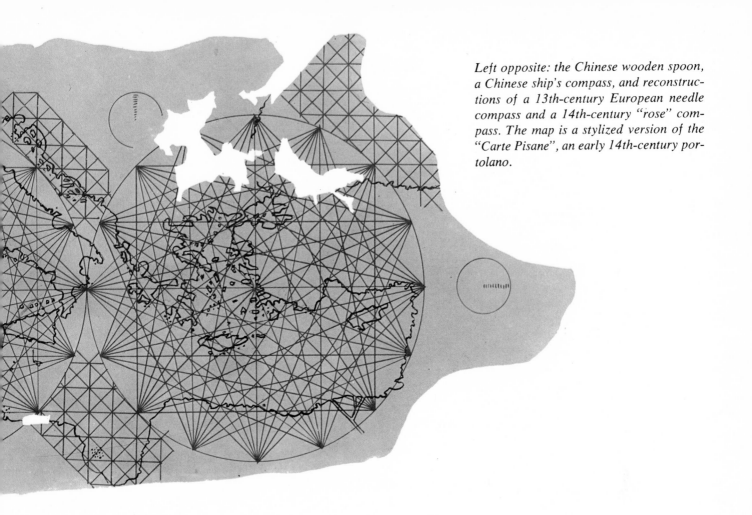

Left opposite: the Chinese wooden spoon, a Chinese ship's compass, and reconstructions of a 13th-century European needle compass and a 14th-century "rose" compass. The map is a stylized version of the "Carte Pisane", an early 14th-century portolano.

hand round from right to left: the needle follows round after it. Then they take it away quickly, and the needle turns until it points north and south. I have seen this done with my own eyes, on a voyage from Tripoli in Syria to Alexandria."

When people could fix the various directions more exactly with the compass, the old navigational descriptions were supplemented with maps. Medieval maps or charts, mainly drawn by Italians, were called portolanos —the Italian *portolano*, like the Greek *periplus*, means "sailing description" in the form of narrative, chart, description of harbours etc., and illustrations. The oldest surviving portolanos date from the early 14th century, and, unlike contemporary maps by learned cosmographers, they show land contours, in particular those around the Mediterranean and the Black Sea, which are almost perfectly correct. They are not drawn to a grid-system of degrees, but are based on compass courses and estimated distances. Auxiliary lines, of help to the mariner as well as the cartographer, were known as "loxodromes"; they were drawn through the quarters on the compass rose.

Ptolemy's *Almagest* was translated from Arabic to Latin as early as the 12th century, and the geocentric theory—with the round Earth suspended in the middle of the Universe and the "planets" rotating in their spheres round the Earth, with the fixed stars in the outermost Heaven—gradually came to be accepted by the learned of the Middle Ages. At the beginning of the 15th century, Ptolemy's geography also became available to the geographers of Europe, and people began to draw maps on his projections, generally based on a system of lines of latitude and longitude.

The Pole Star had long been the fixed point by which mariners had navigated, and its height above the horizon—measured, for instance, in fractions of a spear-shaft, or in handsbreadths—gave them some idea of their position in the north-south line. The astronomers' astrolabe was a star-map, a table and an instrument for measuring angles at one and the same time. With the aid of the alidad, a rotating arm in the middle of the instrument, it was also possible to measure accurately the height of the Pole Star above the horizon in degrees of an arc. It was now accepted that the earth was a sphere, and the position of any point on this sphere could be fixed by the network of latitudes and longitudes which began to appear on the maps. With minor corrections, the height of the Pole Star is the same as the latitude

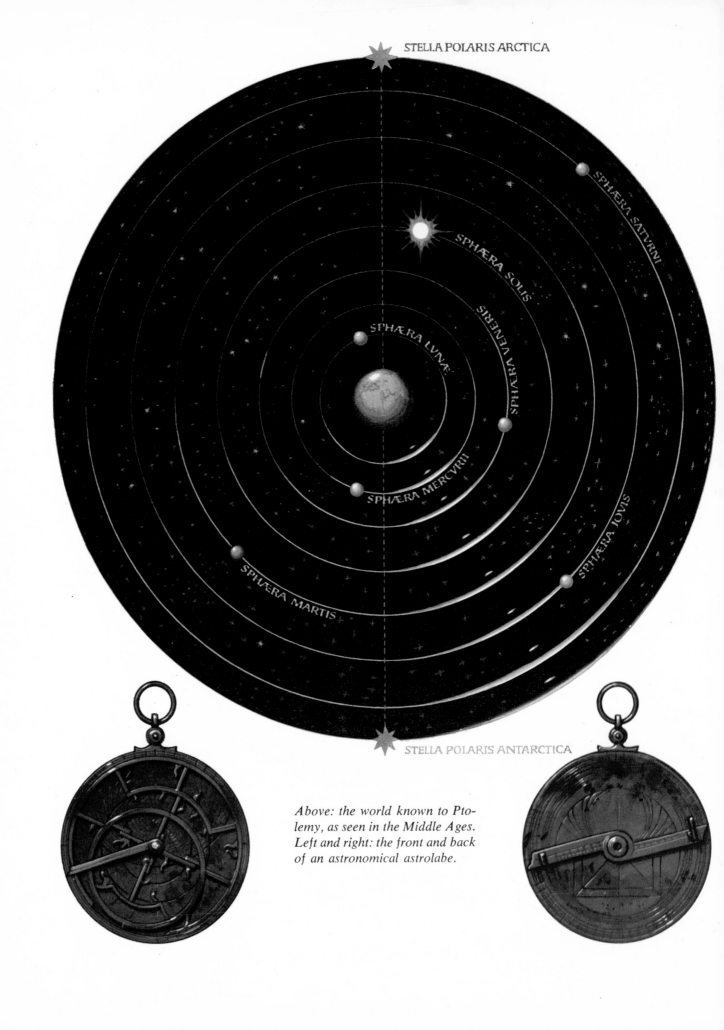

STELLA POLARIS ARCTICA

SPHÆRA SATVRNI

SPHÆRA SOLIS

SPHÆRA VENERIS

SPHÆRA LVNÆ

SPHÆRA MERCVRII

SPHÆRA JOVIS

SPHÆRA MARTIS

STELLA POLARIS ANTARCTICA

Above: the world known to Ptolemy, as seen in the Middle Ages. Left and right: the front and back of an astronomical astrolabe.

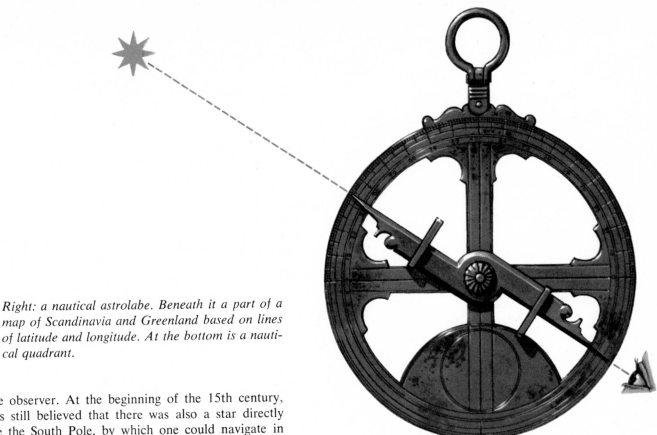

Right: a nautical astrolabe. Beneath it a part of a map of Scandinavia and Greenland based on lines of latitude and longitude. At the bottom is a nautical quadrant.

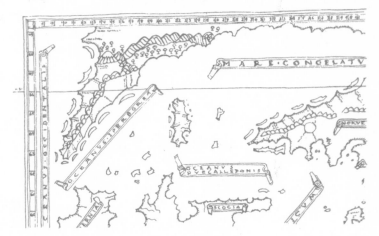

of the observer. At the beginning of the 15th century, it was still believed that there was also a star directly above the South Pole, by which one could navigate in the Southern Hemisphere.

For use at sea, a simplified astrolabe was constructed which consisted only of the graduated ring and alidad with a dioptric sight. But it was found necessary to construct an even handier instrument, and so the nautical quadrant appeared. This too was a simplification of a complicated astronomical instrument. It consisted of a quarter-circle, graduated from 0 to 90. Along one side ran a dioptric sight, and a weighted thread showed the height directly.

But 15th-century navigators seldom thought in degrees of latitude, and they often simplified the quadrant so that instead of degrees they marked various place-names —capes, rivers and towns along the Atlantic coastline— and in this way homebound seafarers, blown out of sight of land, could take a simple measurement of the Pole Star and read directly off the quadrant when they were, for example, in the latitude of Lisbon. Then they would only have to steer due east by compass.

This was the theory, and we have evidence that such manipulations were indeed carried out in practice, especially if any sufficiently educated person was on board. But as we shall see later, the records show that even experienced mariners did not always use the quadrant. It was only towards the end of the 15th century and the beginning of the modern era that it became common practice to try to determine one's position at sea with the aid of the stars and the available instruments. It was the plumb, the compass and the look-out which showed the way to India.

The Kingdoms of the Iberian Peninsula

When the Mohammedan Empire was at its largest, the Mediterranean lay in a pincer-grip between the Infidels in the west, in the south and in the east. After the fall of the Visigoth Kingdom in the Iberian Peninsula, most of the population, already a complex racial mixture, surrendered readily enough to the "Moors", as the Christians called the Arabs of Spain and north-west Africa: the word "Moors" or "Mauri" originally denoted the inhabitants of Mauritania. But a large section of the Visigoth ruling class withdrew to the north-west corner of the peninsula, where, together with Celtiberians and Basques, they soon formed the Kingdom of Asturia. Before the end of the 8th century they had begun to attack the Moors, whose empire was weakened by internal conflict almost as soon as they arrived. Moreover, the Franks pushed down from the north across the Pyrenees, and by the early years of the 9th century they had conquered all the land north of the Ebro (conventionally known as the "Spanish March") together with its capital, Barcelona.

The most important city in Asturia during the 9th century was Leon, which was later to give its name to a kingdom. By repeated aggressions, the kingdom expanded in the south, and, in order to secure the border, a series of forts or castles was built; that is why the region was called Castile. During the 11th century, Moorish Spain was split into a number of small kingdoms, and this made things so easy for the Christians that they could force their way far across the Douro, and in 1095 a Burgundian count was given the administration of the northern part of modern Portugal under the King of Leon. Less than a hundred years later, the Governor of Portugal, with the

assistance of Templars and Knights of the Order of St. John, had taken Lisbon, made the Tagus the southern border and Portugal a separate kingdom, independent of Leon and subject to the Pope alone. More than half the peninsula was now in Christian hands. The north-west corner and the part nearest Portugal composed the Kingdom of Leon. Between this and Aragon, which had developed out of the Frankish mandate of the Spanish March, lay Castile, and, right up against the Pyrenees, the little Kingdom of Navarre.

From time to time, Castile and Leon had had the same ruler, and in the 13th century they were finally united. They took large areas from the Moors, including Cordova and Seville, and moved the border far south of the Guadalquivir. The Portuguese pushed forward at the same time, taking the province of Algarve and thus bringing the kingdom to approximately its present-day shape. Aragon, too, expanded in the south, taking the Balearic Islands and, later on, Sicily and Sardinia. After a long war in the 14th century, Castile, with the help of the other Christian

152

kingdoms, managed to take Gibraltar. All that then remained of Moorish Spain was Granada.

Naturally these six hundred years did not consist of one long series of wars; at times there were such friendly relationships between the Moorish and Christian Dynasties that marriage alliances were agreed to. Contact with Arab culture was even more fruitful for the Spanish Christians than it had been for the Crusaders. Many Christians studied at the Moorish universities, and the inhabitants in the Christian kingdoms were a healthy mixture of Celtiberians, Basques, Visigoths, Franks, Jews, Arabs and Berbers.

The Canary Islands and Madeira

Merchants from all over the Christian Mediterranean traded with the Arabs in North Africa, but they never went further than the ports; the caravan routes which led from these to the countries somewhere beyond the desert were closed to them. The information that some of the routes led to a land where gold was to be found may have come from Jewish merchants, who were more conversant with the facts and enjoyed greater freedom; further details may have been wrung from Moorish prisoners: in any case, the demand for gold in Europe was great, and we hear of expeditions that were sent out as early as the 14th century with the aim of reaching the gold, the "River of Gold" somewhere on the dangerous west coast of Africa.

A Portuguese expedition to the Canary Islands in 1341 reported what was thought to be a vast lateen sail on the top of the Pico de Teyde on Tenerife.

It was perhaps on such an expedition that Lanzarote from Genoa rediscovered the easternmost of the Canary Islands in 1312. But we hardly know anything of him or his voyage.

Alfonso IV of Portugal, however, had learned, like others, of his discovery, and as he considered that the islands lay closest to his kingdom he claimed them for himself and sent out an expedition led by a certain Anghelino de Tegghia, a Florentine, to take possession of them. In a manuscript which is said to have been written by Boccaccio (1313—1375) we find the following: "In the year of the Incarnation 1341 there came letters to Florence, written on 14th November of that same year, by certain Florentine merchants in Seville, a city in farthest Spain. They related the following:

"Two ships fitted with all necessities by the Portuguese King left the city of Lisbon and sailed out into the high seas in July of this year, and with them a small well-armed vessel manned by Genoese, Castilians and other Spaniards. With them they took horses, weapons and various war machines so that they might be able to take cities and castles, and they set out to find these islands which were generally known to have been rediscovered. Favoured by a good wind they landed there on the fifth day. At the end of November they returned, carrying with them the following: four people, inhabitants of the islands, together with great quantities of goatskin, tallow, blubber, sealskin,

153

The dragon's-blood tree, which grows on the Canaries, produces a red resin (or "dragon's blood") which is said to have been used as a cosmetic by Roman ladies in classical times. During the Middle Ages its chief use was in medicine, and it was considered to be a cure for leprosy, among other things.

red dyewood which colours almost like verzino [brazil or sappan wood which was obtained from the Sunda Isles through the Arabs], even if those who have knowledge of this do not consider it to be true, furthermore bark for dyeing red, red earth and other things.

"Niccoloso da Recco of Genoa, the pilot of the expedition, said when asked that the archipelago lay almost 900 miles from the city of Seville, but if we calculate from the place which today is called Cape St. Vincent the islands are much nearer the mainland, the first of the islands discovered lying about 140 miles away. [In actual fact there is not much difference in the distance.]

It was a barren mass of rock, but rich in goats and other animals and full of naked men and women who were like savages in their way of life. He added that he and his companions took most of their cargo of tallow and hides on board here, but had not dared to go deeper inland. They had sailed past yet another island which was much larger than the first, and had seen numerous inhabitants who had hurried to the shore to meet them. These men and women were also nearly naked. Certain of them seemed to give orders to the others; and these wore goatskins painted red and yellow. From a distance, we thought these furs to be very fine and soft, sewn together very skilfully with gut. By what can be understood from their demeanour, they have a chieftain to whom they show great respect and obedience. All these islanders made signs showing their readiness to meet and trade with the seafarers, but when the boats approached the shore, the men understood nothing of their language and did not dare to go ashore. Their language is very soft, and their manner of speaking is vigorous and excited, like that of the Italians. When the islanders saw that the mariners did not intend to land, some of them tried to swim out to them. Four of these were kept on board; these were they who were taken back to Portugal.

"When sailing along the coast in order to circumnavigate the island, they found that the north side was far

found had many birds and good water. There, too, were many trees and wild grapes of which they ate, after having brought them down by beating the vines with sticks and throwing stones at them. They were larger than our grapes, and yet tasted as well, if not better. They saw many hawks and other birds of prey. But they did not venture to go ashore as the island seemed completely uninhabited.

"They saw yet another island before them whose rocky mountains rose to a great height and were almost completely covered in snow. Rain is always falling there. But the part which is to be seen in clear weather they thought very pleasant, and they believed it to be inhabited. They saw other distant islands, some of which were inhabited and some not, thirteen in all, and the farther they sailed

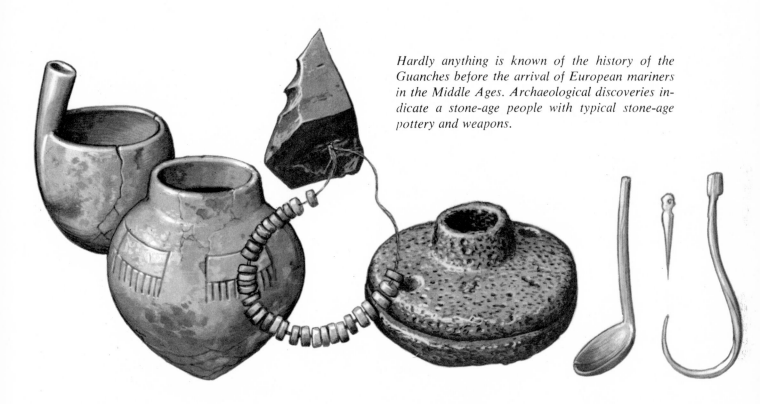

Hardly anything is known of the history of the Guanches before the arrival of European mariners in the Middle Ages. Archaeological discoveries indicate a stone-age people with typical stone-age pottery and weapons.

better cultivated than the south. They saw many small dwellings, fig-trees and other trees, palms which bore no fruit, and yet others, and gardens with cabbages and other vegetables. Here they decided to go ashore. Twenty-five sailors betook themselves well-armed to the shore, searched the houses, and in one of them found thirty completely naked people who ran away in terror when they saw the weapons . . . As they passed on from that island, they saw many others at a distance of five, ten, twenty or forty miles. They steered towards a third on which they noticed a large number of tall trees almost reaching to the sky. Then they sailed past another which they

the more they saw. The sea between them is calmer than along our coasts and affords good anchorage, although the islands have few harbours. But they all have good supplies of water. Of the thirteen islands they visited, five were inhabited, but not all to the same extent. They also said that the language used by the inhabitants was so strange to them that they were unable to understand anything of it, and moreover that there are no forms of shipping whatsoever there. It was only by swimming that the people could go from one island to the other.

"One of the islands they came across contained something so strange that they did not go ashore. They say that on it is a mountain which according to their reckoning was thirty miles high or more, and can be seen at a great distance. There is something white on its top, and this white thing looked like a fortress; and indeed the whole island is rock-girt. A very sharp crag on the peak is fitted with a ship-sized mast, together with a yard-arm and lateen sail. This sail, which is filled by the wind, is shaped like a shield upside-down and bellies out quickly. Now and again the mast lowers itself of its own accord, like the mast of a galley, then raises itself, falls once more and raises itself again. They sailed round the island and saw this phenomenon repeated from all sides. Since they believed it to be the work of a sorcerer, they did not venture ashore.

"They also saw many other things of which the aforementioned Niccoloso did not wish to tell. But the islands cannot have been rich, for the mariners were hardly able to cover the costs of their voyage."

The news of the journey aroused considerable interest, and the following year three ships sailed from Aragonian Majorca to the islands. The Canaries were never recognized as belonging to Portugal. The Pope granted them in 1344 to Luis de la Cerda, a great-grandson of Alfonso X of Castile, and when he died a year later, the islands, in spite of Portuguese protests, were considered to be Spanish possessions.

The story of the 14th-century discovery of Madeira and Porto Santo is rather fantastic, but Europeans certainly knew about this island group before 1350, since it is clearly marked on maps and mentioned in writing. The tale is to be found in its clearest form in *Tratado dos Diversos e Desvayrados Caminhos,* written by one Antonio Galvano in the 16th century: "At that time, the island of Madeira was discovered by an Englishman called Macham who was sailing with his wife from England to Spain. He was driven off course by a storm, came to the island and anchored in the harbour which today is called Machico. Since his wife was seasick, he went ashore with his retinue. Meanwhile, his vessel drifted out to sea and was carried away, leaving them behind. His wife died of grief at this. Macham, who loved her greatly, built on the island a chapel or burial-place, called it the Chapel of Jesus, and wrote or carved her name and his own, as well as the cause of their coming there, on her gravestone. He then built himself a boat entirely out of timber, for the trees there are very large, and sailed out to sea in it with his countrymen who had stayed there with him. He managed to reach the coast of Africa without sail or rudder. The Moors who were there considered this to be a miracle and took them to their ruler. He was amazed at the happening and sent them to the King of Castile."

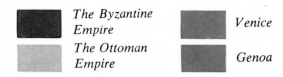

The Byzantine Empire

The Ottoman Empire

Venice

Genoa

The Latin Empire came into being in 1204, when the Crusaders and the Venetians took Constantinople; in 1261 Michael Palaeologus recaptured the city and the empire became Byzantine again: Genoa then took the place of Venice as the most favoured State. But the Byzantine Empire had been too weakened to hold out much longer: threatened at first by Slavonic Serbs to the north, almost the whole empire succumbed before 1400 to the Ottoman Turks, who swept across the Dardanelles and most of Greece. In the 15th century Constantinople controlled nothing but a narrow territory round its own walls, a few islands in the northern Aegean, and about a third of the Peloponnese. Venice and Genoa could still send ships to the Black Sea ports.

Portugal Goes to Sea

The Catalans of Aragon had long been a seafaring people, and the position of the country and its possessions on the islands in the Mediterranean soon made it a great trading power. Like the Venetians and the Genoese, the Catalans obtained privileges for themselves in Constantinople, and even sailed the waters of the Black Sea; in fact their ships reached Britain and Flanders before those of the Genoese. Castile did not enjoy these initial advantages. During the 13th century the people there had to employ shipbuilders and pilots from Genoa and Pisa to build, equip and lead the fleet which protected their coast from the Moors and later took the offensive, forced a passage up the Guadalquivir, and took Seville. The Castilians gained further experience of the sea when, in alliance with the French, they fought against their English mercantile competitors in the north.

The Portuguese were mainly a farming people, and it was their princes who lured or forced them out into the unfriendly ocean, where they were later to perform such amazing feats. The war with the Moors had mainly been fought on land, but a fleet was needed to defend the

157

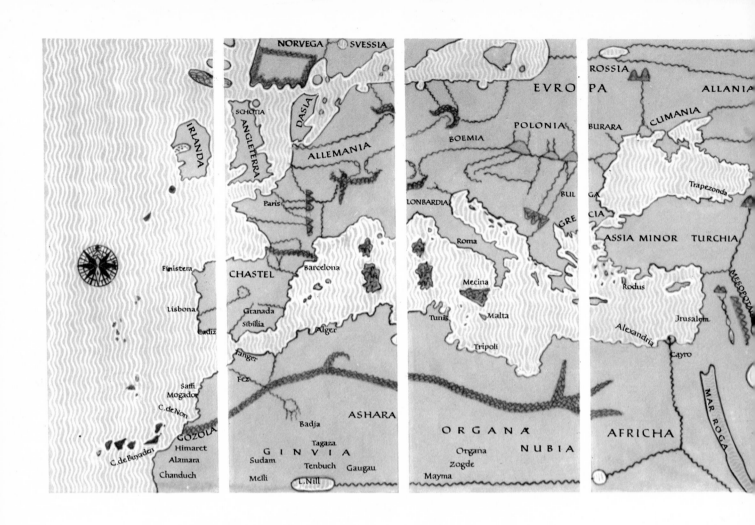

country thenceforward. Before it had reached its full strength, however, Portugal was twice defeated at sea off Lisbon by Castile; the Castilian vessels even went so far as to force their way into the mouth of the Tagus and pillage the suburbs of Lisbon itself.

It is said that King Diniz was the first to realize that Portugal's future lay on the sea. Even before his time there existed a modest mercantile fleet which dealt mainly with northern markets in Normandy, Flanders and Britain. In 1293 he issued a Statute of Commerce which had been suggested by the mariners themselves—strangely enough, for among other things it imposed a tax on exports. He laid the foundations for the excellent trading connections with Britain which have lasted till our own times. In 1317 he appointed Manoel Pessagno from Genoa as Admiral of his fleet, and with him other Genoese as captains of many of the ships. The description of the expedition to the Canary Islands discloses that he also had Florentines and Castilians in his service. In order to encourage the art of shipbuilding, he knighted his foremost constructors, and in order to ensure his supply of timber he planted forests.

During the reign of his successor, Lisbon grew into a great international port where many hundreds of vessels, most of them foreign, lay at anchor. Ferdinand I, known as Ferdinand the Fair, who was the last of the Burgundian kings of Portugal, wanted to build a strong domestic merchant navy, and no monarch has ever done more for seafaring than he. Any Portuguese who wanted to build a vessel of at least 100 tons was given free timber from the royal forests and also the right to import, duty-free, anything else he might need for the building of his ship. On their first voyage to a foreign country, Portuguese mariners were exempted from all export duties on their cargo, irrespective of whether the goods belonged to them or to someone else. If the ship foundered, the owner was granted the same privilege for a further three years. In order to promote trade with Flanders and France, the king halved the duties on the goods brought back from those countries, chiefly cloth and timber. He granted the mariners many privileges and exemptions connected with military service and rates of interest, and his initiative gave rise to an insurance system which reduced the financial risks of seafaring.

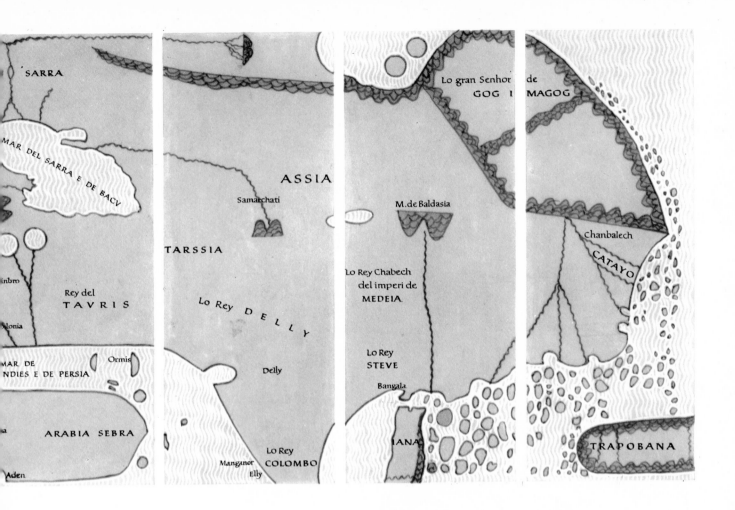

SARRA

MAR DEL SARRA E DE BACV

Samarchati

ASSIA

M. de Baldasia

Lo gran Senhor de GOG I MAGOG

inbro

Rey del
TAVRIS

TARSSIA

Lo Rey D E L L Y

Lo Rey Chabech
del imperi de
MEDEIA

Chanbalech

CATAYO

ilonia

MAR DE
NDIES E DE PERSIA

Ormis

Delly

Lo Rey
STEVE

Bangala

a

ARABIA SEBRA

IANA

Aden

Manganor
Elly

Lo Rey
COLOMBO

TRAPOBANA

*Abraham Cresques, a Jewish map and instrument
maker, drew his "Catalan Atlas" in Palma de Mallorca in 1375. It is an eight-page world atlas, and
is still in existence today. The coastlines are very
faint, but castles, people, flags and other decorative
elements on it are comparatively clear. To do Cres-*
*ques justice as a cartographer, the decorations have
been eliminated, as have all but the most important
of his place-names.*
*Below: a detail from the last page of the Catalan
Atlas, showing the island of "Trapobana" = Ceylon.*

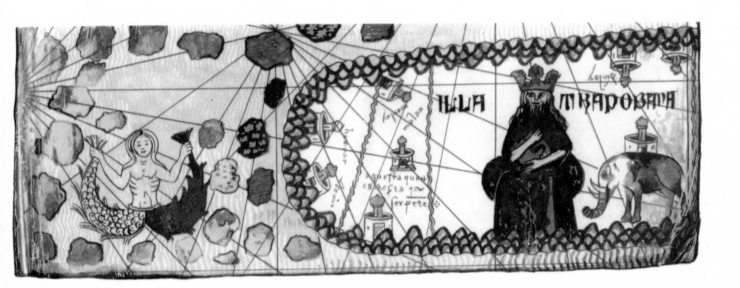

ILLA TRAPOBANA

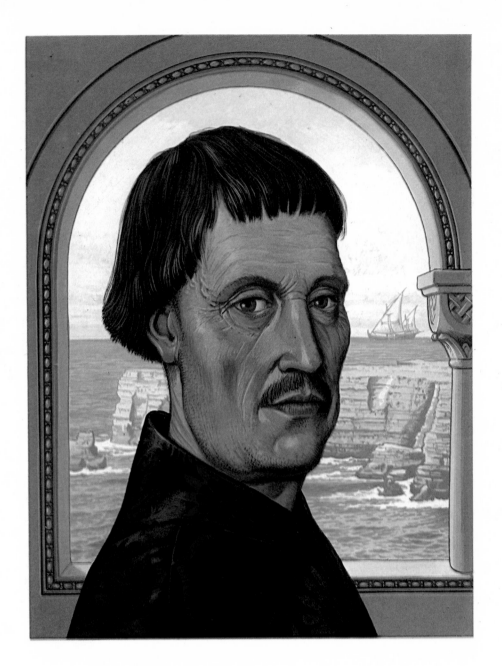

Henry the Navigator, from Nuño Gonçalves' polyptych in Lisbon.

Henry the Navigator

John I of the House of Aviz, who succeeded Ferdinand I on the throne of Portugal, had to fight a war of succession against the King of Castile, and settled the matter to his advantage by his brilliant victory at Aljubarrota in 1385. The following year, he married the English princess Philippa of the House of Lancaster, and according to the chroniclers their marriage was one of the happiest

known to history. She bore him eight children, of whom five boys and one girl lived long enough to come of age. Duarte, the eldest son, succeeded John. The third son, Enrique, is known to us as Henry the Navigator. His own voyages were not much more extensive than those of his brothers, but he was more important for the history of exploration than any other man who ever lived. Historians have regarded the brothers as an exceptionally gifted and loyal and deeply religious family.

The taking of Ceuta by the Portuguese in 1415 began

the great age of discovery. Many draw the dividing line between the Middle Ages and the modern era at this date, and consider that Columbus merely followed up what Henry the Navigator had begun.

Ceuta, one of the Pillars of Hercules, was a Moorish city and fortress on the coast of Africa opposite Gibraltar. The Portuguese expedition has been described as a crusade, and it is said that after the war with the Christians of Castile was over, King John "wanted to wash his hands in the blood of the Infidels". As far as the Portuguese were concerned, the war of conquest against the Moors had come to an end almost two hundred years before, and, unlike the Castilians and Aragonians, they had no common frontier with the Infidels where they could win honour in skirmishes and raids.

King John equipped a fleet of two hundred vessels of varying size, hiring a number of them from England, Flanders and Biscay, against payment in salt. The invasion force consisted of 20,000 men, many of whom were foreign knights with troops of their own. It is said that Ceuta was taken by guile, that the large fleet first sailed past the city into the Mediterranean so that the relieved commander sent away his reinforcements. The victory won by the Christians was described as being very glorious, but the fighting cannot have been hard, since only eight of the 20,000 fell. It is also said that the greater part of the army, after the main assault had been made, did nothing but loot the very rich city, leaving Henry, the hero of the day, with only seventeen men when he forced his way forward to the citadel—which he found abandoned by its defenders.

It was a comfort to the Christian world that a great victory had at last been won over the Infidels, and there was much rejoicing in Europe. Although sudden raids on African ports in the Mediterranean were by no means unusual, the towns being looted and their inhabitants taken away to be sold as slaves, such attacks were never made against large, well-defended cities. The Portuguese could moreover now hold Ceuta, important both strategically and as a symbol. This was where Tarik the Conqueror had gathered the invading army which pushed up into the Iberian Peninsula to threaten Europe seven hundred years before.

Much has been written about the reasons which later led Henry the Navigator to spend nearly all his declining years in encouraging and supporting travellers and organizing expeditions to explore West Africa and the Ocean. Even before the taking of Ceuta it was known that there were caravan routes from the city to the gold and other riches in the heart of Africa, and the costly booty found in the city gave clear evidence of the facts. The unfavourable balance of trade with the Arabs had brought little gold to Europe, and Portugal was no better off than other countries in this respect. One good explanation for

A Portuguese warrior.

Henry's activities is to be found in a statement by Diogo Gomes, one of his intimates who led several expeditions himself. He says: "The sea of sand is a thirty-seven-days' journey wide and separates the whites and the blacks from one another. The Carthaginians, whom we now call Tunisians, travelled across this in caravans, which often consisted of seven hundred camels, to a place now known as Tambuktu [Timbuktu], and to another country which is called Cantor, for the sake of the Arab gold which is to be found there in great quantities. It often happens that only one-tenth of these people and animals manage to return. When My Lord Prince Henry heard this, he was persuaded to send expeditions to these countries over the paths of the seas in order to trade with them."

It can be said that Prince Henry had no other choice if he wanted to reach the gold for Portugal. Ceuta was not the key to riches as long as the Moors controlled the

People also knew that Ferrer the Catalan had sailed out into the Ocean from Majorca on St. Lawrence's Day, 1346, to reach the River of Gold. He had never come back.

Henry the Navigator's decision to reach the Land of Gold by sea absorbed his entire fortune, taxed his amazing patience and needed all the vast amount of knowledge

Sea-monsters of the kind still feared by ocean-going seamen in the 16th century.

surrounding country, and even if it had been possible to send an expedition by land to Timbuktu and Cantor, the Portuguese were such a small nation that no prince would have dared in the long run to expose his men to such a high proportion of losses, not even for the sake of gold. It was probably discovered in Ceuta that Cantor lay on a river, not far from the Western Ocean, and people spoke of a whole land of gold called Ganuja—or Ghana—which lay on the coast somewhere in the south.

Posterity has ridiculed the doubts, the fears, and the disappointing achievements of the Portuguese at sea under Henry the Navigator, but their misgivings were not unique. Nearly all seafarers feared and avoided the Ocean beyond Cape Nun, i.e. "Cape No", and even though ships had already reached the Canaries, it was generally believed that the sea south of this point was not navigable. Educated men knew that the world was round, but many of them still believed that it was divided between habitable and non-habitable zones; and it was thought that the sun passed so close to the Equator that all the land there was scorched and the sea boiled. The great wastes of the African desert and the blackened people who lived beyond it were clear enough evidence for the Mediterraneans. Most of them believed in the fabulous animals and monsters which were portrayed on the maps, both on land and in the sea, and even the foremost Arab geographers, who were well-read and much respected by their European colleagues, advised against sailing in the Ocean.

he was gradually to gain. When Ceuta fell he was only 21 years old, and after the fighting was over he was knighted, together with both his elder brothers, and made Duke of Viseu. He dispatched his first expedition the following year, and Diogo Gomes tells us about it: "The following year, the Lord Prince Henry sent a noble cavalier called Gonzalo Velho out along the sea coasts past the Canary Islands, for he wanted to know the reason for the powerful currents in the ocean there. Gonzalo sailed past the islands and found a calm and peaceful sea off the coast of Africa or Libya. He came to a place which today is called Terra Alta. Along the coast of this country was nothing but sand." — Gonzalo Velho probably reached the vicinity of modern Cape Juby. The expedition can hardly be said to have been remarkable in any way, and neither do we know what the Prince had expected of it.

In 1418 the Moors tried to retake Ceuta, but the city was successfully defended by the Christians, and when Henry arrived with a relieving force, the attackers fled. On his return to Lisbon, he was appointed governor of the southern province of Algarve, and there he built a residence for himself at Sagres near Cape St. Vincent, the most south-westerly point in Europe.

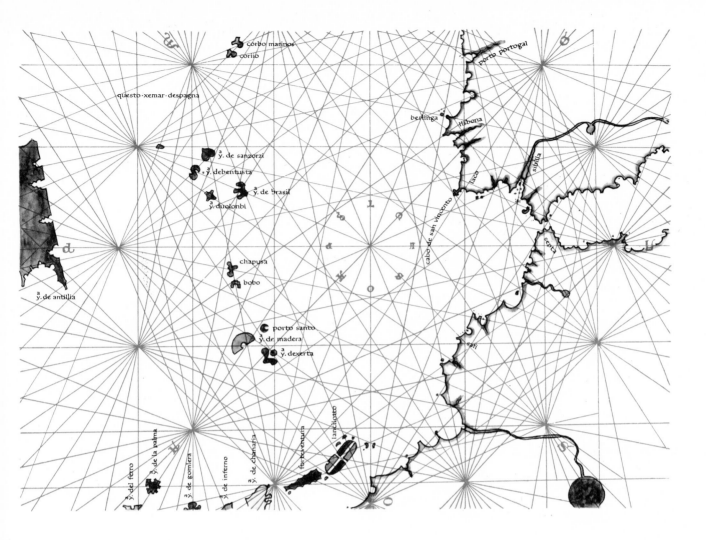

The Discovery of the Azores

It is often said that the Portuguese discovered Porto Santo and Madeira in 1418, but we know that their existence was common knowledge as early as the middle of the 14th century. It is probable that the Portuguese first reached Porto Santo in 1418, but that was certainly not its discovery. It may well have happened as Valentin Ferdinand describes in the 16th century. He says that João Gonçalves was lying in wait for Castilian ships off Cape St. Vincent when a Castilian in his crew suggested that they sail across the sea to Porto Santo in the hope of finding booty. In spite of the objections of an apprehensive crew, they sailed to the island, where they discovered traces of other seafarers who had been there only a few days before. Gonçalves returned to Sagres and suggested to the Prince that the island be colonized, which was indeed done.

This section of a map drawn in 1436 by Andrea Bianco, a Venetian, shows the Spanish Peninsula, Mauritania, the Canary Islands and the Madeiras. All the islands north of Madeira are figments of the imagination, copied from older maps. The island of Lanzarote, named after its Genoese discoverer, was marked with the red cross of Genoa on older maps — presumably Andrea Bianco changed the colour for patriotic reasons. Only the most important place-names are shown here.

The Canary Islands were a bone of contention between Portugal and Castile for nearly the whole of the 15th century. At the beginning of the century, a Norman adventurer called Jean de Béthencourt had colonized a few of the islands with the permission of Castile, and this concession was later sold by his nephew to a Spanish nobleman. It is uncertain whether any Castilians were

163

living on the islands when the Portuguese began to show an interest in the gold of Africa, but they were often visited by ships from Castile. Since Portugal did not wish her rival to have a foothold so close to the Land of Gold, she sent out at least two expeditions to occupy the islands, but both of them failed—officially because of the resistance of the inhabitants and the lack of provisions.

It was only natural that Henry the Navigator should also be interested in these undertakings. Each year he dispatched new expeditions along the coast to the Land of Gold, but met with little or no success until 1432, when the Azores were discovered. It is probable that Portuguese activities at sea were not yet very extensive, and that the Prince was more occupied with preparing himself and his men for their task. He had become Grand Master of the Order of Christ, and could thus get his hands on money for his costly expeditions. We read that it was now that he built an observatory and founded a nautical academy at Sagres, built a shipyard and designed his seaworthy caravels in the neighbouring port of Lagos, and that he gathered around him all the foremost astronomers and geographers in Christendom.

His work is none the less important even when we discover that the nautical academy was only a training school for pilots, that there were caravels before his time, and that we can only find the name of one geographer and cartographer who worked for the Prince at Sagres. This was Jafuda Cresques, son of the great Abraham Cresques, the Jew who had drawn the "Catalan Atlas". We must understand that Jafuda trained Portuguese pilots and cartographers, made astrolabes, quadrants and compasses, and, together with the astronomers who were found at every court in those days, taught the mariners how they should measure the angle between the Pole Star and the horizon in order to find their latitude. Prince Henry was given some Venetian and Danish maps by his brother, Prince Pedro the Voyager, and it is said that he also obtained a copy of Marco Polo's book.

His acquaintance with the geographers and their maps

The caravel, which played such an important part during the great age of discovery, was probably a development of a Portuguese fishing vessel. It was lighter and faster than the round-bellied merchant ships; originally rigged with lateen sails and not drawing much water, it was especially manageable in changing winds and shallow waters. The caravel shown here has the cross of the Order of Christ painted on its sails.

Becalmed caravels off the island of São Miguel.

broadened his mind and his plans, and we are able to surmise the extent of them in Diogo Gomes' description of the discovery of the Azores: "As Prince Henry wanted to learn more about the remoter parts of the Western Ocean in order to see whether there were *islands or a mainland* outside Ptolemy's world, he sent out caravels at a certain time to look for land. They sailed away and found land three hundred hours out from Finisterre. When the crew realized that this consisted of islands, they went ashore on the first and found it uninhabited. They searched it and found many hawks and other birds. Then they visited the second, which is now called São Miguel, and found that this too was uninhabited and full of birds and hawks. There they also found many natural hot sulphur springs. From this island they saw another, which is now called Terceira [i.e. 'The Third']. This too, like São Miguel, had many trees, birds and hawks. There they saw yet another island, which is now called Fayal, and two hours further on a fifth, which is now known as Pico. On this island is a mountain which it takes seven hours to climb. The inhabitants often light their lamps, thinking it is night, while the sun can still be seen from the top of this mountain. Then the vessels returned to Portugal and their master was informed of the news. This made him very happy."

This probably occurred in 1432, and according to an almost illegible note on a portolano of 1439 the discoverer was "Diego of Seville [Sunis? Funes? Guullen?], Pilot to the King of Portugal". Prince Henry sent a new expedition to the islands under the command of the same Gonzalo Velho who had led the first expedition along the west coast of Africa. They took domestic animals—pigs, cattle and poultry—to the islands, and in 1439 both people and "horses from Germany" were sent there, and Diogo Gomes reports that wheat and other agricultural products would soon be sent from São Miguel to the home country.

It is often suggested that the Italians discovered the Azores as early as the middle of the 14th century, and maps with many islands drawn in roughly the position of the Azores are shown as evidence of this. But these maps also have many other islands which no one has yet been able to discover. It was common practice both then and later for cartographers to copy slavishly what others had earlier drawn by chance or in speculation, and, as other seafarers were later to look for Antilia and St. Brendan's Isle and the mysterious island of Brazil, so too Henry the Navigator looked for the small islands he saw drawn on the maps—and, in fact, he found some of them. Before his time the islands are not mentioned in any documents, and we have no reliable evidence whatsoever that the Azores were known earlier in the Middle Ages.

It is not out of the question, on the other hand, that the Carthaginians had known of them in the classical era. On Corvo, the westernmost of the islands, which, together with Flores, was first discovered in 1475, a jar was uncovered in the 18th century. This contained a number of coins, the latest of which were from the period 330—320 B.C. It is possible that a Carthaginian ship had been carried out to the islands by a storm, but even if it did manage to return to Carthage it is hardly likely that the visit was repeated, since there was no one to trade with there. The Azores—the word means "Hawk Islands"—were uninhabited when the Portuguese arrived, and no traces of any earlier inhabitants have been found.

165

Cape Bojador, the low sandspit which Henry the Navigator's captains long regarded as the southern limit of the habitable world: beyond this point it was feared that there was nothing but burnt lands and boiling seas.

From Cape Bojador to Cape Verde

It is difficult today to understand how mariners who had sailed from Portugal to Flanders, the Azores and Madeira could be seized by fear and panic as soon as they approached the waters off the coast of West Africa. It is true that they had ventured round Cape Nun, but when there appeared to be nothing dangerous there they immediately persuaded themselves that imagined dangers were now lying in wait for them round Cape Bojador. They swore that all the horrors of the deep lay beyond that cape, and those who had been far enough told of a powerful southerly current which made it impossible to return. But what the mariners took to be the violent eddying of currents was nothing but surf above a reef off the cape; the tidal current there, which alternates between north and south, moves at a speed of half a knot at the most.

The chroniclers write that Henry the Navigator sent out ships to round Cape Bojador for twelve years without any success, and that the men spoke in this fashion: "Why should we be forced to pass the boundaries drawn up by our forefathers? What can the Prince gain from the loss of our bodies and souls?" In 1433 Prince Henry equipped a ship, appointed his own shield-bearer, Gil Eannes, to be captain, and ordered him to round the cape. But he was seized by the same fear as the others and got no further than the Canaries, where he took some prisoners, and then returned to Sagres.

The following year, the Prince re-equipped the same vessel and spoke severly to Gil Eannes. From what may be deduced from the scanty references to this, it seems that the shield-bearer feared the Prince more than the cape after this conversation. And he did in fact round it without meeting anything terrifying and without being impeded by any currents on the return journey. He did not venture far beyond the cape—only far enough to be able to say that he had rounded it—but he was nevertheless welcomed as a hero at Sagres and in time was finally knighted. The following year he tried again with orders to push further south this time. He sailed a mere fifty miles south of Cape Bojador, and when landing there found tracks of horses and camels, but none of people.

In 1436 Alfonso Baldaya sailed a little further south, coming to an inlet which he took to be the mouth of a river. In his joy he believed he had reached the long coveted River of Gold, the Rio d'Ouro—the modern Rio de Oro. But he also found people. The chronicler Azurara writes: "There he sent ashore two horses and two young noblemen, neither of whom was over seventeen, to look for a [native] habitation. When they had gone seven miles inland, they met nineteen men, who were armed with spears. These wounded one of the youths in the foot and then fled to some rocks. The youths returned to the ship in the evening. The one was called Eytor Homen, the other Diego Lopez Dalmeyda. The ship was loaded with seals [i.e. skins and blubber] which they found there on an island in the river. From there they sailed a further fifty miles to the port of Galee."

Castile did not take kindly to the Portuguese advances and activities in Africa. She considered herself to have at least as much right to the land of Africa and tried to persuade the Pope to recognize the Moorish zone of Tangier as Castilian territory. In order to forestall this, King Duarte—or Edward—, who had succeeded his father on the throne of Portugal in 1433, decided to conquer

A map of the West African coastal strip explored by the Portuguese, 1416—1446. The broken red lines are Moorish caravan routes.

Tangier. His brother Pedro and a large section of the nobility protested, saying that Portugal had not got the resources for such an undertaking, but Prince Henry supported him, and it was he who later led the expedition. The unwillingness and low morale of the army can be deduced from the fact that a third of them deserted even before reaching Ceuta. Needless to say, the expedition was a total failure. The attacking Portuguese were themselves surrounded and threatened with annihilation, and the only way Prince Henry could buy himself and his army free was to promise to restore Ceuta and guarantee a ten-year peace. As security for the keeping of the agreement, the Moors detained the Prince's youngest brother Fernando. But Ceuta was never returned, and Prince Fernando was sacrificed. He died after eleven years in Moorish captivity.

King Edward died of the plague in 1438, and dissension arose between the Queen and Prince Pedro as to who should be regent during the minority of the heir apparent, Prince Alfonso. Prince Pedro won in the end, and when things had more or less settled down in the kingdom, Henry the Navigator was gradually enabled to continue the activities which lay closest his heart. But Portugal was still impoverished and disunited, and he was much criticized for wasting money on expeditions that led to nothing.

In the spring of 1441 he dispatched two caravels. First his young chamberlain Antão Gonçalves sailed with orders to catch seals at Rio d'Ouro, but since he "sought honour more than profit", as it says in the records, mere seal-hunting did not satisfy him: he pushed inland and managed to capture a man, and later a woman. When he returned to his ship with his men and the captives, he saw to his joy that another Portuguese ship was lying at anchor in the inlet. This was the Prince's second expedition, which was led by the knight Nuño Tristão. A Moorish interpreter with him tried to interrogate the two captives, but he could not understand their language.

167

Later, the two captains set out one night with twenty men on a slave-hunt. They managed to creep up on a camp and stormed it with cries of "Portugal" and "São Tiago". They killed three natives and took ten prisoners, including a chieftain named Adahu. When the glorious battle was over and done with, Nuño Tristão knighted young Gonçalves. When the prizes had been divided, Gonçalves sailed home, while Tristão moved on south, reaching a point of white sand which he called Cape Blanco.

Now that there was evidence that people really did live in these parts, Henry the Navigator succeeded in persuading the Pope to sanction these expeditions as crusades and promise the forgiveness of sins to all who took part in them. From his brother, Prince Pedro, he also obtained the sole rights of trade and seafaring along the west coast of Africa in the name of the infant King. Chief Adahu wanted to buy himself and two of the other captives free, promising to pay with ten other slaves, so Prince Henry, considering it a better bargain to save ten souls than two, sent Gonçalves back to Rio d'Ouro the following spring to effect the exchange. Adahu escaped without fulfilling his part of the agreement, but the two others bought their freedom with ten black slaves, and Gonçalves for his part managed to obtain a little gold-dust, an oxhide shield and several ostrich eggs, returning in triumph with all these things to Sagres. The chronicler assures us that the Prince thought the ostrich eggs tasted exactly like fresh hen's eggs, and goes on to say: "It is very likely that no other Christian prince has ever seen such a dish on his table. Yet the Prince must have been even more pleased to hear that there were merchants on this coast who sold gold, the same gold that was transported by the caravans of camels which he had heard of in Ceuta."

When Nuño Tristão the following summer sailed past Cape Blanco to Arguin Bay, he and his men saw something close to the shore which they first thought was a flock of giant birds, but which later turned out to be twenty-five canoes of natives. The whites immediately began to chase them, managing to capture fifteen natives before their boat was full. On one of the islands in the bay they took another fifteen, and on another island they made a successful capture of nesting herons.

A good price was paid for the slaves, and it was found that the expeditions were beginning to make a profit. Furthermore, since one of the islands in Arguin Bay had good deposits of salt and had long been an objective for merchants from Timbuktu and other cities inland, this region gradually became a source of much gain for Portugal. Prince Henry made over the salt island to a Portuguese trading company, and in 1448 a fortress was built there to protect the colony. Thanks to the Papal Bull, which gave the expeditions the semblance of crusades, it was doubly advantageous to sail to Prince Henry's

new land, and in the summer of 1444 a fleet of five caravels under the command of Lançarote sailed in the name of the Cross to Arguin Bay, captured a considerable number of natives, and returned to Lagos. A few of the strongest slaves were given to the Church, one youth was sent to a monastery to be brought up as a Franciscan, and the rest were sold.

The chronicler Azurara exclaims: "At last, it pleased God, Who rewards all good deeds, to give them a day of victory for the great hardships they had suffered in His service, to give them honour for adversities and recompense for their losses, for in all they took 165 men, women and children." And he goes on to relate about the day the slaves were led ashore at Lagos: "On the following day, the eighth in the month af August, the crews put the boats in order at an early hour because of the heat and led the captives ashore. It was truly a wonderful sight to see them all standing there, for some were fairly white and well-formed, some were as yellow as mulattos, and some were as black as Ethiopians and so revoltingly ugly and misshapen that one regarded them as creatures from a lower world. But who would have been so hard of heart as not to feel pity for them in their distress! Some lowered their tear-splashed faces, others bewailed themselves loudly and turned their eyes to the heavens, and still others struck themselves in the face and threw themselves to the ground. There were those who sang lamentations, and although we did not understand the words, the melodies told of their great sorrow... The Prince also came. He was mounted on a magnificent war-horse and was accompanied by a great following. Forty-six slaves were allotted him, but it was his wish to save their souls and not to profit by them. Nor was he disappointed. No sooner did the natives understand our language than they voluntarily adopted Christianity. And I who have written this narrative have seen in the city of Lagos the children and grandchildren of the first captives grow up to be such good honest Christians that it might well be thought that they were directly descended from those who were first baptized in the days of Christ."

Like other princes in southern Europe, Henry the Navigator was convinced that Prester John was to be found somewhere in the depths of Africa, on the side which was called India, and he had long cherished the hope that he would be able to reach the river which was indicated on many maps, and which might perhaps be a western arm of the Nile. Along this it might be possible to make contact with the priest-king and persuade him to attack the Moors in the rear. Rio d'Ouro had been a disappointment, but in the summer of 1445 Lançarote found a real river in the land of the Azenegs. The river was named the Çanaga (Senegal), and it was hoped that this was the western arm of the Nile, or at any rate the true River of Gold. Nuño Tristão also set off that same

169

summer, sailing further to the south and suddenly coming on a Green Country—a paradise of palms and green trees after the wastes of the desert coastline. A strong wind prevented him from going ashore, but he saw dark-skinned people on the beach who appeared to be waving in a friendly manner, and he immediately set sail for home to tell of the good news.

Ten ships were sent out in the summer of 1446, partly to sail up the river and partly to explore the Green Country, but there appears to have been only one positive result. Diniz Fernandez, a citizen of Lisbon who did not belong to Henry the Navigator's circle of captains, obtained the Prince's permission to sail to the newly discovered country. Outside the mouth of the River Senegal he saw

Nuño Tristão's caravels off the coast north of Cape Verde.

some negroes fishing from canoes, four of whom he captured, but since he had sailed "for glory rather than profit", he did not stay to hunt for more slaves, but pushed on and reached the Green Country and a tall wooded promontory, on the other side of which the coastline turned towards the south-east. He went ashore and erected a cross on one of the two hills there, and he called the place Cape Verde, which means the Green Cape.

South of Cape Verde the Portuguese often met
strong and systematic resistance: their heavy casual-
ties at the Battle of the Rio Grande may have been
caused by their unwillingness to wear adequate
armour in the extreme heat.

Juan Fernandez Enters Africa

It seems at this stage as if Henry the Navigator was less
interested in moving further south than in pushing deeper
into Africa along the rivers in the hope of making contact
with Prester John and perhaps the Land of Gold. The
year after the discovery of Cape Verde, the indefatigable
Nuño Tristão had sailed far to the south-west, probably
all the way to Cape Verga, discovering a river which he
named the Rio Grande, today known as the Geba. He
rowed up the river in the ship's boat with twenty-two
men and came to a village, but there they were attacked
by natives who shot at them with poisoned arrows. Pursued by the natives, they rowed back to the ship, but
all but two had by this time been wounded, and a further
two were hit on board the vessel when unfurling the sail
for flight. The wounded died in agony, and not a single
officer survived, but the five who survived out of the
whole crew managed to sail the ship back to Portugal
after many hardships.

A nobleman called Juan Fernandez had learned the
language of the Azenegs from a slave in Portugal, and in
order to learn something of the country inland, where
according to all rumours there was much gold, he was
left at his own wish with some Azenegs on the shores
of Rio d'Ouro. It was Gonçalves who had taken him
there, and in the early spring of 1447 he reminded Henry
the Navigator of this in a letter: "Your Highness knows
that your caballero Juan Fernandez is in Rio d'Ouro with
the object of finding out all that he can about this country,
things both great and small, so that you may have knowledge of it, which he knew to be your wish. You also
know that he has served you there for many months. If
Your Grace is now willing to send me to fetch him, then
I will be most ready to carry out this task in your service
and return with the caballero. The outlay for this voyage
can certainly be covered."

Gonçalves was of course given permission by the
Prince. He sailed with three caravels to Arguin Bay and
went slave-hunting to cover the costs of the voyage. And
he did find Juan Fernandez, who was so sunburned that
they first mistook him to be a native. But Fernandez had
not discovered any Land of Gold, and the narrative of
his journey, which is to be found in Azurara, among
others, speaks mostly of hardship and shortages: "When,
seven months earlier, he was left with kinsmen of a native
who had been removed to Portugal as a hostage, these
kinsmen immediately removed his clothes, gave him a
mantle in their stead, and took him with them to their
country, a land partly flat and partly undulating which

consisted entirely of pure sand with the exception of a few oases where they grazed their sheep. The only trees to be found there are palms, and the only water is in wells.

"As Fernandez wandered from place to place with those nomads he learned much about the inner regions of West Africa. The people there consist of Arabs, Azenegs and Berbers, who live in tents and are supported by what their flocks produce. They obtain bread and other goods from the Moors, supplying them in return with black slaves. They often move camp, never staying for more than eight days in one place. Their primary form of nourishment is milk, with which they also feed their horses and hounds. Nevertheless they do eat solid food now and again, supplementing it with roots and the seeds of herbs. Wheat they consider a delicacy, in the same manner as sweets are to us Portuguese. And those who live on the coast eat nothing but fish, both raw and dried.

"The men wear vests and trousers of skins. The more important among them wear a burnous, and they also have good mounts and complete saddle accoutrements. Women and girls hide their faces behind veils, but apart from this run about quite naked, which is evidence of their animal nature. If they had a little intelligence they would surely follow the laws of nature? It is seldom one sees jewellery. Only the wives of the rich wear rings of gold in their ears and noses. As there are no roads there, the herdsmen whom Fernandez accompanied followed the stars and the flight of birds. In accordance with his wishes, they took him to Sheik Ahude Meymom, but since they did not have sufficient water and the heat of the sun was merciless, they suffered greatly on the way. Fernandez was hospitably received by Sheik Ahude, who ruled over about one hundred and fifty men. Yet during the whole of his stay there he was given nothing to drink but milk, which clearly did him no harm, for he was well-nourished when the caravels found him.

"Since it is very difficult to walk in the deep sand, the wealthy nomads always travel on horseback. Those who have no horse use a camel, and among these there are several white animals which can run 50 leagues a day [i.e. about 180 miles!]. It is a common thing for them to have black slaves. Men of rank also have considerable quantities of gold, which comes from the Guinea Coast . . . Fernandez often saw great flocks of ostriches and gazelles, and he observed that the swallows which migrate from Portugal spend the winter in the sands of this region, while storks fly still further south."

Juan Fernandez had not had his fill of hardship, heat and sand. In 1448 he left with Diego Gilhomen, who under Prince Henry's orders was to negotiate with the Moors around Cape Nun, and once again he allowed himself to be persuaded to seek more information. But from that expedition he never returned, and no one knows what happened to him.

A Dane in Africa

A friendly relationship and a certain amount of co-operation existed between Portugal and Denmark during the 15th century, and we hear of Danish knights who fought side by side with the Portuguese against the Moors in Africa. A Danish nobleman, referred to as Vallarte in the Portuguese annals—perhaps his real name was Vollert—, commanded an expedition to the country around Cape Verde in 1448, and although the voyage did not result in anything positive, it is described in such detail by Azurara that I should like to quote him. The year before, four ships had sailed to the same region, only one of them returning with any prizes—forty-one slaves and a live lion—while the three others returned with empty holds after having suffered losses in battles with the warlike natives. For some reason or other Henry the Navigator believed that the king of this country was a Christian, and since he presumably hoped that he might be one of Prester John's many vassal kings, he was eager to make contact with him.

Azurara writes: "When the report of these activities spread to the various parts of the world, it also reached the court of the King of Denmark, Norway and Sweden [Christopher of Bavaria]. We have seen that noblemen, driven by desires to experience and take part in such activities, have hazarded their lives. Thus it happened that in this case a nobleman at the court of this King, who wanted to see the world, was given his master's permission and so came to our kingdom. When he had spent a considerable time at the Prince's court, he one day approached him and begged him the favour that a caravel might be equipped for him so that he could sail in it to the land of the blacks. The Prince, who was easily moved to help a brave man to win honour and respect, gave orders that a caravel should be carefully equipped. He then gave him the task of sailing to Cape Verde and of obtaining reliable information about the ruler of the country, for he had been told that this man was a mighty prince. He was to take a letter to him from the Prince, and in the Prince's name inform him of all kind of Church matters and of the True Faith, for the Prince had been told that this ruler was a Christian. He was convinced that all who truly confessed to the teachings of Christ would be only too glad to lend support in the fight against the Moors in Africa . . .

"All was soon in readiness. The aforementioned nobleman, whose name was Vallarte, went aboard the ship, and with him there was a Knight of the Order of Christ, Fernandaffonso by name, who was a servant and friend of the Prince. This knight accompanied the vessel since Vallarte was a foreigner and as such not sufficiently conversant with the customs and habits of the crew . . .

At anchor in a Cape Verde inlet.

"When they reached the outermost point of the cape, a place which the inhabitants of the country call Abram, a boat was lowered and rowed ashore. Vallarte landed with several others, and they soon met with a few of the natives of the country. Vallarte then commanded them to hand over one of their company as a hostage, saying that he in his turn would do likewise with one of his men, so that in this way they would be able to negotiate peacefully and safely. They replied that they could not do this without the permission of him who acted as governor of the country there. His name was Guitanye. When he heard what was wanted, he came to them in person and readily agreed to the proposal.

"When one of the natives was now taken on board the caravel, Fernandaffonso, since he had better command of Portuguese [the interpreter naturally knew only Portuguese and the native's language], immediately began to interrogate him in the following manner: 'The reason why we have demanded that you should come aboard the ship is that you are to inform your master that we have told you that we are subjects of the great and mighty Prince of Western Hispania, and that we have come here at his command in order to negotiate in his name with the great and good king of this country.' Then they showed him some of the letters they had brought with them. These were read to him through one of the interpreters so that he could inform his master, who had sent him, of their contents. He replied: 'However much you may wish to speak with our great King Boor [*boor* or *bor* = king], you cannot at present obtain any message from him, for he is sure to be far away fighting another great chieftain, who would not obey him.' Fernandaffonso then said:

Cape Verde is of volcanic origin, and the adjacent beaches consist mainly of black rocks and sand.

'How many days would it take to send a messenger to him from us and to return with his answer, were he now at his residence?' 'Six or seven days at the most,' the man from Guinea believed. 'Good,' answered Fernandaffonso. 'It would then be best for you that you tell your master that he is to send a man with a message to him, informing him of everything that we have just told you. If your master does this, he will be doing the king a great service and his country a good deed.' 'Good,' replied the man from Guinea. 'I shall tell Guitanye of all these things myself.' A meal was laid before him, and he ate and drank. Then they gave him one of the letters they had brought with them so that he could show it to his master. He was to tell him that the letter contained all that they had said to him and that it had been given to him as a token of friendship . . .

"Vallarte was a man of little prudence, and one day he wished to go ashore. It might well be thought that he would have known what had happened before. It is certain that he was warned, but he longed to go ashore, as if Fate had decreed that he himself should decide the hour of his undoing. As he drew close to the beach, a native appeared carrying a gourd of water or wine, and indicated that he wanted to give this to him. Vallarte then ordered the men to row closer, although they told him it was not wise to go too near. But to their sorrow they had to obey his order. While Vallarte was watching a group of natives who were standing in the shade of a tree, Affonso, one

of the interpreters with them, made as if he wanted to fetch the gourd, suddenly jumping out of the boat. The others saw this and now wanted to push the boat away from the shore, but just at that moment a large wave came in and capsized the boat. The natives rushed in to the attack immediately, throwing their spears so that of the entire crew that rowed to the shore only one man returned. He threw himself into the water and swam away.

"As to what happened to the others we do not know. The man who had saved himself by swimming told us that he had seen only one dead, and on looking back three or four times had seen Vallarte sitting in the stern of the boat. But while we write this narrative, several captives from the same stretch of coastline have fallen into the Prince's hands, and they have related that four Christians had lived in a guarded region in the depths of the country, and that one of them had died. The three others were still alive, however, and there are some who believe that, to judge by native reports, these must be the lost men.

"Because of this sad occurrence, and since there was no other boat with which to row to the shore to look for the others, Fernandaffonso weighed anchor and returned to Portugal."

Usodimare and Cadamosto

Vallarte's ill-starred journey brings Azurara's chronicle to an end. He sums up by saying that a total of forty-one caravels had sailed beyond Cape Bojador during the four-teen years which had passed since Gil Eannes had rounded it. He adds that 927 slaves had been taken and that of these "the majority had been directed along the true path of salvation".

There now followed an interval of seven years, during which no official voyages were made to Guinea. This was partly because Prince Henry, who was undoubtedly no thrifty man, was deeply in debt, and partly also because Portugal was once more engaged in political struggle with Castile, ending in open war. In 1449, in order to acquire some of the African trade, the King of Castile gave the stretch of coast between Cape Ghir and Cape Bojador to the Duke of Medina-Sidonia, and Prince Henry, whose King had given him the monopoly of all voyages beyond Cape Bojador in 1443, now received in addition the sole right to coastal trade between Cape Cantin and Cape Bojador. The situation became even more complicated when Portugal repeated her claims on the Canaries and sent out forces to conquer them. This led to open warfare, which lasted from 1451 to 1454.

But in 1453 all Christendom was shaken by the news of the fall of Constantinople, and the contending parties on the Iberian Peninsula begged the Pope to mediate. In 1455 Nicholas V issued a Papal Bull, decreeing that the Canaries were to belong to Castile for all time, whereas all land in Africa, both discovered and undiscovered, was to belong to Portugal. Part of the bull runs as follows: "Since it became known to the Prince that within the memory of man no seafaring had been customary on the waters of this ocean towards the southerly and easterly coasts, and since we Westerners were so ignorant that we had no certain knowledge of the peoples in that

175

part of the world, he thought that he would prove his devotion to God by making the sea navigable, by his industry and courage, even unto the Indians, of whom it is said that they profess the name of Christ, in order to make firm ties with them and to win them as allies for the Christians in their struggle against Saracens and other enemies of the Faith."

Some people have tried to take this as meaning that

Usodimare and Antonio de Noli, both from Genoa, and Aloisio Ca' da Mosto, a Venetian. Usodimare had run away from his creditors in Genoa. Prince Henry put him in command of a caravel. He sailed south, met Ca' da Mosto before reaching Cape Verde and then accompanied him to the River Gambia. He achieved nothing remarkable in the way of exploration, but he did write a morbidly humorous letter to his creditors in Genoa, explaining that

Two low green hills, extinct volcanoes, by which Cape Verde can be identified from the sea.

the object of Henry the Navigator's expeditions was to find a way to India—the real India—by circumnavigating Africa. But from what we know of his life, there is not a single statement, or any other piece of reliable evidence, which might indicate that he ever held any such plans. His main interest was in Africa's gold, and many authorities bear this out. Then there is more evidence that he wanted to make contact with Prester John in the part of Africa which contemporary Europe generally knew as India. This was doubly important now that Constantinople was in the hands of the Turks.

Prince Henry resumed his explorations in Africa as soon as the Pope had effected the mediation, and it is now that we hear of three Italians in his service: Antoniotto

although they could not expect any money from him, the least he felt he could do was to tell them something of his experiences. It is written in a woeful Latin which is at times very difficult to understand; nevertheless I should like to quote a rather remarkable part of it. He describes his stay in Africa, and then goes on thus: "But be assured that it is really less than 300 leagues to Prester John's land—not to his residence but to the boundaries of his kingdom. Had it been possible, I should also have met the King of Melli's Minister, who spent six days in our part of the country with 100 men, and together with him some Christian subjects of Presbyter John V, and I have spoken with men in his army. — Here I came across a fellow-countryman. I believe him to be a descendant of one of the crew of the Vivaldo galleys which left the country 170 years ago. This he told me in person, and except for him not one of their descendants has survived,

questions about things which were entirely unknown to the natives, and in this way obtained extempore "confirmation" of almost anything. Presbyter John V may not have been entirely a figment of Usodimare's imagination; the general European estimate may well have been that by this time the successors of Prester John I should have brought the number up to five. That Usodimare's "fellow-countryman" was a descendant of the Vivaldo

Cadamosto of Venice and Usodimare of Genoa sailed up the River Gambia together.

a fact which the Secretary also confirmed. Another man told me of elephants, unicorns [rhinoceroses], civet-cats and other rarities, likewise also of people with tails who eat their own offspring, a thing which may seem incredible to you. May you know that if I had gone on for one day more, I should have lost sight of the Pole Star."

This was neither the first nor the last time that language difficulties had led to curious misunderstandings. Through the mouths of ignorant interpreters, the Christians asked

travellers was very likely mere wishful thinking—some light-skinned man had probably been ready enough to answer "yes" to all questions,—unless, of course, Usodimare cheerfully made up the whole story to entertain his disappointed creditors at home.

Aloisio Ca' da Mosto, or Cadamosto as he is usually called, wrote a description of his travels which begins as follows: "In the year 1454, when I, Aloisio, was in Venice, the city of my birth, I was 21 years old. Having already travelled round all the coasts of the sea which is called the Mediterranean, we decided to journey to Celtic Gaul [Flanders], which I had formerly visited for purposes of trade."

Cadamosto sailed from Venice and out into the Atlan-

177

tic. There he was driven by storms to Lagos, where he came in contact with Henry the Navigator's men. These tried to interest him in a voyage to Africa, and when he asked on what conditions a foreigner could trade in Guinea, the Prince's secretary replied: "If a caravel is equipped and loaded at one's own expense, a fourth part of all profits is to be paid to the Prince on one's return. If the Prince pays for the ship and the mariner for the cargo, the profits are divided. Should the expedition bring no rewards, then the Prince defrays all costs." And Cadamosto was told that they would be glad to see him make the voyage, since they hoped to find spices in Africa, and felt that as a Venetian he would understand such things better than the Portuguese.

The result was that the Prince equipped the caravel and Cadamosto supplied the necessary cargo of goods for bartering. It was usual that ships destined for Guinea first put in at Porto Santo to take on provisions, and

Cadamosto did the same. From there he went on to the Canaries, and he relates that four of those islands were inhabited by Christians, but that Grand Canary, Tenerife and La Palma were still held by the Guanches. He also mentions litmus, the dyestuff which was exported to Cadiz and thence to eastern and western markets. From the Canaries he sailed to Cape Blanco and Senegal, where he did some peaceful trading, and was told that people living further south on a river called the Gambia could pay with much gold. North of Cape Verde he caught sight of two caravels, one commanded by a Portuguese and the other by Usodimare, and the three vessels sailed on together round the Green Cape to the great River Gambia.

They sent an interpreter ashore to make preliminary contact with the natives, but he was killed immediately. Nevertheless, they ventured up the river, sailing with the smallest caravel in the lead and armed men in the boats. Cadamosto told them to avoid all fighting as far as possible, since they were only there to trade. Four miles up river they were met by a group of fifteen canoes. Cadamosto writes: "Sitting in each of them were eight to ten warriors, imposing figures in white cotton robes and white head-dresses which were decorated with a wing on each side and a feather in the middle. The man farthest forward in the bow carried a shield, probably of leather. They all lifted their paddles up in the air and stared at us in silence, as if we were ghosts. Suddenly, without any provocation from us, they laid down their paddles, took up their bows and shot a cluster of arrows at us. We immediately replied with gunfire. This helped, for the natives dropped their bows in amazement and stared in terror at the stone balls which sent up cascades of water. But no sooner had the noise stopped than their courage returned. They came boldly towards the ships and shot at us once again. Then our crossbowmen came into action. They took careful aim, and the first bolt shot hit a native in the chest. When their losses increased, the canoes attacked the smallest and most weakly manned caravel. To protect this outnumbered vessel, the two larger ships drew up on either side of it, but a salvo from our bombards was needed to persuade the canoes to retire. When all was over, we chained the three vessels together and anchored with a single anchor."

The captains now wanted to push even farther up river in the hope of making contact with less warlike natives, but the crews thought that they had had enough adventures, and so the three ships returned to Portugal.

The following year Cadamosto and Usodimare each equipped a caravel for a new voyage to the same waters, and Prince Henry sent a third caravel along with them. Off Cape Blanco they were struck by a violent storm. This drove them south-west for three days and two nights, and on the third day to their surprise they sighted land.

Cadamosto writes: "We put out a boat and sent two men to explore the land. This they did and could report that they had seen two large islands. On hearing this we gave thanks to God, Who in His infinite mercy had chosen to reveal to us unknown new lands, never yet seen by any man in all Hispania. In order to explore the lands which God had shown to us, we now felt curious to try our luck, and so we steered towards the aforesaid islands. It was not long before we reached them, and seeing them at closer range, we noticed that they were very large. We sailed on until we had found suitable anchorage, but before anchoring we dispatched a well-armed boat to find out whether the island was inhabited. Our men went ashore and saw neither men nor any sign of them . . .

"When this was ascertained, our curiosity increased, and on the following morning I let ten of my men arm themselves with spears and slings, that they might

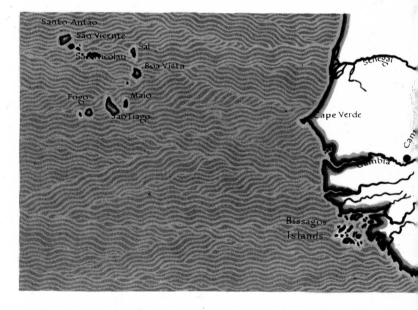

Between 1456 and 1458, Aloisio Cadamosto and Antonio de Noli discovered the five Cape Verde Islands now known as Sal, Boa Vista, Mayo, São Tiago and Fogo. Cadamosto saw other islands further west but did not explore them; Noli was the first governor of the Cape Verde Islands, and he was probably the first to explore the whole group.

179

Cadamosto was an experienced mariner and navigator, but the report of his observations at the Gambia shows that he did not use either an astrolabe or a quadrant. We must therefore presume that only a few specially trained mariners could use those new instruments.

Cadamosto writes: "During our stay at the mouth of the river, we only saw the Pole Star once; and then it sank so low that it seemed to touch the sea, apparently standing only one third of a spear-shaft above the water.

There we also saw six large and wonderfully bright stars. We measured them [i.e. their direction] with the compass. We believed them to be the Great Bear of the Southern Hemisphere. It is not contrary to reason that we saw this constellation before we lost the Pole Star; that is, before it disappeared from our sight. At the beginning of July, when it is extremely hot in those parts, we measured the length of the day to be 13 hours and the length of the night to be 11."

There can be no doubt that Cadamosto had seen the four stars of the Southern Cross (see p. 139) together with the two stars known today as Alpha and Beta Centauri. Like others before and after him, he thought that there was a southern Pole Star to guide mariners in the Southern Hemisphere. Time on board was usually measured by a half-hour-glass. The youngest man on each watch had to keep an eye on the glass, turn it at the right moment, and call out the half hours.

Of the negroes at the Gambia, Cadamosto writes: "The men often go out hunting. Armed with assegais and poisoned arrows, they crouch in the trees and wait for their quarry. When they have made a hit, they jump from branch to branch in pursuit of the fleeing animal. In this manner they even kill elephants, of which there are many." — To the right Cadamosto's "horse-fish".

penetrate to the inner parts of the island to see whether there might be men behind the hills that rose there. They set off and went over the hills, but all they found were pigeons and birds of almost every kind. The pigeons allowed themselves to be taken by hand without difficulty. Nor did they fear the sight of men, which was something hitherto unknown to them. And so our men caught as many as possible, killed them with sticks and brought them back to us.

"In another direction they had sighted a further three large islands which we had not seen, for they lay to the north of us. Also to the west they saw two other islands out in the open sea. These they could hardly see because they were so far away, and we could not see them at all. But it was very important that we should complete the voyage which we had begun, and which had been our original purpose. As there was not much time left, we were afraid of wasting it on uninhabited islands.

"While I was exploring these four islands, the others found ten smaller ones. When they went to them they found nothing but birds and giant fish. Wishing to return to the place from which we had been driven off course, I put out to sea from the islands, and lo, there were another two! I explored the coast of one of them and found the mouth of a river. We went ashore, thinking that we might find drinking-water there. The most beautiful trees of all kinds were growing on it. While looking for a spring, we found small white lumps of salt beside the river. We collected as much of the salt as might be useful for the rest of our voyage . . . I may add that the first island we saw we called Boa Vista . . . But another of the four islands was named after St. James, for we first saw it on the day of St. Philip and St. James."

Cadamosto and his followers had discovered the Cape Verde Islands. It is believed that he, or one of the transcribers of his manuscript, made a slip when writing that he found them on the day of St. Philip and St. James; instead he should have written on the day of St. James and St. Christopher. If so, the discovery was made on 25th July 1456.

The three caravels then sailed east from the islands, and made their first landfall between Senegal and Cape Verde; then they went on as planned to Gambia. On this occasion they sailed up the river without meeting with any resistance, and they were soon able to begin trading with the natives. They did not obtain as much gold as their Senegalese informants had led them to expect: the eager natives who swarmed over the caravels

paid them chiefly with cotton cloth, civet-cats, baboons, marmots and a great deal of fruit, mostly dates. About the novelties they saw, Cadamosto says, among other things: "Everywhere there are great trees which, although very thick, are not correspondingly high. For example, I saw a hollow trunk with shady foliage, and its circumference at ground level was seventeen arm's-lengths [the baobab tree]. Apart from elephants, we discovered an even stranger animal in Gambia, which the natives call a horse-fish [hippopotamus]. It is more than ten feet long and has very short legs with cloven hooves. In its head, which is like that of the horse, it has like the wild boar two tusks, which are each almost as long as a fore-arm. This horse-fish rises out of the water and walks about like other four-footed animals. We also saw some giant bats—the breadth between the tips of their wings was often three hands or more—together with parrots of many kinds and innumerable fishes unknown in Europe."

But the heat on the Gambia was too much for the white men, and many of them caught fever. After eleven days of trading they returned to the mouth of the river, and, as their food and water supplies were plentiful, they decided to try their luck farther south. They sailed right down to the Bissagos Islands and anchored there. Cadamosto has this to say about the violence of the tide: "Here the ebb and flow do not last six hours each as in Venice: the flow lasts four hours and the ebb eight. The flow is so strong that three anchors were hardly enough to hold each caravel."

They had no success with the inhabitants of the Bissagos Islands, however, since their interpreters could not understand their language. And as they felt that they would meet with the same difficulties further south, they decided it would be useless to continue and turned for home.

A civet-cat.

Nothing is mentioned about the running aground of ships in the short reports of the Portuguese expeditions, but we must presume that they did occur, then as now. When it was necessary to repair a bad leak, the vessel was careened, i.e. heeled over with ropes and tackle from the mastheads so that the damaged boards came above the waterline.

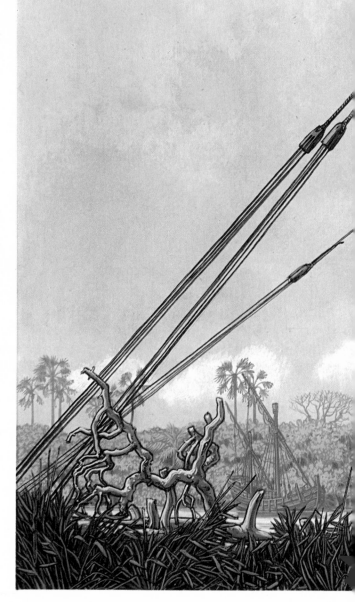

Gomes in the City of Gold

Diogo Gomes, the Prince's friend, took three caravels to the same waters in the summer of 1457. He found the same strong currents as Cadamosto had, and these frightened the crew, who refused to sail any further; but he traded with the natives and bought some cotton cloth and ivory, and it is said that he was also given a little pepper in exchange for his goods. They then sailed back to the north and turned into the River Gambia. Gomes, who was apparently less timid and more diplomatic than most, made alliances with the native chieftains and pushed far up the river in one of the caravels in order to reach the golden city of Cantor. But the river became too narrow for the vessel, and so he sent messages to the city saying that he wanted to trade.

Gomes says: "We made peace with them, and all over the country the news spread that Christians had come to Cantor. People flocked there from all directions, from Timbuktu in the north and from Serra Geley in the south, and people also came from Quioquia, a large city which is surrounded by a wall of baked bricks. I was told by these that there was an overabundance of gold in that country and that caravans with camels and dromedaries come there with goods from Carthage and Tunis, Fez and Cairo and all the Saracen lands to fetch gold; for there is a store of gold there which comes from the mines in the Gelu Mountain . . . They said that the king's name was Bormelli [= the King of Melli], that the whole negro territory on the right bank of the river was controlled by him, and that he himself lived at Quioquia. They said that he also controlled all the mines; and that outside the entrance of his house there was a block of unwrought gold, just as it had come out of the earth, so large that twenty men could hardly move it, to which the king regularly tethered his horse . . . My men were growing weak from the heat. So we turned back and searched for the other two caravels. On the vessel which we had left at Ollimansa I found that nine men had died, that Captain Gonçalalfonso was very weak, and that the others had also grown weak; only three men were still in good health. I found the other caravel fifty leagues lower down towards the ocean, and in it five men had died. We immediately set sail towards the sea."

It was probably the year after, in 1458, that Diogo Gomes, in company with Antonio de Noli of Genoa, "discovered" the Cape Verde Islands on his way back from Guinea. Cadamosto, their true discoverer, was above all a determined businessman, and though he writes that they had given thanks to God for having shown them those new islands, he maintains that, as there was nobody to trade with on the islands, it was more important to go on to Gambia as originally intended. On this occasion, Gomes and Noli wanted to get the credit for, and the profits of, the discovery. Gomes says: "After this we put

in at Palma Island in the Canaries, and then at the island of Madeira. When trying to sail from there to Portugal with an unfavourable wind, I was blown off course to the Azores. Antonio de Noli stayed at Madeira, and reached Portugal before I did. He asked the King for the governorship of the island of São Tiago, which I had discovered. This the King granted him, and he lived there for the rest of his life. I myself returned with difficulty to Portugal and Lisbon."

All the other sources say that Noli discovered the islands. João de Barros writes in the 16th century: "We have found that about that time the islands which are now called the Cape Verde Islands were discovered by a Genoese nobleman called Antonio de Nola. Because of certain dissensions in his native country he came to our kingdom with two large ships and a barinel, together with his brother, Bartholomeus de Nola, and his nephew, Raffael de Nola. The Prince gave him permission to set out on a voyage of discovery. — Sixteen days after their departure from Lisbon they reached the island of Mayo, as they named it, for they found it on that day [30th April]. On the following day, that of St. Philip and St. James, they found two islands which now bear the names of those saints."

IMPERIO
e triumpho
nobilissimo
bel chataio

chambaluch

OCEANVS ATHLANTICVS

NORVEGIA
SVETIA
FILLANDIA
Lifilant
Gothia
Bergen
Islant
Scan dinabia
Xo de Rossia
Xausta

ROSSIA over SARMATIA
Nuovograt
SINVS GERMANICVS
Rgol
Solistat Riga
Grap
D.nzech
Lobag Maxaveri
Mariaburgo
PRVSI

POLANA
Praga
Bohemia
Saxonia
Fl.Ren
Bavaria
ALEMAGNA
VNGARIA
F Danubio
Vlachia
Crovatia
SERVIA
Bologna
Cagora

Solant
Ischandia
Islandia

TIBERNIA
Scot

ANGLIA
Bersil
Pareisi

GALLIA
Bordeus
Marsel

ITALIA
Venicia
Roma
SINVS ADRIATICVS
ALBANIA GRETIA
MACEDONIA

ISPANIA
Burgos Barcilogna
Minorica
CORSICA
SARDENIA
Malorica
Lisbon
Cadis
Zibiltera
MARE GADITANVM
Barbaria
Catagna
NVMIDIA
Termesen
Fessa
Capsa

Porto santo
I.de Madeira
I.Fortunatas
Palma
Tenerif
I.Gomera
Lancelot
I.d.Preterite
Canaria
C. Bojedor
Marocco
M. Athlas

Rio d'or
Prom.
montium

MAVRITANIA
Melli

C.Verde
Regana
Fl.Mas

SINVS ETIOPICVS
Fundan
DOLCARMIN
Daan GARBI
CETOSCHAMAR
BENICHILEB

Dafur
GARBI

ETHYOPIA OCCIDENTALIS

Coroscana Curbi Calen
Tambutut
Mergi
Palude
Almaona
Mella

GARAMANTIA
Gana
ARABIA DESERTO
ORGANA

NVBA

DAXO
ALMAONA
F.Tagus

Regno de SABA
Gozan
Rg.Gogam
FONTE
Vinzu
Sadai

HAMARA
Badabedi
Digena

ABASSIA
Vuasech
F.Amara
Xixeira
Nadaber
Chrunoch
Dauaro
Facagar
Ziacia
Mason

ABASSIA
ETHYOPIA

ETHYOPIA AVSTRAL quasi salvaza
Fl.Xebt
Fl.Galla
DIAB

186

PERMIA
Rostabo
Megriphel
Mera
Cimarchia
Mostal Quier
Marobala over
Volga
Moschouia
Canbach
Noagra
Alan
Fl.Eca
Fl.Edil
ROSSIA NEGRA EVROPA
LITVANA
Lech
Cartana
ROSSIA ROSSA
Mesenexe
Raxan
Podolia
Epicuo vecchio
RVENIA
Gothia
Chumania
Fl.Coxucu
TARTARIA

PERMIA EVROPA

Cimano
Zimacis
Nagonico
Regalli
SIBIR
Batima
Alich Nef
SARMATIA IN ASIA
Fl.Boch
Castryn
Saray
Fl.Iaincho
ORGANCA
Chiava
CAGA
Amaxobii
MARE BIANCHI
SCITHIA

MARE CHASPIVM
Tana Hircania
Acetrecham
Fl.Tanay
Archo Noe
SIROAN
Mingrel
Tephilis
Siamichu
Bachu
Siguiar Nu
Thaurus
SOLTANIA
Nassabor
Sab
Spahan

PONTVS EVSINVS
Constantinopli
Pontus
Aidin M.s Thaurus
Nichia ASIA MENOR
Philadelphia
Casarie
Tarso
ARMENIA
PARTHIA
ASSIRIA
Sirax
Chasc
MEDIA

Antiochia
Alepo
Sermin
Damasco
Hierusalem
SIRIA
PALESTINA
EGYTO
Babilonia Arabia Petrea
Masuet
Chajero
Merdis M.
Caoruis M.
Fl.Canysu
Lor Chreman
Babilonia
SVXIANA
Suca
Chaheria
Fl.Tigris
Fl.Eufrattes
Mosel
MESOPOTAMIA

DESERTO
MARE RVBRVM
SINVS ARABICVS
Mecha
Thasi
ARABIA FELIX
Arabia Sabea
Aden
Misira

CIPRO
CRETA
Rodus
Lodus
MARE MEDITERRANEVM
M.LIBICVM M.EGYPTICVM
M.d Barcha
LIBIA
Marmarica
Cirenaica
TEBAIDA
ARABIA
Saito
Siene
Fl.Nilo

SINVS PERSICVS
Tarna
MARE ARABICVM
Mogicesur
Congapu
Zilla
Hatsum
Tegre
Ebebereti
ADEL
MARE PERSIC
MARE I

Mancoro

Nobilistar
GW

SICILIA
MARE AFRICVM

Fra Mauro's Map

Fra Mauro, a Camaldolese monk from Venice, was regarded as the most prominent geographer of his time—"cosmographus incomparabilis". In 1457—1459, at the wish of Alfonso V of Portugal, he drew a map of the world, together with a duplicate which has been preserved and can be seen today at the Biblioteca Nazionale Marciana in Venice. It is usually described as "the masterpiece of medieval cartography", and it is without doubt the most beautiful of all existing maps. What is shown here is a greatly simplified version—the duplicate in Venice is over six feet in diameter and drawn with the south at the top. In the spaces between rivers and placenames Fra Mauro drew cities with walls and towers—e.g. Chambalech, the capital of China, at the top left corner of the opposite page. In a footnote Fra Mauro says that he drew the cities in Asia so large because there was more room there than in Europe.

In addition to all the knowledge of the world which travellers had brought back to Venice, Fra Mauro had also received from his royal patron full information about the African countries explored by the Portuguese. He reproduces the proportions of the various parts of the world with remarkable accuracy. He did not believe that the Indian "Sea" was surrounded by land; like the Greek geographers before Ptolemy, and like the Arabs, he shows the continents as surrounded on all sides by the Ocean. We can be sure that he did not see the earth as a disc. The circular form of the map was his way of depicting a sphere.

There are many "legends" on the map, short observations and descriptions of events. One of them, near the southern extremity of Africa, says among other things this: "About the Year of Our Lord 1420, a ship, what is called an Indian junk [*zoncho de India* in the original], sailed from the Indian Sea to the Isles of the Men and the Women, past Cape Diab and between the Green Isles out into the Sea of Darkness, on the way west, in the direction of Algarve. Nothing but air and water was seen for forty days." — His "Indian" must be taken as meaning "Arab". The Arabs had regular trade connections with places far to the south in East Africa, and it is not unlikely that a vessel may have rounded the Cape of Good Hope and sailed out into the Atlantic, which the Arabs had long been calling the Sea of Darkness.

Fra Mauro, then, would not be convinced by Portuguese optimism that the southern tip of the continent had nearly been reached. He had come to an approximately correct conclusion about the size of Africa, and he portrays the sea outside the recently discovered Guinea Coast merely as a large gulf, the Sinus Ethiopicus, cutting deep into the long coastline.

187

The Death of Henry the Navigator

In order to protect Christendom in its hour of danger after the fall of Constantinople, the Pope summoned all the kings of Europe to a crusade, and sent a call for help to the priest-king in Abyssinia. But the Christian kings took no notice of his appeal. Only in Portugal was any attempt made to equip a crusading army and fleet, and even these were meant not to fight against the Turks in Constantinople, but to be used against the ever-present threat of the Moors, who were then attacking Ceuta.

At the beginning of October 1458, the crusading army and fleet lay in readiness off Sagres, waiting for Henry the Navigator, who then led the initial operations and took the town of Alcacer. But he was sixty-four years old when he took this revenge for his defeat at Tangier, and two years later he fell ill and died at Sagres.

Private Adventurers in the Fifteenth Century

It has already been pointed out, and it can hardly be sufficiently emphasized, that of all the earlier expeditions only an extremely small number were recorded in writing. Most travellers did not write any reports—many of them were illiterate—and of the reports that were written, most have disappeared: at best, we have nothing but poor copies, or summaries, of them. If an expedition was official or planned on a large scale, it might appear in the chronicles; but many men set out as commercial spies, or as private adventurers—or simply because they longed for adventure and wanted to see the wide world. And of these men we know nothing.

From Arab and Jewish merchants, Europeans had come to know of rich countries and cities far inland in Africa, and we have seen how the efforts of Henry the Navigator were directed at reaching them. In spite of control measures in North African ports, a few Europeans managed to get through; we know three of them by name, and we may presume that there were many more.

Diogo Gomes wrote of the rich city of Quioquia, and it is likely that this was the same city on the Niger which al-Idrisi had written of in the 12th century and called Gao—others call it Kaukau or Gago. Al-Idrisi said that it was the best and most populated trading city in negro country, that the inhabitants were Mohammedans, and that merchants came there from all the surrounding countries and from western Morocco. — There was a Frenchman who lived in Gao for many years in the early 15th century. No one knows how he got there, but it has been suggested that he went with Béthencourt to the Canaries and crossed over to Africa from there. He wrote a description of his experiences which was still in existence

in the 18th century, but has since been lost. All that is left are two summaries; I will quote the one written by one of his contemporaries.

In his 15th-century *Histoire Chronologique des Parlements de Languedoc*, Guillaume Bardin writes: "In 1413, Anselm d'Ysalguier, a distinguished citizen of Toulouse, returned home. He had spent twelve years travelling in Europe and Africa, and, when among the negroes in Africa, he had married a girl called Salam-Casais. With him came his wife, his daughter and his two sons. Salam-Casais was of noble birth and came from the city of Gao; so far had Anselm travelled. Since he was much attracted to the young girl, and desired the riches of gold and precious stones which she had inherited from her father, his passion for her was great, and she was joined to him in wedlock. Certainly I cannot believe that he could have married her without abandoning his faith. Eight years later they took ship and sailed over the Mediterranean to

Gao was still under the control of Melli in the early 15th century. It was older than Timbuktu; an important trade centre from early times, it had its greatest period from 1465 to 1588, as the capital of the great Songhai Empire. If it is the same as Quioquia, we know that it was once surrounded by baked brick walls, but nothing of the old Gao remains today except for a few foundations. The picture above is only meant to show a typical city of the western Sudan. The woman belongs to the Fulani race.

Marseille, accompanied by three black eunuchs and the same number of black maidservants. From there they went to Toulouse, where they became Christians. Their six-year-old daughter was christened Martha."

We have a letter, written in 1447 at the Oasis of Tuat,

on the Timbuktu trade route, by a Genoese called Antonio Malfante, who had probably been sent by a Genoese firm to obtain some commercial information. Let me quote a few passages from it: "Merchants live in complete security here, at least in much greater security than in cities under monarchical government, such as Tlemcen and Tunis. I am a Christian, and yet no one has shown me any discourtesy. Nobody here had ever seen a Christian before. It is true that the curiosity of the people was annoying at first. Everyone wanted to see me, and they cried in surprise: 'He is a Christian, and yet he looks just like us!' For they had imagined Christians to be quite different from themselves. But their curiosity soon died down. Now I walk about alone, without ever hearing an unfriendly word. — There are many Jews here. Although they are dependent on many masters, their lives run a very smooth course... It never rains here. If it did, their houses would collapse, for they are built of salt and reeds. And there is hardly ever any frost here. But the summers are uncommonly hot, so that nearly all the people are black.

"Through these countries [in the south] flows a very large river which floods the regions lying along it at fixed seasons. This river [the Niger], which flows past the walls of Timbuktu, is the same as that which flows through Egypt and out into the sea at Cairo. Merchant ships sail on it. It is believed that it would be possible to sail all the way to Egypt along this river if it did not hurl itself over a cliff 300 cubits high at one place... From what I have been able to learn, the inhabitants here are neighbours of the Indians. Indian merchants come here and make themselves understood with the assistance of interpreters. These Indians [Abyssinians] are Christians who pray to the Cross. There are said to be 40 different languages in the countries of the negroes, with the result that their inhabitants are often unable to understand one another."

We can get some idea of the extent of medieval caravan traffic in the barren Sahara from the report, given by the Arab historian Ibn Khaldun, that 12,000 dromedaries passed the Ahaggar Mountains every year at the beginning of the 15th century. And there were other routes than this. The "Indians" (i.e. Abyssinians) mentioned by Antonio Malfante probably travelled along a route which passed south of Lake Chad and then north of Kano to Gao, Timbuktu and further north (see the map on p. 218). As we have seen earlier, the whole of the Sahara and the Sudan were criss-crossed with trade routes. Gold came mainly from the south and copper from the east; and to the rich land of Melli came silk, damascened swords, and horses from Egypt and the Mediterranean countries. The usual articles of payment were pieces of gold and copper, cowries from the Red Sea and salt, a commodity so plentiful in Tuat that the houses there were built of blocks of it.

Finally, at the National Library in Florence we find a few curious lines in a manuscript from 1470 which was written by a traveller called Benedetto Dei: "I was in Beirut the year I sent a serpent with a hundred teeth and four legs to Florence, in Jerusalem the year I brought home a number of relics for my sister and my cousins, in Carthage the year I brought back a chameleon, which lives on air... in Oran and Archudia, where they sell monkeys of both sexes, which they carry trussed like fowls... and I have been in Timbuktu, a place in the kingdom of the Berbers, in the hottest parts of the world. Men do much trade there and sell thick cloths, serge and loose material which are made in Lombardy."

190

Hans Schiltberger, a young Bavarian nobleman, was one of the many thousands who were taken prisoner and sold during the wars against the Turks. In 1427, after spending 32 years as a slave in Asia, he managed to return to Christendom, and wrote a book about his experiences. He says that ten thousand prisoners were beheaded by the Turks after the battle of Nicopolis in 1396, but that all who were under twenty years of age were spared and enslaved; he himself was not more than fifteen at the time. He came into the Sultan's possession and served him as an outrider, but a few years later both he and the Sultan were taken prisoner by Tamerlane, who removed them to Samarkand. After first having served as a slave of Tamerlane's son, Hans passed from master to master until he came to the Mongol Prince Chekra, whom he accompanied on a campaign in the Urals and Siberia. After Chekra's death, a Mongol official called Manshuk became his master, and when, on another campaign, they had to withdraw as far as the Black Sea, Hans Schiltberger and several other Christian slaves managed to escape to a ship which brought them to Constantinople and liberty.

In 1444 Pope Eugenius IV was visited by Nicolo Conti, a Venetian, who wished to be given absolution, for while in Egypt he had found himself compelled to go over to Islam. The wise Pope listened to his explanation and promised him the absolution of his sins if he first, as a penance, described all his adventures to the Papal Secretary. He had to give an account of twenty-five years in India and China, and Poggio Bracciolini, the secretary, listened and wrote; and the written narrative, of which only sections are preserved, begins in this way: "One Nicolo, a Venetian who had been to the interior of Asia, came to Pope Eugenius—who was at that time in Florence—that he might seek absolution of him, for while on the homeward journey from India, on the borders of Egypt and the Red Sea, he was forced to abandon his faith. This he did, not so much from fear for his own death as from the danger in which his wife and his children, who were with him, found themselves. I was most eager to speak with him, for I had heard many remarkable things about him. Both at my own house and at conferences of learned men I questioned him carefully about all manner of things that seemed to me to be worthy of note and of recording . . . In his youth Nicolo lived as a merchant in the Syrian city of Damascus. He learned

During and after the Middle Ages, travellers returning from Africa often brought with them stuffed "dragons" or "serpents". One still hangs in one of the cloisters of the Cathedral in Seville.

A cobra-masked devil-dancer scaring away evil spirits in southern Ceylon.

Arabic and then set off in the company of six hundred other merchants, in what is called a caravan, through the deserts of Arabia Petraea and through Chaldaea to the Euphrates."

After this, we have to try to follow Conti, in what remains of Bracciolini's description, on his journey along the Euphrates to Basra and across the Persian Gulf to Ormuz. He stayed for a while at a port on the Indian Ocean, learning Persian among other things, and then sailed with some other traders to Cambay in India. From there he moved south along the coast to the vicinity of Goa and then straight inland to Vijayanagar, which was the capital of the Kingdom of Deccan. It is uncertain

whether he came back the same way, and then sailed round Cape Comorin to the east coast, or whether he continued the journey by land right across the Indian Peninsula to Mailapur, where St. Thomas the Apostle was said to be buried. Be that as it may, he ascertained that St. Thomas' supposed converts were scattered all over India, just as Jews were scattered all over Italy. It was probably at Mailapur that he married a Christian Indian, who afterwards accompanied him on all his travels.

He visited Ceylon, and was the first European to describe the cultivation of cinnamon on that island. He stayed there for a year, and then sailed across the Bay

A cargo ship on the Irrawaddy.

of Bengal, past the cannibal-haunted Andaman Islands, to Tenasserim in Burma, and later sailed on to the Ganges. After sailing fifteen days up this river, which according to him was so broad that it was impossible to see the banks from midstream, he reached the beautiful city of Cernove, probably somewhere near Rajmahal.

Bracciolini's narrative continues: "After leaving this place, he sailed up the Ganges for three months, leaving many renowned cities unvisited on the way, and came to Maarazia, a wonderfully rich city where aloes, gold, silver, precious stones and pearls were to be found in abundance. From there he moved on to certain mountains in the east to buy the precious stones called carbuncles

A cargo ship on the Irrawaddy.

which are to be found there. He spent fifteen days on this journey, then returned to the city of Cernove, went to Buffetonia and left that place also, reaching after almost a month the mouth of the River Racha [the Lemro in Burma]. He sailed up this river, and after six days came to a very large city which bore the same name as the river. He left the city and travelled for seventeen days across completely barren mountains, then a further fifteen days across flat country until at last he came to

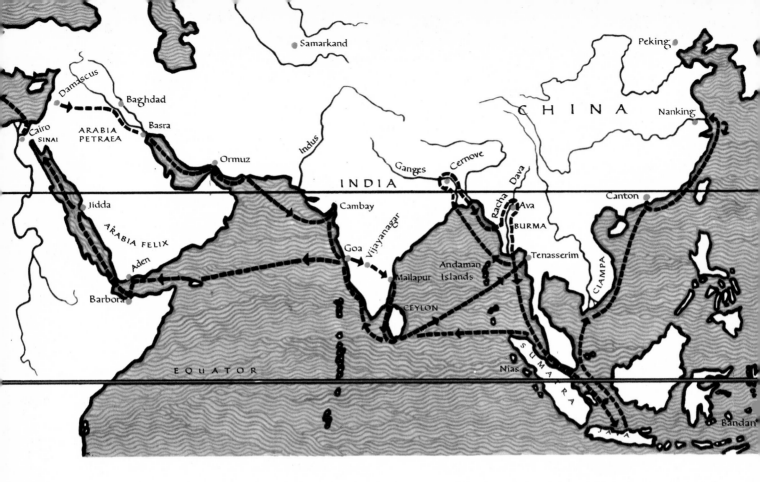

The broken line on the map shows the approximate routes taken by Nicolo Conti during his twenty-five years of travel.

a river which was even greater in size than the Ganges; the inhabitants called it the Dava [Irrawaddy]. He sailed down this for a whole month and came to a city called Ava, which is more splendid than all others and fifteen miles in circumference."

Nicolo Conti had reached the same parts that Marco Polo had visited about one hundred and fifty years before in the service of Kublai Khan. The former capital of Burma, Pagan, had just been sacked by the Grand Khan's troops: Ava, the new capital, lay further upstream, near modern Mandalay. Among other things, Conti could tell of tattooed men, of an elephant hunt, of rhinoceroses and pythons.

It is probable that he sailed from Burma to "the two islands of Java", i.e. Java and Sumatra. Bracciolini writes: "Here he stayed with his wife and children, who accompanied him on all his travels, for nine months. The inhabitants of these islands are more inhuman and cruel than any other people ... If one sails from these islands for fifteen days to the east, one comes to two others. The first is called Sandai and the second Bandan." Conti said that it was from there that cloves came. Sandai might mean the Sunda Isles; Bandan must be the Banda Islands south of the Moluccas, this being the only place where cloves grew at that time. It is possible that the Banda Islands, which produced nutmegs and other spices, were

such an important centre of commerce that the cloves were exported from there to Java and so further west.

After this we find Conti in a place called Ciampa, which was probably somewhere in Indochina, and some believe that he moved on from there to China and Nanking, which was then its capital. We know that he once again visited the Indian Peninsula and traded there. He spent two months on the island of Socotra and could report that most of the people there were Nestorian Christians.

About the last stage of the journey home from Aden Bracciolini writes: "Then he steered towards Ethiopia, which he reached after seven days, and cast anchor in the harbour of Barbora [Berbera in Somaliland]. After a month on the Red Sea he came to a port called Gidda [Jidda], and thence to Mount Sinai. In order to reach this place on the Red Sea he needed two months because of the difficulties of sailing. He then passed through the desert to Carras [Cairo], a city in Egypt, together with his wife, four children and numerous servants. In this city

194

he lost his wife, two children and all his servants, who died of the plague. At last, as fortune would have it, after all his journeys by land and sea, he arrived with his two surviving children at his native city of Venice."

Nicolo Conti's travels were almost as extensive as those of his countryman Marco Polo, and it is very likely that they were far more dangerous, for he was not able to travel under the protection of any powerful prince. As far as we know, he was the first European ever to enter the Indian Peninsula, and the first since the beginning of the Arab hegemony to sail right down the Red Sea. He returned to Venice thirteen years before Fra Mauro began to draw his map of the world, and we may take it for granted that the great geographer filled out his information about all the land that was called India with what Nicolo Conti was able to tell.

Yet another protracted journey to India is described by the Russian traveller Athanasius Nikitin from Tver. He was a merchant on whom fortune did not smile: when he left his native city, the modern Kalinin, and sailed down the Volga in 1466, he and his companions were robbed by Mongol brigands, and it seems as if the remainder of his travels were more a tale of adventure than of commerce. He was at Ormuz and in India proper, although it is likely that he got no further than Bidar, near Hyderabad. When, after six years of absence, he returned to Russia, he no longer had the strength to make the journey home to Tver. The narrative of his travels is unfinished, and it is believed that he died of illness in Smolensk.

After the middle of the 15th century, when the Turks, inveterate enemies of commerce, had blocked the approaches to the Black Sea, the Venetians made particularly vigorous attempts to reopen the trade routes. They even persuaded their old trading allies, the Mohammedans of Persia, to attack the Turks in the rear, and they tried to induce the Poles and the Hungarians to do the same. They still maintained their good trade connections with Egypt and could import goods from India and China that way, but since the alternative route through Persia was blocked by the Turks, the wares became extremely expensive. It is true that a certain amount of Chinese silk was transported from Samarkand to Moscow and from there to the rest of Europe, but that did little good to Venice. Josaphat Barbaro, who was the Venetian Ambassador in Persia, recommended his countrymen in the 1470's to re-open the old route along the Indus and the Amu Darya, and he encouraged them to negotiate with the Russians for a route across the Volga and the Caspian. At the beginning of the 16th century, when the trading cities of Italy were rapidly approaching disaster, the Genoese commercial house of Centurione approached the Tsar in Moscow about this matter, but the Russians mistrusted the foreigners, and no agreement was reached.

A warrior from the island of Nias, off the west coast of Sumatra. Conti says that the inhabitants of Java and Sumatra were more cruel and inhuman than any other people.

195

In Guinea and Sierra Leone the Portuguese met a stone-age people who, it appeared, had no connection with the Mohammedan negroes round the upper Niger and the Gambia. Hardly anything remains of their civilization. The stone figure above comes from Sierra Leone and has been dated to the 16th century. The medicine-man's mask from Simo in Guinea has been used in the present century.

From Sierra Leone to the Equator

The year after the death of Henry the Navigator, a certain Pedro de Cintra sailed with two armed caravels to Sierra Leone and the Grain Coast. Cadamosto was still in Portugal at the time, and a former secretary of his accompanied Cintra and was able, on his return, to tell Cadamosto of the details of the voyage. As was the practice, they probably first sailed to Porto Santo or Madeira to take on provisions, timber and water. The King had ordered them to sail as far along the coast of Africa as possible, and first they went to the islands off the mouth of the Rio Grande (the Geba). Cintra's men found wooden idols in huts on the beach, but they had no interpreter who could understand the language of the islanders, so

A caravel off the "roaring" Sierra Leone.

they immediately sailed on past Cape Verga to coasts which were new to the Portuguese. A promontory, which was the highest they had ever seen, they called Cape Sagres in honour of their dead prince.

Here they found negro tribes which had never had any contact with the trading peoples in the north. Their tools and weapons were made of wood, they were dressed in short aprons of raffia, and they worshipped carved wooden idols; but their canoes were larger than any seen before, thirty to forty men being able to stand and paddle in them. Of the voyage to Sierra Leone Cadamosto writes: "Two hundred and four miles beyond Cape Verde they discovered a new cape, which they called Cape Ledo, meaning 'comely', for the cape and the beautiful green stretch of coast were a joy to behold. Rising behind this was a great mountain range which was completely covered with large tall trees for fifty miles of its length.

Where it came to an end they found three islands eight miles from the shore, of which the largest [Sherbro Island?] was 10—12 miles in circumference. These they called Salvezze and the mountain range Sierra Leone [Lion Mountains]. They gave it this name because of the great roaring that is to be heard there which comes from the thunder of the clouds that constantly envelop the mountain peaks."

They sailed on past Cape Mesurado in modern Liberia and saw beacons lit along the coast, as the natives spread the news about the two amazing winged ships that had appeared. Here the high trees came right down to the shore, and when they anchored, some naked men came

197

A highly developed civilization is found in the Kingdom of Benin, north-west of the Niger Delta. The bronze head dates from the early 16th century and is said to represent a queen mother. The wooden figure below is from the Gold Coast — modern Ghana — and is still worn by newly married women to make them fertile. Is it a coincidence that it is like the Egyptian hieroglyph "ankh" — the red figure — which is the symbol of life, or can there have been some ancient connection between the peoples of the Nile and the peoples south of the Niger?

out to meet them in canoes. Three of them ventured aboard Cintra's vessel, and, as the King had instructed, he detained one of them. Later, when they reached home, this prisoner was interrogated by other black slaves.

Nine years were now to pass before any further advance was made along the west coast of Africa, and it is probable that Pedro de Cintra's voyage was accomplished only because it had been planned by the dying Prince. Everything connected with later Portuguese discoveries was kept very secret, and if Cadamosto's description of Cintra's voyage had not come down to us, we should have known nothing of that either. The King, fully occupied fighting the Moors, had neither the money nor the organization to continue his uncle's work, but in 1469 he sensibly decided to put it all into the hands of Fernão Gomes, one of his uncle's noblemen. Gomes was given a five years' monopoly of the Guinea trade, subject to an annual payment of 500 ducats and an obligation to advance at least 100 leagues—about 375 miles—along the coast every year, starting from Sierra Leone.

We know practically no details of these secret voyages, but Fernão Gomes did his best to keep his part of the bargain, and the results were good. Antonio Galvano writes of the whole affair in this way: "The next year, 1472, Fernando da Póo discovered the island which now bears his name. Also discovered at that time were the islands of São Tomé and Principe, which lie on the Equator, and the mainland where the Kingdom of Benin is situated and which stretches as far as Cape St. Catherine. This cape lies 3° on the south side. The man who made this discovery was in the service of the King, and his name was Sequeira."

The newly discovered coasts were found to be more profitable than all the rest of Africa, as far as it was yet known, put together. On the Malaguetta Coast in modern Liberia they found pepper, and although in quality it could not compare with the pepper which came from India, it nevertheless brought the Portuguese much profit on the Flemish market. The inhabitants on the stretch of coast between Cape Palmas and Cape Three Points

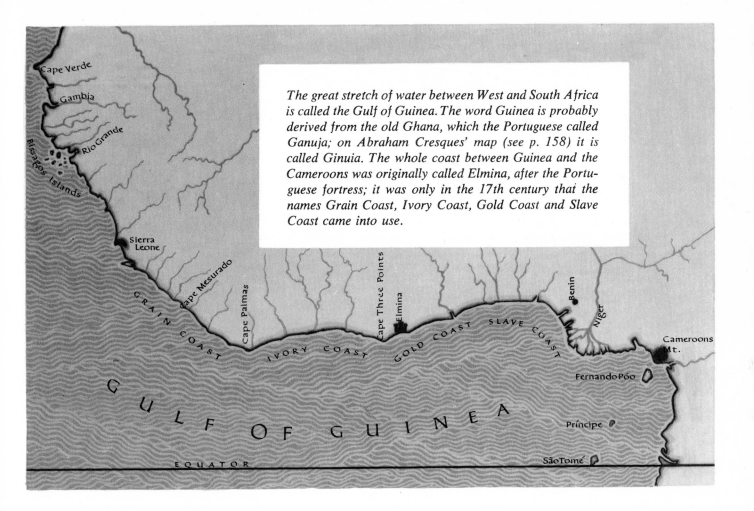

The great stretch of water between West and South Africa is called the Gulf of Guinea. The word Guinea is probably derived from the old Ghana, which the Portuguese called Ganuja; on Abraham Cresques' map (see p. 158) it is called Ginuia. The whole coast between Guinea and the Cameroons was originally called Elmina, after the Portuguese fortress; it was only in the 17th century that the names Grain Coast, Ivory Coast, Gold Coast and Slave Coast came into use.

were extremely hostile, but even so, it was gradually found possible to buy large quantities of elephant tusks from them (later on, this region came to be called the Ivory Coast). Most important of all, however, was the country discovered by João de Santarem and Pero de Escolar beyond Cape Three Points—later known as the Gold Coast. It was here that the Portuguese first came in direct contact with the source of the gold: they saw how it was washed from the rivers and dug from the mines, and even though the mines remained in the hands of the negro kings, the gold trade became highly profitable.

It was probably also Santarem and Escolar who discovered the Benin coastline, in modern Nigeria. There they found good pepper, of the same quality as the Indian, but the climate was bad and the cultivations cost many lives, so the inferior Malaguetta pepper long continued to dominate the market. The most lucrative business in the Bight of Benin was the slave trade, and the whole coastline as far as the Niger Delta came to be called the Slave Coast. Slaves were no longer taken to Portugal with

the excuse of saving souls for Christianity; they were now captured, or bought cheap, in Benin and sold at a high price on the Gold Coast. It even happened that slaves who had already been baptized were sold to Mohammedan traders along the Gambia. And the price of slaves rose. In 1446 twenty-five slaves had to be paid for an old horse on the Senegal, but on the Gambia thirteen years later an equivalent article fetched only twelve. On the Malaguetta Coast the price of a slave rose in a few years from two brass shaving-bowls to five. It is stated that at that time 3,500 slaves passed through Portuguese hands every year.

Fernão Gomes' agreement with the King expired in 1474, and the Guinea monopoly now came into the hands of Prince João, the nineteen-year-old heir-apparent. But the discovery that the coast turned south after the Cameroons was a great disappointment, and almost ten years were to pass before new voyages of discovery were undertaken in Africa. Portugal now began to look for land in the west.

199

Westward to the East

Long ago, Aristotle had said: "The regions round the Pillars of Hercules are in connection with the regions round India, and between them there is nothing but sea." Strabo believed that by sailing with an easterly wind in the western ocean one "could reach the Indies". About 120 A.D the Roman philosopher Favorinus wrote that the same ocean which the Greeks knew as the Atlantic Sea was known in East Asia as the Great Sea. Roger Bacon and Albertus Magnus put forward similar views in the 13th century.

Crates, who made the first globe in 180 B.C., believed that many unknown continents lay in the great world ocean, and the same opinion was held by the learned archbishop Isidore of Seville in the 7th century, by the Arab genius Ibn Sina, known in Europe as Avicenna, in the 11th, and by the Spanish missionary and philosopher Ramundus Lullus in the 13th. But in the 14th century, when Petrus of Albano and Cecco d'Ascoli actually taught that the earth was round, like a ball, the Church called them heretics and handed them over to the temporal authorities to be burned at the stake.

Although it is true that the 15th-century Church officially maintained that the earth was flat and had four corners, exactly as the Bible said, it allowed cosmographers and other scholars to have their own opinions and to make maps and globes which showed the true shape of

At the end of the Middle Ages almost all cosmographers agreed that nothing except the Great Ocean separated the West from the East, and Europe from Asia. The Atlantic was regarded as the source of the tempest: this was only natural, since nearly all the storms that ravaged the coasts of western Europe came from its direction. It was also natural for cosmographers to draw pictures of sea-serpents and other monsters: man has always imagined the unknown as something evil and frightening. But only a minority among scholars thought that the Ocean was not too broad to cross: only the most experienced of the mariners (who had never seen any seamonsters) were led by the hope of great profits to brave the dangers of the journey.

the earth. We do not know whether Henry the Navigator thought it possible to sail westwards to Asia or whether he believed in undiscovered continents. Diogo Gomes wrote that he had sent out caravels to find out whether "islands or a mainland" were to be found there. His captains did find islands, but they were not ready for longer voyages across the uncharted ocean.

There were doubtless many in the 15th century who held and expressed the same ideas that Aristotle and

Strabo had suggested before them, and one who often discussed the matter was Paolo Toscanelli, a Florentine scientist. One of his friends was Fernan Martinez de Roriz, a Portuguese canon who later became King Alfonso's confessor at the Court in Lisbon. It is probable that some time about the beginning of the 1470's, the canon had come to discuss geographical questions with the King, or with Crown Prince João, who was more interested in geography, and then happened to mention Toscanelli's theory about a passage to India across the ocean to the west. At that time the Portuguese believed that they had already reached the southern extremity of Africa, and that the way to the riches of India already lay open before them. But then came the disconcerting news that once past the Cameroons the coast again turned south, and continued to do so for mile upon mile; it seems almost as if all hope of ever being able to circumnavigate Africa was abandoned. It was in this situation that the King instructed his confessor to write to Toscanelli and ask him to explain his plans more clearly. Toscanelli answered at some length, enclosing a map of the sea which divided Europe from Asia.

I shall quote this most important document in its entirety:

"To Fernam Martins, Canon of Lisbon, Paulus the Physician [i.e. Toscanelli] sends greetings.

"It pleased me to hear of your intimacy and friendship with your great and powerful King. Often before have I spoken of a sea route from here to India, the land of spices; a route which is shorter than that via Guinea. You tell me that His Highness wishes me to explain this in greater detail so that it will be easier to understand and to take this route. Although I could show this on a globe representing the earth, I have decided to do it more simply and clearly by demonstrating the way on a nautical chart. I therefore send His Majesty a chart, drawn by my own hand, on which I have indicated the western coastline from Ireland in the north to the end of Guinea, and the islands which lie along this path. Opposite them, directly to the west, I have indicated the beginning of India, together with the islands and places you will come to; how far you should keep from the Arctic Pole and the Equator; and how many leagues you must cover before you come to these places, which are most rich in all kinds of spices, gems and precious stones. And be not amazed when I say that spices grow in lands to the west, even though we usually say the east; for he who sails west will always find these lands in the west, and he who travels east by land will always find the same lands in the east.

"The upright lines on this chart show the distance from east to west, whereas the cross lines show the distance from north to south. The chart also indicates various places in India which may be reached if one meets with a storm or head-wind, or any other misfortune.

"That you may know as much about these places as possible, you should know that the only people living on any of these islands are merchants who trade there.

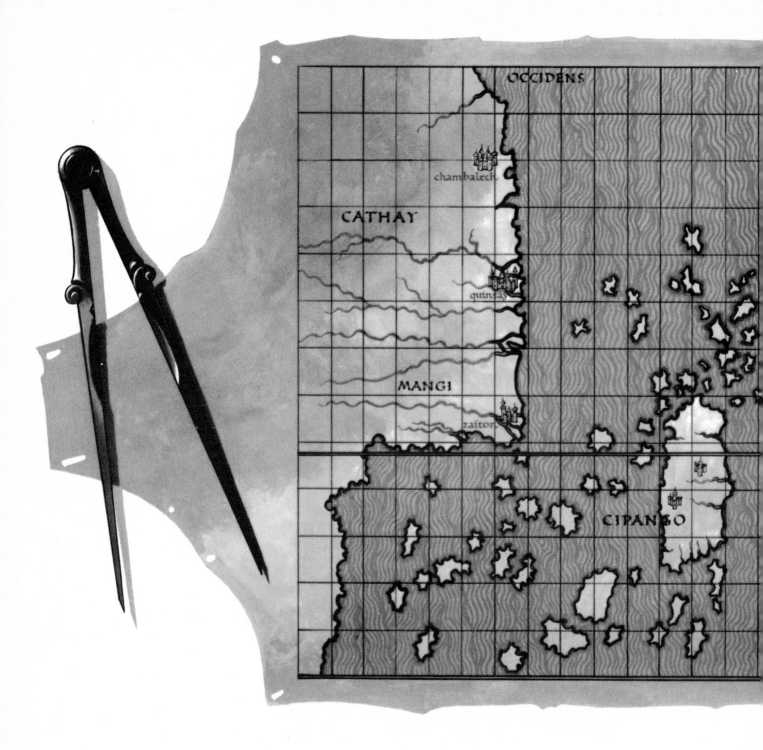

There are said to be as many ships, mariners and goods there as in the rest of the world put together, especially in the principal port called Zaiton [Marco Polo's Zai-tum] where they load and unload a hundred great ships of pepper every year, not to mention many other ships with other spices. That country has many inhabitants, provinces, kingdoms and innumerable cities, all of which are ruled by a prince known as the Grand Khan, which in our language means 'The King of Kings', who mainly resides in the province of Cathay. His forefathers greatly desired to make contact with the Christian world, and some two hundred years ago they sent ambassadors to the Pope, asking him to send them many learned men who could instruct them in our faith; but these ambassadors met with difficulties on the way, and had to turn back without reaching Rome. In the days of Pope Euge-

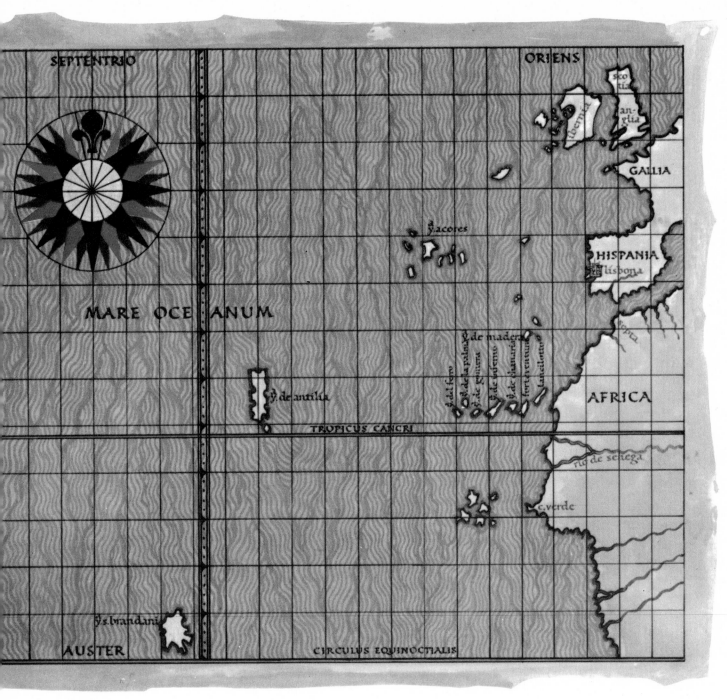

Map labels (clockwise/as positioned):

SEPTENTRIO · ORIENS

scotia · anglia · ibernia · GALLIA

ỹ.acores · HISPANIA · lisbona

MARE OCE ANUM

ỹ.de madera · ỹ.de palma · ỹ.de gomera · ỹ.de inferno · ỹ.de diamargo · forteventura · lancilotto · ceupta · AFRICA

ỹ.del fero

ỹ.de antilia

TROPICUS CANCRI

rio de senega

c.verde

ỹ.s.brandani

AUSTER · CIRCULUS EQUINOCTIALIS

nius, there came an ambassador to him, who told him of their great feelings of friendship for the Christians, and I had a long conversation with the ambassador about many things: about the vast size of the royal buildings, about the amazing length and breadth of their rivers, and about the great number of cities on their banks—so great a number that along one river there were two hundred cities with very long, wide bridges of marble which

The map which Paolo Toscanelli sent to Alfonso V of Portugal has disappeared. This is a reconstruction, based partly on Toscanelli's own description, and partly on a copy of a latitudinal and longitudinal grid which was found among his belongings. It was a rectangular projection of one half of the circumference of the earth — 180° — and each horizontal line on the projection represented 5 degrees of longitude. The coasts and islands are mainly taken from Martin Behaim's globe, which is still in existence and was probably much influenced by Toscanelli's map.

203

were adorned with many pillars. This country is richer than any other yet discovered, and not only could it provide great profit and many valuable things, but also possesses gold and silver and precious stones and all kinds of spices in large quantities—things which do not reach our countries at present. And there are also many scholars, philosophers, astronomers and other men skilled in the natural sciences, who govern that great kingdom and conduct its wars.

"From the city of Lisbon to the west, the chart shows twenty-six sections, of two hundred and fifty miles each —altogether, nearly one-third of the earth's circumference —before reaching the very large and magnificent city of Kin-sai. This city is approximately one hundred miles in circumference, possesses ten marble bridges, and its name means 'The Heavenly City' in our language. Amazing things have been related about its vast buildings, its artistic treasures and its revenues. It lies in the province of Manji, near the province of Cathay, where the king chiefly resides. And from the island of Antilia, which you call the Island of the Seven Cities, to the very famous island of Cipango are ten sections, that is 2,500 miles. That island is very rich in gold, pearls and precious stones, and its temples and palaces are covered in gold. But since the route to this place is not yet known, all these things remain hidden and secret; and yet one may go there in great safety.

"I could still tell of many other things, but as I have already told you of them in person, and as you are a man of good judgement, I will dilate no further on the subject. I have tried to answer your questions as well as the lack of time and my work have permitted me, but I am always prepared to serve His Highness and answer his questions at greater length should he so wish.

"Written in Florence on the 25th of June, 1474."

It is clear that Toscanelli obtained most of his information about Furthest "India" from Marco Polo's book, but he also mentions that an "ambassador" visited Pope Eugenius. Poggio Bracciolini, the Papal Secretary who wrote about Nicolo Conti's travels in India, adds at the end of Conti's narrative: "There came a man from the northern parts of Upper India to the Pope, wishing, on the instructions of his Nestorian Patriarch, to learn of the Christians in the countries of the West. He told of the Grand Khan and of his dominion over nine powerful peoples." This man was probably the ambassador mentioned by Toscanelli, and we shall have to presume that Conti and other travellers who are unknown to us today gave Toscanelli further valuable information.

Toscanelli probably based his very exaggerated idea of the size of the world on what Marinus of Tyre had said; this was later to have some very remarkable consequences. The 6,500 'miles' of open sea which divided Europe from Asia seems to have appeared a short and

204

easy voyage to the sober eye of an Italian scientist, but to the superstitious Portuguese mariners they were a terrifyingly great stretch of water.

Perhaps it was to break the long voyage into stages that people began to look for Antilia and the other imaginary islands that Toscanelli and earlier geographers had drawn on their maps. Antilia, which was supposed to lie half-way between Lisbon and Cipango [Japan], had long been found on the maps and in the wishful thinking of mariners, and was long to remain so, and under Antilia on Martin Behaim's globe there are the following words: "In the year 734 after the birth of Christ, as it was calculated, when the whole of Hispania had been taken by the Infidels from Africa, the above-shown island of Antilia, called the Seven Cities, was colonized by an archbishop from Oporto in Portugal, together with six bishops and other Christians, men and women, who had fled there from Hispania by ship with cattle, goods and belongings. — In 1414 a ship from Hispania sailed close to it."

In a document dated the 28th of January 1475, King Alfonso granted to a certain Fernam Tellez a group of islands, called the Foreiras, which shortly before were said to have been discovered by Diogo Deteive and his son, who then made them over to Tellez by contract. The document says that Tellez was to visit these islands, but he never found them. — Bartolomeo de Las Casas

The Portuguese mariner Corte-Real presumably went to Labrador in 1476 with the Danish expedition led by "admirals" Pining and Pothorst. The voyage must have been made in summer: we may presume that it met with the inconvenience of ice carried down from Greenland by the Labrador Current.

tells in his *Historia de las Indias* of a Portuguese pilot called Vicente Diaz who, on the way back from Guinea, sighted an island, or at any rate thought he did. On Terceira, an island in the Azores, he told a friend about it, and they decided to equip an expedition together and take possession of the island. Las Casas writes: "When the King of Portugal gave his consent to this, Lucas [the friend from Terceira] instructed his brother Francesco de Casana, who lived in Seville, to equip a vessel and hand it over to the aforementioned pilot, Vicente Diaz. But Francesco ridiculed the plan and refused to cooperate. When the pilot returned to Terceira, Lucas undertook to equip the vessel himself. Vicente Diaz sailed out three or four times to look for the aforesaid island, and reached a distance of as much as a hundred sailing hours from his point of departure, without discovering anything, with the result that he and his employer at last began to doubt that there was anything to discover."

King Alfonso's successor, John II, announces in a document of 30th June 1484 among other things the follow-

205

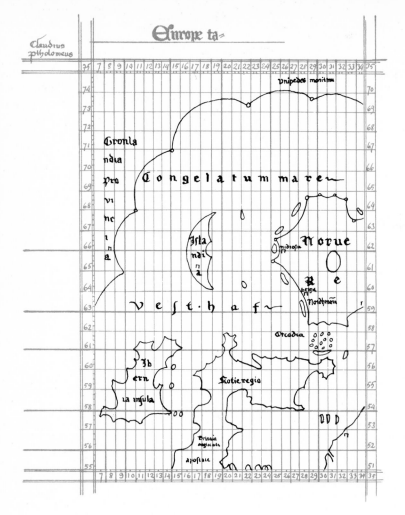

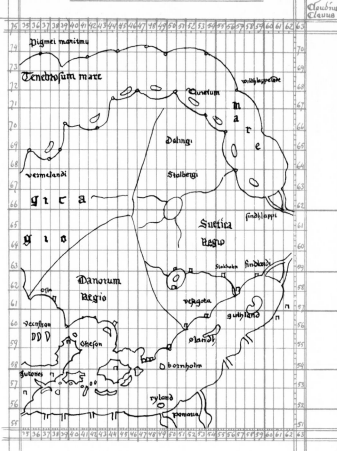

ing: "Let all who read this know that it is Our pleasure that Fernão Domingues de Arco, who lives on the island of Madeira, shall, if he discovers the island which he is now setting out to find, be made Governor of this said island."

It seems as if King Alfonso, perhaps inspired by Toscanelli's letter, entered into some form of partnership with King Christian I of Denmark during the 1470's in order to find a passage across the North Atlantic—perhaps to India. There is no complete report of such a combined undertaking, but certain passages from various documents do lend coherence to the picture. In a letter dated the 3rd of March 1551, the Mayor of Kiel wrote to Christian III of Denmark, telling him of a chart which had appeared in Paris: "There it is observed that Iceland is twice as large as Sicily, beneath Italy, and that the captains Pining and Pothorst, whom Your Royal Majesty's grandfather, King Christian I, on the request of His Royal Majesty of Portugal, had dispatched to seek for new islands in the north, set up a great sea-mark on the cliff of Hvitserk in front of Greenland, which lies across the sea directly opposite Snefellsjokul . . ." The chart which the mayor refers to is Gourmont's 1549 map of Iceland,

Prince Pedro, Henry the Navigator's brother and a great traveller, returned from a protracted journey in Europe in 1428, and the gifts he brought back for Prince Henry included a map of Scandinavia, which had probably been drawn in Venice some years earlier by the Danish geographer Claudius Clavus. The map is not extant, but it may have been a copy like the above — which is still in existence at Nancy — and it is possible that it encouraged the Prince, and later his nephew King Alfonso, to look for "islands and a mainland" in the western ocean.

Claudius Clavus based his work on Ptolemy, but he corrected Ptolemy's latitudes for Scandinavia. Ptolemy's figures are on the left of the above maps, and Clavus' on the right. In his description of his map Clavus says: "The peninsula of Greenland is connected in the north with a country which is inaccessible and unknown to us on account of the ice. But as I have seen, savage Karelians come to Greenland in great numbers every day, doubtless from the other side of the North Pole." — Had Clavus been there? And had he seen Eskimos?

206

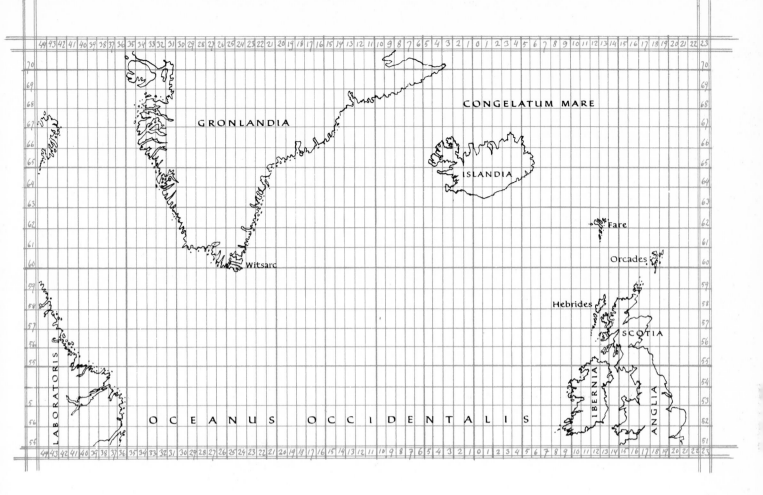

This map of the North Atlantic is drawn on the same projection as Claudius Clavus' map. The coastlines are modern.

showing a small rock to the north-west of the island. Written under the rock are the words: "The great mountain, called Witsarc, on the top of which a sea-mark was set up by the two pirates Pining and Pothorst, to warn mariners about Greenland."

Many sources speak of the pilot Johannes Skolp in connection with the discovery of Labrador on the mainland of North America, and his nationality has been given as Danish, Norwegian and Polish. In the 17th century, a certain Georg Horn wrote: "Joh. Scolnus Polonus, in the service of Christian I, King of the Danes, discovered the Anian Straits and the land of Laboratoris in the year 1476." But Portuguese sources mention quite a different name in connection with the discovery of Labrador. In a manuscript by one Gaspar Fructuoso, from the end of the 16th century, we read: "From the voyage of discovery to the new land of Bacalhãos [= Stock-Fish Land = Labrador] came João Vaz Corte-Real, who at the orders of the King became governor at Angra on the island of Terceira."

All this may be taken as showing that it was a question of one expedition alone, undertaken on the initiative of King Alfonso. The expedition was led by the two master mariners—at times called "admirals"—Pothorst the Dane and Pining, probably of German birth, whereas Johannes Skolp was simply the steersman. Skolp was of course a comparatively well-educated man who may well have been in contact with the cosmographers and who would therefore receive greater mention than the others. Corte-Real accompanied the expedition as a Portuguese observer. It was quite natural to choose to sail across the ocean in the north, for the Portuguese had the map drawn by Claudius Clavus, a Dane, and probably other charts and globes too, which showed that the sea was narrower in the north and might contain islands which could be used as stages on the journey. It is true that they found the inhospitable Labrador, which they naturally took to be an island, but what Corte-Real was able to report to his master was not very encouraging for those who were looking for a passage to India.

207

Diego Cão's Voyages to South-West Africa

When Henry IV of Castile died in December 1474, and was succeeded by his sister Isabella, who was married to Ferdinand of Aragon, a war of succession broke out between Portugal and Castile. This claimed Alfonso V's attention to such an extent that he was unable to give much thought to voyages of discovery. Ferdinand and Isabella quickly seized the opportunity to encroach on Portugal's lucrative African trade, letting it be announced that Isabella's royal forefathers "had always had conquests in Africa and Guinea close at heart, and had received a fifth of the wares which were obtained in those parts". They also pointed out in the same document how important it was that the gold from Guinea should come to their countries and not be taken to others. They encouraged the merchants of Andalusia to send ships to Guinea, sold privileges to them for a fifth of the value of the cargo, and gave them an escort of warships for the dangerous voyage. In 1478 thirty-five caravels sailed from Seville and other Andalusian ports to trade along the Gold Coast; a navy began to be equipped to drive the Portuguese away from the coveted coasts; and Castile even appointed a governor over Guinea.

But it was not the Castilians alone who exploited Portugal's temporary weakness: Flemish ships, too, were employed in trading with Guinea, and the chronicler Duarte Pacheco tells of such a vessel which had sailed to the Gold Coast in 1475: "God ordained that it should

On a rocky promontory at the mouth of the small River Beya on the Gold Coast Azambuja founded the fortress called Elmina, "The Mine", in the hope that the gold of Africa would pass through it to Portugal. By an agreement with the local chieftain, guaranteeing peace and friendship, he was allowed to build the fortress; it was only used for the protection of trade, and never as a base for conquest. — Elmina is shown on Cantino's map of the world in 1502 (below), and this is probably the oldest picture of the fortress.

end in disaster: for it foundered, and the entire crew of thirty-five men were eaten by the negroes."

Then the Pope mediated again. By the Treaty of Alcaçovas in 1479, it was once again decided that the Canaries were to belong to Castile, whereas Portugal was guaranteed the sole rights of trade and navigation to Guinea and the countries beyond. Ferdinand succeeded to the throne of Aragon that same year, and from then on Castile and Aragon were united under the rule of Ferdinand and Isabella.

Alfonso V of Portugal died in 1481. He was succeeded by his son, John II, who as early as December of that year dispatched a large expedition to the Gold Coast with instructions to build a fortress there to protect Portuguese traders; for they were still being molested by Spanish ships in spite of the treaty. All Portuguese captains were given instructions to throw overboard the crew of any foreign ship that was found in Guinea, and to take the captain to Lisbon to be tried and executed as a common criminal.

The expedition was led by Diogo de Azambuja, a veteran of the wars. It consisted of nine caravels and two transport ships, five hundred soldiers and one hundred craftsmen; and the name of one of his captains was Diego Cão. They began to build the fortress, which was called São Jorge da Mina, towards the end of January, and it soon became such an important place for trade that in 1486 it was enlarged into a city. The chronicler Pacheco has this to say about São Jorge da Mina, or Elmina as it was usually called: "By the grace of God, trade has so flourished in this colony that it is now possible to export 170,000 dobras of pure gold to Portugal each year. Negroes, belonging to various tribes and coming from distant places, barter there for wares of divers kinds. The profit is five to one, or more; but the country is unhealthy because of its fevers, and white men die there very quickly."

Diego Cão then sailed south from the newly built fortress. He moved down along the coast with the object ot discovering new territories. The voyage, against an increasing current, and with winds which varied from southerly and easterly to northerly, was long and difficult. Past Cape St. Catherine—modern Cape Lopez—the country was unknown. It is probable that the vessels anchored in what we today call Loango Bay on 4th August 1482, St. Dominic's Day, for we know that they called the bay Praia Formosa de São Domingo, and it was usual at that time to name capes and islands after the saints on whose days they were discovered.

The Portuguese used to erect wooden crosses bearing inscriptions on the newly discovered coasts that they claimed in the name of their king, but when later travellers noticed that these rotted away quickly in the tropical air, they came to be replaced, in the reign of John II, by stone crosses brought from Portugal for the purpose. They bore the names of the king and the discoverers, and also a text in Portuguese and Latin. Some of them are still in existence, and on the stone cross erected by

Diego Cão at Cape Agostinho—the modern Cape Santa Maria Benguela—we can still read the following: "In the Year of the World 6681, and the year 1482 after the birth of the Lord Jesus Christ, at the command of the glorious, most powerful and excellent King John II of Portugal, this country was discovered and this cross erected by Diego Cão, a knight at his court."

This cross — padrão in Portuguese — was erected by Diego Cão at Cape Cross in 1485, and was rediscovered in 1893.

Once past the Gulf of Guinea the Portuguese found practically no traces of civilization. Idols, cult-objects and implements were presumably made of wood for the most part, as in later centuries; and this mask from Gabon on the Equator, which was used to frighten away witches and evil spirits, is from modern times.

miles out into the salty ocean, as the mariners to their joy could see from the eddies. He prevailed against the current of the river and saw the black heathen Ethiopians, who in mind as in behaviour are amiable. By giving them small gifts and making friendly gestures, he persuaded them to go aboard his ship. Their movements were confident and fearless, and he treated them well. By sign-language he was able to understand that they were ruled by a very powerful king who resided far inland at a royal city, and that this could be reached along the river. He sent a few Portuguese to the king with gifts, gathered information about the country and its people, and then returned to Portugal with four Ethiopians who came of their own free will, after he had promised them on his word of honour that he would restore them unharmed to their country."

On this one voyage Diego Cão had discovered more new land than any other man in the service of Portugal had done before, and in recognition of this he was knighted by the King and given a pension for life and the right to carry two crosses on his coat-of-arms.

About that time, in 1483 or 1484, John II was visited by a certain Christopher Columbus, a Genoese mariner who had spent the last eight years in Portugal. His brother was a cartographer in Lisbon, and it was probably through him that he had learned of Toscanelli's letter and chart, and later corresponded with Toscanelli about the western route to India. But he believed that the passage to India across the great world ocean was shorter than Toscanelli had calculated, and he explained to the King that he knew the best way to get there, and promised to do so if three fully manned ships were placed at his disposal. John II was not learned enough to be able to judge the accuracy of Columbus' statement, so he appointed a committee of scholars to examine the matter. These did not believe either Toscanelli or Columbus, maintaining that the earth was far larger than the two Italians imagined, and that the proportion of land was smaller—with the result that the extent of water between Portugal and India was far too wide to be able to sail across. On the advice of the committee, therefore, the King refused Columbus' request, and it is known that he left Portugal for Castile towards the end of 1484.

And yet it is possible that the King put more trust in Columbus than in his learned men. Among other things, a document drawn up in his name on 24th July 1486 contains the following: "Fernam Dulmo told Us that it was his intention to discover a large island, or many islands, or a mainland, which he thought was the Island of the Seven Cities; and this at his own expense and risk." — In another document, written eleven days later, it says: "With respect to this agreement, the aforementioned Fernam Dulmo, finding himself unable to equip the two caravels necessary for the undertaking, has con-

Cão placed the first of these crosses on the cape immediately south of the estuary of the River Congo. He sailed a short way up the river and found that the natives called it the Zaire, but he named it the Rio São Jorge; it was only later that it came to be called the Congo, after the great chieftain Mani Congo, who allowed himself to be baptized in 1490 and tried to arrange his court on the European model. On this first voyage, Cão got no further south than to Cape Santa Maria Benguela at a latitude of 13° 16′ south, but on the way back he sailed once more up the Congo. Luca Wadding, a chronicler, says: "He came to the enormous river called the Zairis [Congo] which begins at the source of the Nile and with ever increasing force and volume gushes its fresh waters eighty

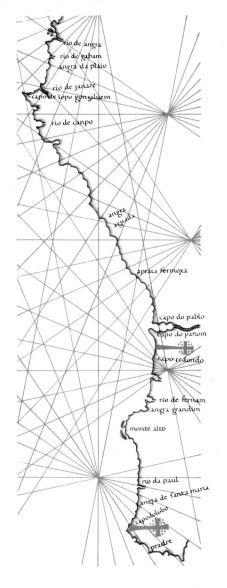

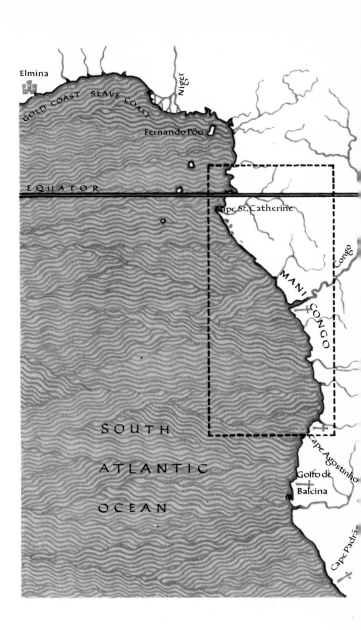

The Portuguese must have drawn maps of their 15th-century discoveries. None has survived, but it is thought that Cristoforo Soligo's 1490 map (left) is a direct copy of one made immediately after Diego Cão's first voyage. It corresponds to the framed section of the modern map (right) representing the coasts explored by Cão. The crosses on both maps indicate the crosses he erected.

sented to Joham Afomso's retaining one half of the island, or islands, or mainland, which may be discovered or reached by the said caravels, irrespective of whether these may be inhabited or not; with the same liberties, privileges and rights as the aforementioned Fernam Dulmo in the said document under certain conditions in the aforementioned agreement. — Here it shall be noted that the said Joham Afomso is to follow the direction and route appointed him by the said Fernam Dulmo, according to instructions he shall be given, for 40 days after his departure from the island of Terceira. But when these 40 days shall have passed, the said Fernam Dulmo shall no longer determine the course to be taken, but shall follow the route, instructions and direction given by the said Joham

Afomso until they are once more back in Our kingdom . . . The above concession shall be valid so long as the islands are discovered within the next two years."

Of Dulmo's and Afomso's voyage we know no more than this. If they ever did set out, the partners would probably soon have tired of trying to make west from Terceira against an unremitting head-wind.

The discovery of the great River Congo and the news that a powerful king resided far inland there naturally brought to life the hope of finding a direct path to Prester John. By that time it was practically certain that his kingdom was Abyssinia in East Africa, and Abyssinian ambassadors had been both to Rome and to Lisbon. A certain Battista d'Imola, who had accompanied a Papal

In order to determine the latitude of places on the new coasts as correctly as possible, people were put ashore to make observations wherever it was practicable. Large wooden astrolabes were often used for accuracy.

delegation across Egypt and the Red Sea to the court of the Negus, returned home in 1483 and was able to tell of many Italians who resided with the Negus, among them the Venetian church artist and organ-builder Nicolo Brancaleone. When asked why they had gone to that foreign country, they had replied: "To find jewels and precious stones. But as the King does not allow us to return, we are all dissatisfied, even though he treats us well, each according to his own station. He likes to speak with us of political matters."

Only a few individuals or small groups of travellers, however, were given permission to pass through Islamic Egypt; and John II wanted surer methods of making contact with the man who was supposed to be the mighty priest-king. Even before Diego Cão had returned from his first voyage, he had dispatched two expeditions, in 1483, to make contact with the inland negro princes in Africa; Barros writes of this: "At that time he sent Pedro de Evora and Gonçalo Eanes to the Prince of Tucurol and the Ruler of Timbuktu. At the same time he also sent Rodrigo Rabelo, a knight at the Court, Pero Reinel,

another knight, and João Colaso, a crossbowman, with others to make up the number of eight, across the River Cantor [the Gambia] to Mandi Mansa, one of the foremost chieftains in this part of the province of Madingo [Melli]. With them they had gifts of horses, beasts of burden and mules, together with suits of armour and other gifts which are much prized in that country, for these things had been requested. The only one of these men to return was Pero Reinel, who had partly managed to accustom himself to the climate. The others died of disease."

When Diego Cão set out once again in 1485 with three caravels, it is probable that he was accompanied by the two astronomers, José Vicinho and Rodrigues, who were to find out whether the sky of the Southern Hemisphere possessed any equivalent of the Pole Star. Navigators in the north could easily find their latitude by measuring the height of the Pole Star above the horizon. South of the Equator this was impossible, and the astronomers could not find any star at the pole of the southern sky; hence they had to use the more complicated method of

Imagine the earth's equatorial plane extended infinitely: the extension would cut the celestial sphere along what is called the celestial equator, and divide it into northern and southern hemispheres. Similarly, an infinite projection of the earth's axis meets the celestial sphere at the celestial poles. The great circles from pole to pole, corresponding to the meridians of the earth, are called circles of declination. Corresponding to the parallels of latitude on the earth, we have the parallels of declination. The position of a heavenly body in relation to the celestial equator is called its declination, and corresponds to latitude on the earth. The declination of the sun varies from a latitude of about 23° north at midsummer, when it is directly above the Tropic of Cancer, to a latitude of about 23° south at midwinter, when it is directly above the Tropic of Capricorn. The declination changes by about one degree every three days, and 15th-century navigators, like those of today, were able to find the variation tabulated in special almanacs.

According to the "Regimento do Astrolabio e do Quadrante", which was probably devised as early as the 1480's,

one can find the latitude by measuring the altitude of the sun at noon, when shadows are at their shortest, in the following way: "When the sun is in the southern signs, which are Libra, Scorpio, Sagittarius, Capricorn, Aquarius and Pisces [i.e. when the sun is in a southerly declination], between the 14th of September and the 11th of March, you shall reckon in this way: you take the height of the sun, as has already been explained, and find its declination for the particular day in the table. You shall then add both these figures together and subtract the sum from 90°. The difference is your distance from the Equator, that is 90 — (h + d). For example, on the 10th of November you take the height and find it to be 35°. To this you then add 19° 35', which is the declination of the sun for the 27th day of Scorpio [10th November], and in this manner you obtain 54° 35'. When you subtract this from 90° you obtain 35° 25', and this is your distance from the Equator."

The drawing above right explains the principles. The line H—H' is the observer's horizon. R—R' is a line through the centre of the earth, parallel to H—H'.

213

Martin Behaim's "Earth Apple" from 1492 is the oldest globe in existence. On the map projection of the eastern hemisphere of the globe we see how the west coast of Africa south of the Cameroons runs, incorrectly, towards the south-east, as on Fra Mauro's map.

measuring the altitude of the sun. Only then, with the aid of the tables in the *Almanach Perpetuum* of the Spanish Jew, Abraham Zacuto, which José Vicinho had translated into Latin, could they calculate the latitude.

Martin Behaim, a German merchant and later cartographer who was then living in Portugal and among other things instructing navigators in the use of an instrument known as Jacob's staff, noted on his globe that he had taken part in Diego Cão's voyage. If this is true, he was a very poor geographer and a very poor map-maker, for on his globe he allows the west coast to run towards the south-east, exactly as on Fra Mauro's map. Nor are his indications of latitude anywhere near right: and this is the more remarkable since in Portugal he claimed to be a specialist in that very subject. He was either an impostor—and in that case his globe would be nothing but a copy of others' maps—or, in his own city of Nuremburg where the globe was made, he tried to win credit for voyages he had never made. I think the latter is more likely.

About Diego Cão's second voyage Luca Wadding writes: "So that the Portuguese visitors [the hostages left by Cão] should not, on account of the long wait, meet with inconvenience at the hands of the Ethiopian ruler, the King ordered Cão to take back the people he had brought with him—these had now been converted to the True Faith and won over by the great friendliness of the King—and to persuade their ruler to renounce his false gods and come to know the one and only God, the Creator of Heaven and Earth. Cão returned to the Congo, faithfully handed over the Ethiopians he had taken, receiving in return the Portuguese hostages, and then sailed on for 200 leagues [750 miles] along the coast of that country to discover yet more lands. On the way home he visited the King of the Congo with a group of selected companions and gave him rich gifts, to the profound joy of his people."

We know that Diego Cão sailed all the way to Cape Cross, at a latitude of 21° 51′ south, and that he erected a stone cross there which still exists today. Some sources say that he died there; according to others he returned to Portugal. It is probable, as Wadding says, that he returned to the River Congo. On a rock face on the right bank of the river—near the modern Matadi, 100 miles inland—there has been found an inscription with the arms of Portugal, a large cross, and the following words: "To this place came ships sent by the magnificent D. João II, King of Portugal: Dº Cão, Pº Annes, Pº da Costa." A little further away it is still possible to read this: "Jº de Santyago † of disease, Jº Alvez †, Dº Pinero,

Gº Alvez—Antuo." There are also a few other crosses and the names Ruys, Farubo and Annes.—Pero Annes and Pero da Costa were the captains of two of the caravels. We know that Pero Annes later fought with Albuquerque in India, and that João de Santiago was the pilot of one of the transport ships on the next great voyage of exploration.

Nothing is known of how Diego Cão met with his fate. Perhaps illness kept him from continuing until the land came to an end, and it is probable that the great mariner died on the way home, for his name is not mentioned after this. Up to the time of his death he was the greatest of Portugal's maritime explorers: he had charted more than 1,500 miles of new coastline.

Part of the inscription made by Diego Cão on a rock beside the River Congo.

The Route to India

The result of Diego Cão's voyages cannot have encouraged the King. He had no doubt been hoping that his men would soon reach the cape, so clearly marked on Fra Mauro's map, which brought the continent to an end; but the coast seemed to continue southwards indefi-nitely, and it was reported that wind and currents were usually against one. The chroniclers say that the King's advisers tried to persuade him to be satisfied with the lucrative trade with Guinea and not to waste money on

The church of Abba Libanos at Lalibela in Abyssinia was cut directly out of a sandstone cliff in the 13th century.

unprofitable expeditions. We know so little about the real motives behind all that occurred. The official objectives were to make contact with Prester John and to spread the Christian gospel. It is certain that the key to the riches of India had long been the chief goal, but it appears as if Portugal, perhaps for political reasons, had not wanted to speak openly of it. In Italy there were those who very probably understood the designs of the Portuguese; after all, Toscanelli had written in his letter about "a sea route from here to India, the home of spices; a route which is shorter than *that via Guinea*". What Barros, the historian, writes is perhaps correct: "The King hoped that Prester John would show him a gateway to India, for many friars who travelled through Portugal had said that Prester

Ivory mask from Benin; early 16th century.

John's kingdom reached from Egypt to the Southern Sea."

At about the same time as Cão's second voyage, a certain Afonso de Aveiro returned from Benin, where he had established a trading station and found good pepper. According to Barros he was also able to report the following: "A twenty-month journey from the coast there lives a king who is venerated by his people in the same manner as the Pope is venerated by the Catholic Christians. The kings of Benin ask him to sanction their election; if he agrees to this he sends them a helmet of brass, a sceptre and a cross, without which the people would not recognize them as proper rulers. When foreign ambassadors wish to pay him their respects, they are never allowed to see his face; a curtain hides him from their view, and when they depart he advances his foot beneath it so that they may kiss it."

It was now calculated that this twenty-month journey into Africa was of 300 leagues—1,125 miles—and it was found on Fra Mauro's map that it led straight to the Kingdom of Abassia, or Abyssinia—the land of the priest-king. At least, so Barros said. But it is not certain that José Vicinho and the other scholars of the court trusted the maps and the estimated distances with so little discrimination. After all, one of their chief duties was to correct mistakes, and we know that their impression of the west coast of Africa had come, as years passed, to differ markedly from Fra Mauro's. They based their impression on true observations and measurements, and even though not a single Portuguese chart from those times survives today, we can see that the results of those

observations—which were supposed to be strictly guarded state secrets—were smuggled out and reproduced on maps drawn in other countries.

All later developments show that the Portuguese navigators calculated distances, measured the length of coastlines and their latitudes, noted down winds and currents, and made rough maps which were then gathered together by the more learned—first at Sagres and later at Lisbon—to be correlated and made into proper maps and navigational instructions for use on coming expeditions. It has often been said that the navigators of those days could not measure the altitude of the sun and calculate their latitude, because some places have been shown with a latitude which was ten or even twenty degrees out. But if the navigators had been as careless as this, they would not have been able to steer their ships time and again to the same island or the same spot on distant mainlands across the ill-known seas. The reports about new countries and their position that were published at that time—and that is virtually the only information that has survived—must have been deliberately misleading so that rival nations should not find the way.

John II now decided that he must obtain definite information about several different things at once. He wanted to know the truth about the power and dominions of the priest-king; he wanted to learn things about India proper, about the goods that could be bought there and from

Abyssinia, the one-time powerful Kingdom of Axum, was isolated from Europe by the Arab Empire from the 7th century onwards, and only a few travellers, mainly friars, received Arab permission to travel to and from the Christian kingdom. Early in the 15th century the Emperor Yeshak tried to establish diplomatic relations with European princes, and we know that among other things he wrote to Alfonso of Aragon, suggesting an alliance against Islam. Zara-Yaqob, his successor, received the answer, and began a further exchange of letters in which he, too, suggested an alliance, this time cemented by marriage. At about the same time, the authorities in Florence tried to persuade some Abyssinian monks in Jerusalem to visit their city, and we know that a Papal delegation was allowed to travel through Egypt and across the Red Sea to the residence of the Emperor Eskender at Tegulet in the 1480's.

whom they could most conveniently be bought; he wanted to know whether the Indian "Sea" was surrounded by land, as Ptolemy thought, or whether it was connected with the Atlantic "Sea", as Fra Mauro thought and the

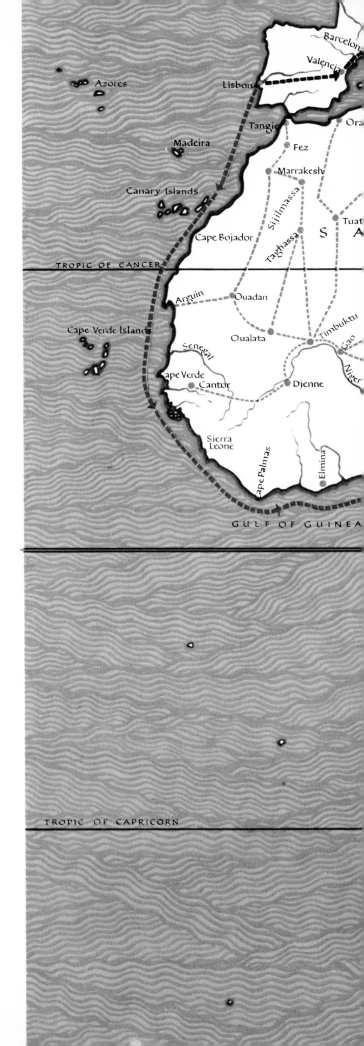

The broken black line on the map shows the approximate routes taken by Pedro de Covilhão on his protracted travels during the years 1487—1493. He sailed the entire length of the Red Sea five times; at last, through the port of Zeyla, he arrived at Tegulet, which was then the city of residence of the "priest-king". The pink area shows the rough extent of Abyssinia at that time. The Arabs controlled the entire Red Sea. — The broken lines in Africa show the most important caravan routes (cf. the map on p. 167). — The broken brown line along the west coast of Africa shows the route taken by Bartolomeu Diaz in 1487—1488, when he reached the southern extremity of the continent.

Portuguese hoped; and finally he wanted to know where Africa ended.

It had come to his knowledge that Abyssinian monks made pilgrimages to Jerusalem, so he immediately sent two Portuguese friars to that country to see what they could learn. It is probable that he also sent spies and delegations in many other directions, but we know nothing of what they managed to find out. On the other hand we do know several details about a certain Pedro de Covilhão's very noteworthy travels in the service of the King. If we bring together the essential points from various sources—mainly Galvano, Barros, Castanheda and Alvares—the following story emerges:

In his youth, Pedro de Covilhão had served under the Duke of Medina Sidonia in Andalusia; hence he spoke Spanish like a native, and John II could use him as an agent in Castile. He had also learnt Arabic, and had been on secret missions to Morocco. When, therefore, he was sent at the age of forty to India and Africa, he was particularly well qualified for his difficult task. His companion was Alfonso de Paiva, a man from the Canaries, who also knew Arabic well. Before their departure the travellers were carefully briefed by the King's geographers, and it is likely that they took with them a little map, which they could later correct and supplement from personal observation.

On 7th May 1487 the King gave them their credentials and a purse of 400 cruzados. In Lisbon they handed over the greater part of the money to the Italian banker Marchioni, who gave them a letter of credit which was to be made good in Valencia. They then rode to Valencia, and thence again on horseback to Barcelona, where they found a ship which took them to Naples. In time another vessel took them to Rhodes, where they were taken care of by two Portuguese Hospitallers, who advised them to con-

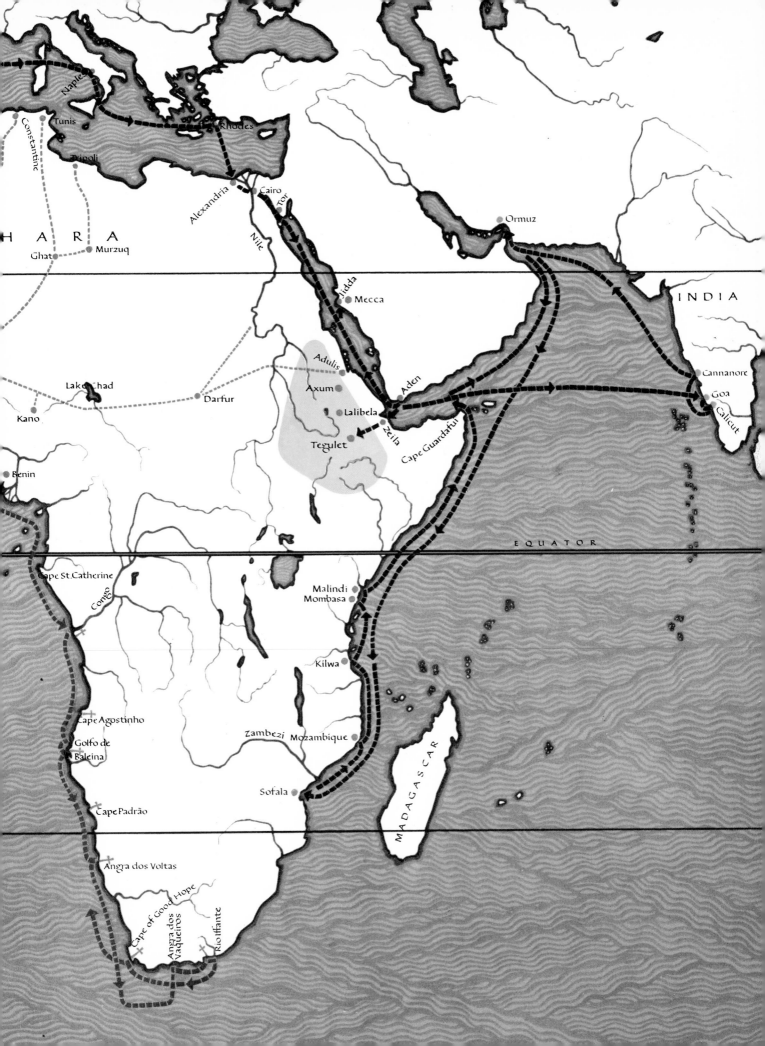

HARA

Constantine

Tunis

Tripoli

Naples

Rhodes

Alexandria

Cairo

Tor

Nile

Ghat

Murzuq

Jidda

Mecca

Adulis

Axum

Lalibela

Zeila

Tegulet

Aden

Ormuz

INDIA

Cannanore

Goa

Calicut

Cape Guardafui

Lake Chad

Darfur

Kano

Benin

EQUATOR

Cape St.Catherine

Congo

Malindi

Mombasa

Kilwa

Cape Agostinho

Golfo de
Baleina

Zambezi

Mozambique

MADAGASCAR

Sofala

Cape Padrão

Angra dos Voltas

Cape of Good Hope

Angra dos
Vaqueiros

Rio Infante

tinue their journey in the guise of merchants. Covilhão therefore bought a quantity of honey, and then they crossed over to Alexandria, where both of them immediately fell ill. While they lay sick there, the honey disappeared; and they were told that the Sultan's chamberlain had taken charge of it because he was convinced that they would never recover. Covilhão nevertheless persuaded him to pay a reasonable sum for it, and with the money they later bought other goods with which they went on to Cairo.

There they tried to make contact with other merchants,

Disguised as a Moorish merchant, Covilhão set out as a spy in 1487 to visit all the ports of importance in Arabia, East Africa and the Indian Peninsula. Later that same year, Bartolomeu Diaz sailed from Lisbon with three ships to circumnavigate Africa.

made friends with two Moroccans who were on their way to India, and sailed from Egypt in their company. First they came to the port of Tor on the Sinai Peninsula, and then to Aden. From this place Paiva was to cross over to Africa on his own in order to visit the priest-king, while Covilhão, still in the company of the two Moroccans, embarked on a ship with pilgrims returning from Mecca and sailed with the south-west monsoon across the Indian Ocean to Cannanore on the Malabar Coast of India. There he was told that the neighbouring city of Calicut to the south was the richest port in the whole of India, and that a colony of Mohammedan merchants were in control of all foreign trade. He went to Calicut and saw that ships from the West arrived there in August and September with wares from Europe, and left in the winter with the north-east monsoon, carrying cinnamon and pepper and cloves, porcelain and silk and pearls and precious stones.

From Calicut Covilhão went to Goa, further north on the coast, the port of arrival for the Arab horses which the Indian princes needed for their cavalry. He probably also visited Ormuz before sailing with the monsoon wind across to Africa right down to the golden city of Sofala. There he received information which convinced him that Africa could be circumnavigated. By this time he felt that his task had been completed, so he turned for home. On the way he visited Mozambique, Kilwa, Mombasa and Malindi. Towards the end of 1490 he reached Cairo, where they had agreed that Paiva was to wait for him.

Instead he was met by two messengers from the King: one Abraham of Beja, a rabbi, and one José of Lamego, a shoemaker. They told him that Paiva had died before

completing his mission, and that the King's orders now were first to take Rabbi Abraham to Ormuz and then to visit the priest-king in Abyssinia. Before his departure from Cairo he wrote a report of his experiences and sent them to the King of Portugal by the shoemaker from Lamego. The report has been lost, but according to the chronicler Francisco Alvares it contained among other things the following: "In Calicut there is great trade in cinnamon, pepper and nutmeg, which come to this place from further east. These Indian cities may be reached from the Sea of Guinea by first sailing to the Sofala Coast, where I have been, or to a great island, said to be three hundred leagues long, which the Moors call Moon Island [Madagascar]. I went to Sofala not to see the gold mines in the interior, but because I wanted to find out whether there was a sea route round Africa to the south."

Covilhão then escorted Rabbi Abraham to Ormuz and crossed the Red Sea once again to Jidda. From there he accompanied some pilgrims to Mecca so that he might see the renowned city and the sacred Kaaba, the black stone which had fallen from Heaven long before the days of Mohammed. After this he continued north, to Sinai and the monastery of St. Catherine—it almost seems as if he wanted to put off his visit to the priest-king. It was not until 1493 that he arrived in Abyssinia. Like so many other European travellers, he was detained there by the Negus and could not send any reports to Lisbon about the insignificant power and barbarous kingdom of the "priest-king". A Portuguese ambassador who visited Abyssinia in 1520 could report that Covilhão was still alive, had an Ethiopian wife and was "generally esteemed and had great influence over Prester John and his entire court".

Preparations for the expedition which was to find out whether it was possible to circumnavigate Africa were already being made at the time Covilhão and Paiva left Lisbon. Diego Cão's protracted voyages had shown that the ships had not been adequately provisioned for the voyage home, and so this time, apart from two fifty-ton caravels, a smaller supply ship was equipped which could stop at a suitable place on the coast and wait for the explorers on their return. As leader of the expedition, the King appointed Bartolomeu Diaz, a man of an old seafaring family, who had sailed many times to Guinea. His pilot was the experienced Pero d'Allemquer, and his first mate a man by the name of Leitão. The captain of the second caravel was João Iffante, and of the supply ship Bartolomeu's younger brother, Pero Diaz. Also on board the vessels were two negroes and a number of negresses, whom Cão and others had previously brought back with them from Africa, and three stone crosses which were to be set up on new coasts.

221

The vessels made their departure towards the end of August 1487. They probably sailed straight to the Congo, where they could buy provisions from the friendly natives, and then moved on to the protected harbour of Angra dos Aldeas, where they left the supply ship and put ashore two of the negroes. These had been baptized and were wearing fine European clothes; their task was to go inland and make contact with the subjects of the priest-king, so that he could be given the news that two Christian ships were on their way to him. The two caravels sailed on past Cão's crosses in the Golfo de Baleina and at Cabo de Padrão—Cape Cross—and put the richly dressed negresses ashore to carry the same message to the priest-king. The rest of the voyage lay along uncharted coasts.

Barros is the only chronicler to describe the journey in fair detail: "Crosses were set up at all important places. They also gave names to bays, capes and promontories, according to the names of the saints on whose days they were discovered, or by reason of other special circumstances. Thus Angra dos Voltas [the Bay of Turns] was so named because they had to tack about there for five days. It lies on a latitude of 29 degrees south. Shortly after this, the squadron was compelled to battle for thirteen days against terrible winds and storms with the sails reefed. When the weather at last improved, they set sail for the east so that they might once more come in sight of land; for they thought that the coastline still ran north

and south as before. But as many days of sailing did not bring them in sight of land, they altered course to the north. They came to a bay which they called Angra dos Vaqueiros [i.e. Cowherds' Bay, the modern Mossel Bay], for they saw that many cattle were grazing there. But they were unable to make contact with the natives.

"Sailing on along the coast, which to their joy continued to stretch towards the east, they found a small island at 33° 45′, which they called Santa Cruz [in Algoa Bay]. The sailors, who were exhausted and much frightened by the recent storm, now began to insist that they had come far enough, for the vessels carried only limited provisions, and all of them might die before any other food could be obtained. It was only with difficulty that Bartolomeu Diaz was able to persuade them to continue for another two or three days along the coast. About 25 miles east of Santa Cruz they came to a river which they called the Rio do Iffante [the modern Great Fish River]. Here they were forced to turn about, for the men refused to be cajoled into going on.

"On the return journey they came at last to the celebrated cape which had remained undiscovered for so many centuries and whose circumnavigation opened the way to another hemisphere. Bartolomeu Diaz called it Cabo Tormentoso [Cape of Storms] because of the terrible weather they had experienced there when first rounding it. But when they returned to Portugal the King gave it the pleasanter name of Cabo da Boa Esperança

[Cape of Good Hope], for he had good hopes of finding the passage to India beyond it."

Certain modern scholars think that Bartolomeu Diaz called the spot the Cape of Good Hope from the very beginning, and that the chroniclers only romanticized the naming of it to honour the King; but there is no definite evidence for this. It looks to me as if Barros' story is perfectly correct, and quite in keeping with Diaz' feelings when he named the cape. Galvano writes: "It may be said that he, like Moses, came to see the Promised Land, the land of India, but was never to set foot in it."

It is thought that the storm swept him past the Cape of Good Hope towards the end of January 1488. By the middle of March the expedition had reached the Rio do Iffante, which was named after the second captain, and they probably first saw the Cape of Good Hope in the middle of August. There they went ashore and put up a cross. On the way back they found the supply ship at Angra dos Aldeas. Its original crew of nine had by now been reduced to three by fever and fighting with the natives; and it is said that one of those with fever had died of joy on seeing the caravels return. The provisions and all of the equipment that could be used were then transferred to the caravels, and the damaged and badly worm-eaten vessel was burned. In the Gulf of Guinea they put in at the island of Príncipe. There they found Duarte Pacheco, the future chronicler, in the throes of fever. He had been sent by the King to explore the rivers

The Cape of Storms — and of Good Hope.

of the mainland, but his vessel had foundered on the island, and he and the other few survivors had given up all hope of being saved when they sighted Diaz' caravels. In order to make the greatest possible profit out of the voyage, Diaz also put in at Elmina and took on board a shipment of gold. After sixteen months' absence, the two caravels dropped anchor in the harbour of Lisbon.

In the margin of one of the pages of Pierre d'Ailly's book *Imago Mundi*, Bartolomeo Colombo, Columbus' brother, wrote the following: "Observe that in December of the year 1488 there came to Lisbon Bartholomeu Didacus [Diaz], commander of three caravels which the King of Portugal had dispatched to Guinea to explore the country. He said that he had sailed 600 leagues beyond the furthest point yet known to man: first 450 leagues to the south, and then 150 leagues to the north, to a cape which he called the Cape of Good Hope. It is likely that this is Cape Agisimba [?]. According to the astrolabe, the cape lay at a latitude of 45 degrees south, and its distance from Lisbon was 3,100 leagues. He recorded the voyage and described it league by league on a map which he was able to show the King. I myself was present when all these things occurred."

223

The last sentence must be interpreted to mean that he was present in Lisbon on the arrival of the caravels, and probably present when Diaz told of his voyage. The Cape of Good Hope lies at a southerly latitude of 34° 22′, and we may be certain that Pero d'Allemquer, Diaz' very skilful pilot who was later to take Vasco da Gama's fleet to India, had not made a mistake of ten degrees but had deliberately, at the express command of the King, published the wrong latitude to deter others. Barros, who did not write his chronicle until later in the 16th century, when the true latitude of the cape could no longer be kept secret, gives the latitude of Santa Cruz as 33° 45′ south—which is fairly accurate.

In 1488 a monk came to Lisbon from Abyssinia, and it is likely that the information the King got from him about the "priest-king" and his kingdom was closer to reality than were the legends which had grown out of a letter forged three hundred years earlier. Early in 1491

the shoemaker from Lamego arrived with Covilhão's report about India and Africa. Henceforward, it is true, nobody could base any confident hopes on the priest-king's help in the war with the Mohammedans which might break out over the trade with India, but now practically the whole of the way to India was known. We do not know why it was not immediately put to use.

On 4th March 1493 a small caravel put into Restello, Lisbon's outer harbour, to ride out a storm. She hoisted a Spanish flag and anchored close to a large warship, whose captain was a certain Don Alvaro Damão. By the following day the storm had passed, and Captain Damão instructed Bartolomeu Diaz, his mate, to row across to the caravel and ask its captain to come aboard. When Diaz saw him, he recognized him as the Christopher Columbus who nine years before had wanted to show the King a western sea route to India. And Columbus told him that the quest for India was now over.

Columbus' arms.

Index

The numbers refer to the page numbers in question. The letter P after a number indicates that a word refers to a picture or its caption. The letter M after a number indicates that the word refers to a map or its caption. Words which occur often, such as the names of continents, countries, etc., are indicated only for pages where they are dealt with in detail, or are of importance for the context.

1 Roman stade = 202 yards
8 stades = 1 Roman mile = 1,616 yards
1 Italian mile = 1,628 yards
1 Portuguese mile = 2,259 yards
1 Portuguese league = 3 Portuguese miles = 6,777 yards

Acknowledgements:

The quotations from Herodotus are taken from Macaulay's translation, Macmillan, 1890.
The Marco Polo quotations are taken from the 1854 revision of W. Marsden's translation.
The quotation from Dante's Divine Comedy in Miss Dorothy Sayers' translation is reprinted with the kind permission of Penguin Books Ltd.
The quotations from Arrian's Anabasis of Alexander in E. Iliff Robson's translation are reprinted with the kind permission of the Loeb Classical Library.

DESIGN BY BJÖRN LANDSTRÖM

TRANSLATED FROM "VÄGEN TILL INDIEN"

BY MICHAEL PHILLIPS AND HUGH W. STUBBS

EDITING: FORUMS FACKBOKSREDAKTION/JAN WAHLÉN

PRODUCTION: INTERNATIONAL BOOK PRODUCTION, STOCKHOLM

SET WITH 10 PT TIMES NEW ROMAN TYPE

BY BOHUSLÄNINGENS AB, UDDEVALLA, SWEDEN,

AND PRINTED BY ESSELTE AB, STOCKHOLM, ON 140 g/m^2 LMB "INDIA"

MATT-COATED PAPER FROM LESSEBO AB, LESSEBO, SWEDEN

PRINTED IN SWEDEN

DATE DUE

MR 30'82			
GAYLORD			PRINTED IN U.S.A